From the Courtroom to the Boardroom

From the Courtroom to the Boardroom

PRIVATIZING JUSTICE IN THE NEOLIBERAL UNITED STATES

Deena Varner

University Press of Kansas

Published by the University Press of Kansas (Lawrence, Kansas 66045), which was
organized by the Kansas Board of Regents and is operated and funded by Emporia State
University, Fort Hays State University, Kansas State University, Pittsburg State University,
the University of Kansas, and Wichita State University.

This book will be made open access within three years of publication thanks to Path to
Open, a program developed in partnership between JSTOR, the American Council of
Learned Societies (ACLS), University of Michigan Press, and the University of North
Carolina Press to bring about equitable access and impact for the entire scholarly
community, including authors, researchers, libraries, and university presses around the
world. Learn more at https://about.jstor.org/path-to-open/.

Library of Congress Cataloging-in-Publication Data

Names: Varner, Deena, author.
Title: From the courtroom to the boardroom : privatizing justice in the neoliberal
    United States / Deena Varner.
Description: Lawrence : University Press of Kansas, 2024 | Includes bibliographical
    references and index.
Identifiers: LCCN 2023041542 (print)
    LCCN 2023041543 (ebook)   ISBN 9780700637119 (cloth)
    ISBN 9780700636594 (paperback)   ISBN 9780700636600 (ebook)
Subjects: LCSH: Criminal justice, Administration of—United States. | Mass
    incarceration—United States. | Neoliberalism—United States.
Classification: LCC HV9950 .V387 2024 (print) | LCC HV9950 (ebook) | DDC
    364.973—dc23/eng/20240205
LC record available at https://lccn.loc.gov/2023041542.
LC ebook record available at https://lccn.loc.gov/2023041543.

British Library Cataloguing-in-Publication Data is available.

The paper used in this publication is acid free and meets the minimum requirements of
the American National Standard for Permanence of Paper for Printed Library Materials
Z39.48–1992.

Contents

Acknowledgments

Shortly after I completed my PhD in 2018, I logged into my Airbnb account and, as I had done dozens of times over the previous five or six years, reserved a place to stay during an upcoming conference. A few days later, I received an email from the company informing me that it had run a background check, and based on the results, was permanently removing me from the platform. I wasn't sure at the time why *this* banishment struck me as particularly egregious. After all, I had been navigating this landscape for fifteen years. For almost my entire adult life, every job application and every apartment rental application has been fraught with the possibility of joblessness and homelessness. My banishment from Airbnb was, in some ways, just one more incident in a long line of incidents reminding me that, at any moment, my life as I know it could cease to exist. But it nagged at me, and it wouldn't stop nagging at me, so I wrote about it. A lot. This book is a result of that writing. So thanks, Airbnb.

Although inspired by Airbnb, the book truly wouldn't have been possible without the help and support of a network of people.

First, I want to thank Bill Mullen, who has read more versions of this project than any person should ever have to read of anything. Bill was my dissertation chair and stalwart cheerleader during graduate school, but since then, I've been blessed to keep him in my life as a trusted advisor, comrade, and friend. His discriminating eye, astute commentary, and kind words over many years and many, many more drafts have made this book possible.

I am especially grateful for Fareed Ben-Youssef, who began reading my writing in 2018 when I drafted one of the first chapters of this book. Over calls, coffees, and chats at the private cinema, Fareed nourished me during the early years of the project with support and kindness. He, too, has read every version of the manuscript from start to finish, and many more partial drafts and starts and stops, always with a joy and excitement that inspired me to continue rethinking and revising.

I am also thankful for the generosity of Ben Golder and James Martel, who allowed me, at a meeting of the Association for the Study of Law, Culture, and Humanities, to invite myself into their conversations. Ben read the entire manuscript during the later stages of the writing and publishing process, and his extensive and nuanced suggestions improved the book exponentially. James read the manuscript as I was preparing to send it off for peer review, and his enthusiasm for the project buoyed me through the final stages.

My colleagues at NYU Shanghai were instrumental in the early stages of writing. Duane Corpis has been a staunch supporter of me and my work, always eager to read new writing and provide incisive commentary. With Tapsi Mathur, I shared many wonderful months walking the streets of Shanghai, exploring, laughing, and working through ideas. Juan Moreno read an early draft of one of the chapters, and we've since spent countless hours supporting each other in the writing process. I also want to thank Saskia Abrahms-Kavunenko, Roslynn Ang, Asli Berktay, Dannah Dennis, Dada Docot, Rebecca Ehrenwirth, Anup Gampa, Quinn Gibson, Brett Goodin, Fang He, Yuan He, Jeongmin Kim, Anne Ma, Rik Ranjan, Cheryl Mei-ting Schmitz, Jing Wang, and Brad Weslake, all of whom were regular participants at various points in the NYU Shanghai Humanities and Social Sciences Colloquium, where we shared our work in progress with each other in the spirit of collegiality and friendship. Responding to drafts of their work and knowing they were doing the same with mine brought us together as a community and made the writing process a joy. Through these colloquia, and often later, over lunches or coffee or KTV, I received so much feedback and support that it would be impossible to quantify.

I also want to thank my editor at the University Press of Kansas, David Congdon, for his support and willingness to ask probing questions and engage in intellectual debate that helped me to better articulate some of the key ideas in the work. I am also, of course, indebted to my anonymous reviewers for their extensive, perceptive, and supportive comments that have substantially shaped the final version of the book, as well as to the other anonymous reviewers who were instrumental in shaping parts of the manuscript, namely chapter 2, which appeared in an earlier form as "Quasi: Adjudicating Guilt, Innocence, and Citizenship in the Neoliberal Prison," in *Cultural Politics* 15, no. 2 (2019): 139–161. The version that appears here does so with the permission of the copyright holder, Duke University Press. Thanks is also due to the Texas Tech Humanities Center, whose generous subvention award contributed to the final production of the book.

I would like to take a few moments as well to acknowledge William Livingston III, whose artwork appears on the cover of this book. When I first encountered Livingston's art in 2019, he had already been incarcerated in Oklahoma for a number of years. Most of the pieces he was creating were silkscreens of album covers and other iconic images of indie bands from the 70s, 80s, and 90s. I've written previously about how, because prisons are sites of total control, inmates are often fashioned as subjects totally controlled, totally *inside*. We often expect them to talk only about prison, or to write or make art only about prison. Livingston's art reminds us that prisoners' interests, politics, and ambitions are both inside and outside the prison, and that the boundary between inside and outside is always more porous than it seems.

The artwork on the cover, "Factotum," is part of Livingston's "Throwaway People" series that he began making at the beginning of his confinement. In our personal correspondence, he cited as inspiration for the piece "the noise, the chaos, the unpredictability and the loneliness while still surrounded by so many." The title, of course, is an allusion to Charles Bukowski's novel of the same name, which, Livingston writes, "is about a man who has lost everything and lives life with no direction." Although the throwaway people inside the honeycomb structure seem to be trapped there, this jail is also porous, visually recalling the way honey oozes out of its comb. *From the Courtroom to the Boardroom* is very much about how the prisoner eventually leaves prison, but it is also about how the prison and its logics ooze out and into our everyday lives, whether we've ever been locked up or not. The rhizomatic quality of the honeycomb, too, evokes the kind of society I imagine when I think about the ways that public and private actors work together to punish. There is no top or bottom, east or west, and no clear direction of the flow of power. We're all inside of it, but it's never quite clear what is the cause and what is the effect.

So thank you, Will, for allowing me to use this piece, and also for eventually finding ways to focus your art and yourself on the music you love.

On a more personal note, I want to thank Susan, Kelly, Kristen, Renee, Mike, Melissa, Jason, Nick, and Lynn for helping me, slowly over a period of time, to believe that life is possible.

While the book benefited from the generous support of so many people, its imperfections are mine alone.

Introduction

On October 27, 2021, a passenger accused of assaulting a flight attendant on an American Airlines flight was detained by police upon landing at the Denver airport. In its statements to the press, the airline suggested that it was working with police to ensure that the alleged perpetrator was prosecuted to the fullest extent of the law. However, it also described the alleged assault as a "disruption" rather than a crime, an example of "unruly behavior."[1] By framing the crime of assault as a violation of company policy or standards, the airline positioned itself as the appropriate body to impose punishment on the passenger, which it did: despite an ongoing FBI investigation, the company took immediate action by banning the passenger from future flights, no investigation or adjudicative process necessary. This reduction in scale, discursively transforming an assault into a disruption, legitimates the boardroom as the appropriate arbiter of crime. Courtrooms, after all, are not the place for adjudicating minor instances of unruly behavior.

While legislatures and courts play a significant role in shaping legal personhood in the United States, it is increasingly not the courts but private, profit-driven institutions that adjudicate and punish institutional infractions alongside illegal and sometimes criminal behavior. This book is about these shifting geographies of justice, from the courtroom to the boardroom. Although arrest and conviction substantially shape the limits and possibilities for exercising citizenship, the private adjudication of crime and imposition of penalties is one way in which companies ensure that they, and not the public, are responsible for defining the terms of the neoliberal social contract. This is a pact in which fewer and fewer activities of daily life can be performed without first paying a company for the privilege of doing so, in which vanishingly few spaces exist in which we are not expected to buy something, and in which all members of society are framed as consumers rather than citizens, bound not by rights under the law but by corporate policies, conditions of carriage, and terms of service.

When the process of defining, negotiating, and punishing the transgression of social norms, institutional misconduct, illegality, and crime takes place behind the closed doors of private organizations and under the veil of non-disclosure agreements, when these negotiations are a matter of institutional or corporate policy rather than law or public policy, public discourse about social and legal norms is gradually relegated to social media comments and chat rooms. Here, the punitive culture of the twentieth century—epitomized by death penalty advocates jubilating outside the prison gates while the lights inside flicker—has been transformed into a different kind of free-for-all: Punishment should be imposed immediately by the private actors involved, prior to any public hearing or finding of guilt by a court, and with no avenue for the accused to respond to charges, confront witnesses, or testify on their own behalf. Responding to the American Airlines incident, for example, many social media commentators seemed uninterested in prosecution, calling instead for the passenger's lifetime banishment from *all* forms of public transportation, effective immediately.

This is not simply law and order run amok but a perversion of the most insidious aspects of US law-and-order culture, which include an excessively punitive and racially motivated attitude towards minor crime, so-called public disorder, and dissent against dominant institutions. Rather, this new type of governance amounts to what this book will call corporate *policy-and-order*. Policy-and-order mobilizes the punitive stance of law and order towards criminality and other perceived misconduct while circumventing legal processes altogether and reducing the rights of people accused—both officially and unofficially—of crimes. Policy-and-order is constituted by the boardroom adjudication and punishment of misconduct alongside illegal and sometimes criminal behavior, as well as by the knowledge that these adjudicative processes produce about criminals and other ostensible bad actors, and the way this knowledge is deployed in both public and private settings—or, as is more likely the case, in the ubiquitous constellation of spaces and institutions that are neither public nor private but public-private.

By the late 1970s, it was clear that neoliberalism, theories of which had been circulating in Central and Eastern Europe since the 1930s, had become ascendant. Michel Foucault argues in his seminal text on neoliberalism, his lectures on biopolitics at the Collège de France in 1978–79, that neoliberalism is not just an extension of liberalism, or of laissez-faire capitalism. Instead, he suggests, theories of neoliberalism propose a radical reorientation of the state to the market—one that alters the role of the legal and criminal justice systems as well as many other institutions. Because "neoliberalism is a political movement with statist objectives," as Mitchell Dean and Kaspar Villadsen have argued, Foucault's analysis of neoliberalism was an analysis of the neoliberal governmentality of the state, governmentality being Foucault's analytic for examining the operations and technologies of the state.[2] These lectures on biopolitics were not, in other words, and did not mean to be, an analysis or critique of the private sector. Perhaps also in part because Foucault was interested in the possibilities neoliberalism offered for disrupting the incessant consolidation of state power, his lectures after 1978–79 did not turn specifically towards the private sector as a new site of legal meanings and operations of power.

In *Undoing the Demos*, Wendy Brown takes up some of the problems of the private sector left open by Foucault at the close of these lectures, presenting a captivating indictment of neoliberalism, which she describes as a "normative order of reason developed over three decades into a widely and deeply disseminated governing rationality" that radically undermines the very foundations of political activity.[3] Her analysis builds on Foucault's lectures to consider how biopower once exercised by the state is increasingly exercised by private corporations. To take one of Brown's examples, neoliberalism has fundamentally shaped the twenty-first-century war machine, whose battles increasingly are fought not by the United States military but by private mercenaries. However, this is not simply a matter of companies like Halliburton waging for-profit wars. Rather, war is indivisible from the "rebuilding" of war-torn regions, and this rebuilding is indivisible from the goal of global domination of the agricultural market for companies like Monsanto.

From the Courtroom to the Boardroom draws inspiration from Foucault's lectures and Brown's political theory by considering how the market ambitions of US companies shape the treatment of ex-offenders in society and what the effects of this treatment are for the exercise of justice and the American political imaginary.

Foucault contends that what is at stake in social and political theory is not the state but government. "Liberal doctrine," he writes, "has never functioned on the basis of, or even by providing itself with a theory of the state. They have adopted principles of government."[4] Governmentality is the rationality or art of government, where government is taken to mean activities that shape, guide, or affect the conduct of people. "The state," in this formulation, "is nothing else but the . . . effect of a regime of multiple governmentalities." Foucault's entire body of work during the 1970s—his genealogies of the prison, sexuality, and psychiatry—was geared towards understanding the process of statification (*étatification*). What was at stake in these genealogies, Foucault argues, "was always the identification of the gradual, piecemeal, but continuous takeover by the state of a number of practices, ways of doing things, and, if you like governmentalities."[5] This book identifies, in contrast, the gradual, piecemeal, but continuous takeover beginning in the late twentieth century of a number of governmentalities by the private sector, especially as they relate to what are traditionally thought of as operations of the law and criminal justice system. Like Foucault's statification, these shifting geographies of justice are spectral: Corporations do not become suddenly or fully responsible for certain aspects of governance. Instead, the state and the private sector work together in increasingly intimate ways to manage the population and its social problems.

For the one hundred million or so Americans with an arrest or conviction record, this system of public-private justice determines where they can live, the kinds of work they can do, and how they can travel and participate in leisure activities. It has also fundamentally transformed how legal concepts such as due process, free speech, and other rights are imagined and exercised. In this book, neoliberalism supplants liberal democratic frameworks, subordinating them to operations of the market and mandating that private entities intervene in the creation, interpretation, and enforcement of law.[6] *From the Courtroom to the Boardroom* thus highlights the deep interconnections between public authorities, such as lawmakers, police, judges, and prison administrators, and private agents, like employers, landlords, and tech platforms, as they forge an American subject compatible with the neo-liberal agenda. In concert with the criminal justice system, questions of individuals' guilt, morality, and risk to society are at the same time negotiated by a private disciplinary wing that produces its own risk assessments, makes moral judgments, and imposes its own collateral consequences for those behaviors it deems antithetical to its own in-terests. The private disciplinary wing examined in this book comprises specific actors who explicitly craft disciplinary policies, activities, and regimes that consolidate their own power. It also constitutes a specifi-cally neoliberal form of social organization: it is formal rather than informal, designed and implemented from above by specific market-based actors, is mandated by the state, and applies putatively apolitical, technical, and managerial expertise to manage entrenched sociopoliti-cal problems.

FROM LAW AND ORDER TO COLLATERAL CONSEQUENCES TO POLICY-AND-ORDER

Massive prison and criminal justice system expansion beginning in the 1970s, a defining feature of the law-and-order society, has gener-ated significant political debate among academics, politicians, policy experts, activists, and the general public. A central aspect of this debate has been how these institutions function as a tool of racial capitalism —that is, how they extract economic, social, political, and symbolic capital from Black people as a constitutive feature of capitalist accu-mulation.[7] Alongside this expansion of the criminal justice and penal systems has emerged a vast system of collateral consequences—a web of state-based restrictions and regulations that people convicted of crimes may be subject to in excess of court-imposed sentences. These interlocking systems degrade legal and political personhood, stripping individuals convicted of crimes of their ability to attain social, sym-bolic, and economic capital and to participate in political activity. This transfer of power has included the partial transfer of responsibility to private, non-state, and market-based actors to make determinations about the appropriate treatment of criminals in society. As a result, landlords, employers, technology platforms, and other private companies now play an outsized role in determining sanctions for people convicted of crimes and shaping normative claims about legal personhood. As a function of racial capitalism, the material effects of these transformations are disproportionately visited on Black people, who, with or without convictions, face discrimination in housing, employment, and the sharing economy. As the primary targets of state-based control and punishment, Black people are then disproportionately surveilled, disciplined, or subject to banishment by the private sector as a consequence of having a criminal record.

The next three sections briefly trace the transition from the racialized mid-twentieth-century law-and-order society to state-based collateral consequences and ultimately to the policy-and-order society.

From Law and Order . . .

Amid the pro-democracy uprisings in Hong Kong in the summer and autumn of 2019, corporate interests in the United States began denouncing and prohibiting certain forms of speech from their employees and customers. In October, the NBA's Philadelphia 76ers ejected fans from one of its preseason games with a team from the Chinese Basketball Association for wearing pro–Hong Kong attire. The ejection came on the back of a controversy in which the general manager of the Houston Rockets published a pro-democracy tweet, which was decried by NBA commissioner Adam Silver. Silver said the tweet—"Fight for Freedom. Stand for Hong Kong"—did "not represent the Rockets or the NBA."[8] It is not entirely clear whether the decision to eject fans from the 76ers game was made by the privately owned 76ers, the privately-owned NBA, or the privately-owned Wells Fargo Center in which the 76ers play. The incident, though, is a valuable reminder that private corporations routinely monitor and censor political speech, and that the constitutional right to free speech in the United States is not guaranteed in privately owned spaces.

US-based firms like Nike and Apple also responded to the Hong Kong uprisings. Nike retail stores in Beijing and Shanghai pulled Houston Rockets merchandise from shelves, and Apple removed an app from its app store that allowed Hong Kongers to track the police. Commenting on these stories, National Public Radio tech correspondent Shannon Bond noted, "These are companies—they're hugely powerful. They're hugely popular. If they can't stand up to China, who can?"[9] In this narrative, multinational corporations like Apple and Nike are much more powerful than any national government or international governing body, including the United States, and they are in fact the *only* bodies that can secure the conditions for freedom and global democracy.

Some media commentators suggested that corporate responses to the Hong Kong tensions implied that China is exporting its authoritarianism to the United States. What it actually shows is that capitalism has no political ideals. It bows not to the authoritarianism of the Chinese state but to a market of 1.4 billion people. It also shows how the neoliberal United States—and precisely not China—already operates as a corporatist-authoritarian form of governance. This is not because the state, properly speaking, restricts speech or assembly or any of the other freedoms that Americans ostensibly enjoy, although it may, but because corporate interests own many of the spaces where public activity might otherwise take place—and with it the prerogative to govern and restrict political speech and behavior.

From the standpoint of neoliberal economics, it is capitalism, and not democracy, that produces the conditions for freedom. For gurus like Milton Friedman, personal freedom can only be realized in the context of the ultra-free capitalist marketplace. In 1992, Friedman remarked on some of the early effects of Deng Xiaoping's economic reforms: "China is still very far from being a free society, but there is no doubt that the residents of China are freer and more prosperous than they were under Mao—freer in every dimension except the political."[10] What is it that constitutes freedom, for neoliberals, if not political freedom? When individuals are free to pursue their own interest, "no external force, no coercion, no violation of freedom is necessary to produce cooperation among individuals all of whom can benefit." By "their own interest," Friedman means economic interest—to acquire wealth largely unimpeded by government and to make choices about consumption from as unlimited a set of goods and services as possible.[11] However, it is through this pursuit of economic interest, and through it alone, that social cohesion and stability are made possible. While he writes that "economic freedom is an essential requisite for political freedom," it is clear from his comments about China that political freedom does not equal and is subsidiary to economic freedom.

Friedman begins *Capitalism and Freedom* by quoting the well-known line from President John F. Kennedy's 1961 inaugural address: "Ask not what your country can do for you—ask what you can do for your country." His critique of Kennedy's exhortation makes clear what Friedman's views are on the role of the state in society and in people's lives. The first half of the injunction, he writes, is "paternalistic," suggesting "that government is the patron, the citizen the ward, a view that is at odds with the free man's belief in his own responsibility for his own destiny."[12] Citizens, that is, should not make any demands on the state, since doing so reflects a lack of autonomy and personal responsibility. The second half implies the reverse, that the state is a master and the citizen a servant. Friedman takes "country" in Kennedy's speech to mean the state, which he distinguishes from the nation: "To the free man, the country is a collection of individuals who compose it, not something over and above them. He is proud of a common heritage and loyal to common traditions," which, for Friedman, are the common heritage and traditions of European liberalism.[13] If neoliberal economists tend to view racism as antithetical to the logic of the free market, Freidman's remarks highlight how nationalist tenets nevertheless are central to the politics of American neoliberalism insofar as they delineate national membership along the lines of heritage and tradition, which are inseparable from race, ethnicity, and class.

The citizen's role, for Friedman, is to ensure that government is limited so as avoid the concentration of power in the hands of a few, and to insist that government carry out only its most essential functions, which are "to preserve law and order, to enforce private contracts, to foster competitive markets."[14] These are not separate functions, as Freidman's omission of the word "and" in the list suggests. Rather, preserving law and order and enforcing private contracts *is* fostering competitive markets, and fostering competitive markets *is* preserving law and order. Neoliberalism therefore reorients the relationship between citizen and state, as well as between state and market, predicating the former on the latter, even as it is undergirded by a nationalist sentiment that privileges the ties borne of racial, ethnic, and linguistic identity over those of heterogeneous political communities and commitments. It also places the criminal justice system at the center of government activity, insisting that the state's primary role is to maintain law and order for the purpose of ensuring citizens' freedom to act in their own economic self-interest. This somewhat paradoxical formulation, insofar as a great deal of crime consists of individuals pursuing their own economic self-interest, is less paradoxical in the context of Friedman's conception of the nation: Citizens are those who share and respect the putatively common heritage of the European social contract. Indeed, freedom should be preserved *"only* for people who are willing to practice self-denial, for otherwise freedom degenerates into license and irresponsibility."[15] Those who are true citizens are signatories to the liberal social contract, meaning that they are capable of self-government, and to the neoliberal social contract, meaning that they agree to pursue their own interest in ways that privilege the accumulation of wealth by capitalists. On the other hand, the very same "paternalism" that Friedman so vehemently denounces in Kennedy's speech "is inescapable for those whom we designate as not responsible."[16] These others require prescriptions and proscriptions on their behavior, which must be mandated and enforced by the state.

It is not especially difficult to draw a line from this premise to mass incarceration—to a third of the adult population having some form of police record, to a third of Black men having a felony conviction, to 2 percent of the population being confined to prisons on any given day, 60 percent of them people of color, to hair-trigger 9–1–1 calls bringing the police to arrest Black men for bird-watching in the park. But if the state's role, in one dominant version of neoliberalism, is to maintain law and order to guarantee the smooth functioning of the free market, which itself is a prerequisite for freedom, how did we also get *here*, to a society in which our support of democracy is so casually censored by our employers, by social media networks, by sports teams and stadiums? In which our use of Uber and Facebook, Instacart and Instagram, United Airlines and eBay all require us to relinquish our legal rights in order to participate in the activities of daily life? In which employers, landlords, and Airbnb are vested with the authority to determine whether we are fit to live and work in the world as a consequence of a criminal conviction or a subpar credit score, and to banish us if they deem us unfit?

This book argues that the neoliberal social contract and cultural landscape are shaped significantly by the complex, arbitrary, and bureaucratic administration of collateral consequences for people convicted of crimes. The current system of collateral consequences has expanded alongside the traditional criminal justice system of the 1970s and beyond, ultimately obscuring the legal system's role in securing the terms of the social contract and becoming a model for private, nonstate, and market-based actors to make determinations about the appropriate treatment of criminals in society.

To Collateral Consequences . . .

Under the capitalist system of wage labor, workers are paid for their labor power, quantified in time, rather than for their labor or the products of their labor. When time is construed as something that can be bought, sold, or traded, the result is a system of punishment that constructs time as a unit of payment.[17] "Just as the wage rewards time for which labor power has been purchased from someone," Foucault argues in his lectures on the punitive society at the Collège de France in 1972–73, the prison sentence "corresponds to the infraction, not in terms of reparation or exact adjustment, but in terms of quantity of time of liberty."[18] Capitalism and this form of penal practice are "twin forms": the wage form of capitalism reorganizes all of social life by introducing "time as measure, and not only as economic measure in the capitalist system, but also as moral measure."[19]

In their Marxist analysis, Dario Melossi and Massimo Pavarini maintain that the value of time in both the workplace and the prison is arbitrary and determined by those who own the means of production. But while the wage earner and the employer may agree, even if only in principle, on a fixed wage that corresponds to time worked, the prison sentence does not function in quite the same way. Sentencing guidelines vary from one jurisdiction to the next, and, as guidelines, they rely significantly on the subjective judgment of prosecutors, judges, and juries. There is no agreement between the sentenced and the sentencer, even in principle, and there is no way to know in advance of committing a crime how much time that crime is worth, since in most cases, its value is expressed in a range of time. The one- to ten-year prison sentence is not uncommon for serious misdemeanors and minor felonies, nor are substantial "tails"—terms of probation that run consecutive to the prison sentence. Neither does the prison sentence satisfy the terms of contemporary punishment. As most anyone convicted of a crime can attest, the completion of a sentence—whether that sentence is a fine, restitution, prison term, or term of probation—rarely represents "payment in full" for the crime committed.

If the relationship between crime and prison term is inherently arbitrary, the unknowability of indebtedness is compounded by the collateral consequences of conviction. The National Inventory of Collateral Consequences of Conviction (NICCC) catalogues state-imposed collateral consequences within each state, Washington, DC, and at the federal level. In total, across jurisdictions, duration, discretion, and offense type, the database lists almost forty-five thousand collateral consequences. Of these, approximately thirteen thousand are mandatorily, automatically, and indefinitely applied. The NICCC notes that while many collateral consequences contain a public safety or regulatory component, others "apply without regard to the relationship between crime and opportunity being restricted, such as the revocation of a business license after conviction of any felony." And while some collateral consequences are temporary and imposed at the discretion of judges or other agencies, others "apply without consideration of time passed between the conviction and the opportunity being sought or the person's rehabilitation efforts since the conviction."[20]

Felon disenfranchisement may be the most visible of collateral consequences, and it is often understood to be the most deleterious. Because voting is one of the very few ways in which American citizens exercise citizenship *as* citizenship, disenfranchisement is often seen as one of the state's most effective mechanisms for reducing or nullifying the legal personhood of people convicted of crimes in order to secure or maintain a privileged social or political regime.[21] Some legal scholars believe that disenfranchisement should be seen as an extension of civil death, which was a formal consequence of felony convictions under English common law that was practiced in some American states as late as the mid-twentieth century.[22] At a time when most felony convictions were punishable by death, civil death acted as an interim period between conviction and imposition of the death penalty during which the condemned's affairs could be put in order. Legal scholar Gabriel Chin notes that people with both felony and misdemeanor convictions may "remain subject to governmental regulation of various aspects of their lives and concomitant imposition of benefits and burdens," and argues that, while disenfranchisement places significant restrictions on legal personhood, it is the larger system of collateral consequences that should be viewed as an extension of civil death.[23]

While some collateral consequences may have negligible effects on legal personhood, such as the requirement in Florida to surrender equipment used for illegal fishing,[24] others have stark implications for how people convicted of crimes are entitled to rights and how they may exercise their rights—often in perpetuity. To take another example from Florida, Chapter 961 of the 2020 Florida Statutes outlines the circumstances under which a wrongfully convicted person will be made ineligible to receive compensation for their wrongful conviction. These include ever having been convicted of or pled guilty or *nolo contendere* to any violent felony in any jurisdiction, to two or more non-violent felonies, or to any violent felony during the period of wrongful incarceration, or serving a felony sentence concurrent to the wrongful conviction sentence.[25] These restrictions on who can collect compensation promote the kinds of practices that make people with felony convictions more likely to be wrongfully convicted in the first place, since, for example, police line-ups are almost always composed of at least some people who have been convicted of crimes, and often of crimes that are similar to the focus of the current investigation. These restrictions also ignore the overwhelming power of prosecutors to produce convictions through plea bargains by threatening to pursue more serious charges—an aspect of the American criminal justice system that UN special rapporteur on torture Nils Melzer calls "a coercive threat scenario that scares defendants into submission."[26] Thus, many people are convicted in the first place by way of threat, intimidation, or coercion, and people who are already in the system are more likely to be convicted again, since investigators consider them suspects in advance of any evidence. Restrictions like the ones outlined in Chapter 961 of the Florida Statutes not only make it impossible for people who have been wrongfully convicted under such circumstances to collect compensation but also remove one of the most important drivers of institutional reform in the United States—civil litigation resulting in monetary loss to the tortious party. In this case, it is not only that wrongfully convicted people are stripped of certain legal rights but that they lose a significant pathway to political participation—since pursuing justice in the civil courts is one of the principal means of effecting social and political change in the United States.

Among liberals, the debate about felon disenfranchisement, and about the appropriate punishment for criminality more broadly, is fundamentally about whether the loss of rights is an appropriate sanction for those who have violated the social contract.[27] But in addition to the question of the appropriateness of such sanctions within a liberal legal order, the system of collateral consequences that exists alongside court-imposed sentences makes the terms of the social contract extremely opaque for people convicted of crimes. Disenfranchisement, as well as some forty-five thousand other collateral consequences of conviction codified in state and federal law, are not considered punishments within the liberal legal framework. Instead, the courts have ruled, albeit with exceptions, that they serve a public safety, regulatory, or preventive function rather than a punitive one.[28] As such, people convicted of crimes may be caught in a web of sanctions—sanctions that fundamentally alter their relationship to the state and their exercise of rights and political activity—that are (often) arbitrarily imposed, difficult or impossible to know in advance, and whose purpose and function are both legally and practically opaque. Such a system not only makes the terms of the social contract incomprehensible for those convicted of crimes; the terms of the social contract and the role the law plays in securing them are, under such a system, also obscure to the broader public.

From the earliest days of American statehood, the terms of the social contract have always been negotiated at least partially within the
criminal justice and penal systems. When the world's first penitentiary
opened in Philadelphia in 1829, it replaced a series of colonial era jails
that had functioned as temporary holding sites for criminals await-
ing corporal or capital punishment. Proponents of the penitentiary
model believed that the penitence it would inspire through isolation
and reflection would rehabilitate the convict who had broken the social contract such that he could eventually return to society as a full
citizen. The penitentiary was not only central to shaping the terms of
citizenship for those who committed crimes. It was also a product of
the longer-standing negotiation of the Enlightenment era social contract during the American colonial period and early statehood. For
many eighteenth- and nineteenth-century prison reformers, for whom
the penitentiary was an expression of universal humanism, the treatment of prisoners was an index of society's deepest values and ambitions, and the abusive and inhumane treatment of prisoners during the
early days of the republic was seen as a reflection of the monarchical
despotism the United States was meant to transcend.[29] Political debates
about transgression and punishment are therefore not simply a matter
of determining what the appropriate treatment of criminals should be.
Rather, they play a central role in defining what social norms are and
what the terms of citizenship and social belonging ought to be. There
has not been a time in American history when these terms have been
conclusively defined or completely transparent, but the increasingly
complex, arbitrary, and bureaucratic administration of collateral consequences in the late twentieth and early twenty-first centuries makes
understanding the terms of citizenship and social belonging extremely
difficult, both for people convicted of crimes and for the broader public.

... To Policy-and-Order

As a legal term of art, collateral consequences refer to those consequences of a criminal conviction imposed by the state. But the actual
consequences of a criminal conviction are far greater in number. One
legal scholar refers to those consequences that "[arise] independently

of specific legal authority" as informal collateral consequences. These include "the gamut of negative social, economic, medical, and psychological consequences of conviction."[30] In addition to the more general phenomenon of social stigma that is attached to a criminal conviction, there is a substantial range of material consequences imposed on people convicted of crimes by public and private institutions. It is not the courts, for example, that determine whether people with criminal convictions may occupy rental units in the private housing market or whether they can be employed at a private company. Individual realtors and employers make these decisions, often with the consent of or mandate from the state but with little or no public oversight. Increasingly, the gig economy is the default employer for millions of Americans unable to find or dissatisfied with traditional, full-time employment. People with criminal convictions of any kind may be temporarily or permanently banned from technology platforms like Airbnb, Task Rabbit, and Uber—making those who are in the most precarious positions in the traditional job market also unable to rent out an extra room in their own home, build Ikea furniture for a neighbor, or drive passengers in their own vehicle. While these activities are not illegal, the near-universal agreement to ban people with criminal convictions from these platforms makes such activities all but impossible.

Private sector banishments are perfectly consistent with the law, which does not view the criminal conviction as a legally protected category. They are also *ideologically* consistent with the law, especially as it relates to the courts' views on collateral consequences, since private employers, landlords, and technology platforms can banish people with any criminal conviction for any length of time they wish, without regard to factors such as the severity of the crime or how much time has passed since the commission of a crime or the completion of a court-mandated sentence. Private sector collateral consequences and their imposition, though, are much more opaque than those codified in law: individual companies' policies regarding whom to banish and for what length of time require no internal consistency; can be made by individuals or algorithms on either a case-by-case basis or on the basis of crime type categories or level of severity, the definitions for which are themselves developed internally and potentially on an ad hoc basis; and do not usually feature a process to contest or appeal company decisions.

Like laws barring felons from collecting compensation for wrongful convictions, privately administered collateral consequences shape the material and political realities of people convicted of crimes. In the private rental market, for example, many landlords deploy blanket bans—meaning that they will not rent to anyone with any criminal conviction. Some also pepper their leases with illegal clauses, including, commonly, one granting them permission to enter rental units for any reason and without prior notice. (I once protested about such a clause in a lease I was considering signing, and the agent had no qualms telling me why it was necessary: how else would the police be able to enter their properties without a search warrant?) On one hand, people with criminal convictions face (legal) discrimination in the private housing market such that we may be unable to find housing at all. On the other, renting an apartment—when we can—may mean consenting to invasions of privacy by our landlords or even warrantless police searches. While a renter's legal rights remain intact, regardless of criminal history, including both their Fourth Amendment rights and their rights under individual states' landlord-tenant laws, many renters, regardless of conviction status, do not have the financial or symbolic capital to pursue litigation when their rights are violated. Landlord-tenant law is a significant political issue in the United States because of the economic and political power imbalance between property owners and tenants. It is a political act to contest the terms of an illegal or unfavorable lease, but because landlords and property managers can ban renters with a criminal history in the very first instance, the material cost of this political activity—including homelessness, being remanded to a community corrections center, or returning to prison—may be too high to brook.

Private sector banishments—and the legal, political, and social impoverishments that accompany them—are made possible in large part by the consumer or commercial background report, an all-purpose risk assessment tool that usually includes information about arrests, convictions, and credit history. A key aspect of neoliberal social organization, the $4.3 billion consumer background report industry is a form of private risk management and discipline that is mandated by the state in the form of the Fair Credit Reporting Act (FCRA), which puts landlords and employers at legal risk when they fail to outsource their background investigations to private, FCRA-compliant companies.[31] Because the consumer background report transforms the criminal record into a commodity to be bought and sold on the open market, the criminal must be framed as a perpetual risk that can be mitigated by purchasing such reports. The risk assessment that the background report ostensibly enables allows potential employers and landlords to make moral determinations not about the past but about the future character, value, or productivity of potential employees and tenants.[32] The logic of collateral consequences in legislation and constitutional cases gives rise to the consumer background report as an ostensibly preventive rather than punitive mechanism, defining the convicted person as "someone likely to commit other kinds of crimes . . . because he has shown himself to be a person without 'respect for the law.'"[33] The person with a criminal record is considered a persistent risk to society, someone who is persistently ineligible for reintegration into society, and someone who should be persistently subject to shifting and arbitrary rules, regulations, exclusions, and banishments.

Even though, as the NICCC notes, "collateral consequences are scattered throughout state and federal statutory and regulatory codes and can be unknown even to those responsible for their administration and enforcement," collateral consequences imposed by the state are codified. Therefore, it is difficult but not necessarily impossible "to identify all of the penalties and disabilities that may be triggered by a particular conviction."[34] While it is at least possible to know what the court-imposed collateral consequences of a criminal conviction *may* be, for example by researching state and federal codes or, more recently, by accessing the National Inventory of Collateral Consequences of Conviction, it is not possible to know all of the many consequences that may be imposed by other, private, institutions. This is because private institutions may develop and implement policies affecting people with criminal convictions at any time, with no notice, and with no public oversight. While some institutions may develop clear and specific policies, others develop ambiguous ones or simply make decisions on a case-by-case basis; and while some institutions publish their policies, others may maintain them only internally. This opacity serves the interests of businesses because it allows them to determine the scope of community membership in apartment buildings, neighborhoods, workplaces, and the sharing economy, ultimately shoring up their symbolic, economic, and political power. This form of policy-and-order not only affects people who have criminal records but also shapes a broader cultural understanding of justice as an aspect of the neoliberal social contract.

SHIFTING GEOGRAPHIES OF JUSTICE

In Ruth Gilmore's formulation, the neoliberal state can be thought of as an "anti-state state." Anti-state, however, describes a rhetorical rather than real political project: the anti-state state is one that grows through its own rhetorical diminishment. Capitalists use the state to accomplish their goals, "to negotiate and guarantee currency and trade, ensure open markets, raise tariffs, seize oil fields, build infrastructure, regulate competition, educate workers, support retirees, open or close borders," while rallying against those aspects of the state that do not serve their interests. Thus, the capitalist state "achieves legitimacy through guaranteeing economic capacities for certain workers or capitalists."[35] Moreover, the transformation from liberal state to capitalist state or neoliberal state includes the definitional transformation of social problems into economic problems whose solutions, largely if not exclusively, can be found in the market. However, as Gilmore explains, neoliberal politicians "have no intention of shrinking the state." They have simply transformed the state into a mechanism for achieving their aims. Thus, the anti-state state is "a state that grows on the promise of shrinking."[36]

The growth of the neoliberal state has included massive expansions of the military, police, criminal justice system, and prisons, which are justified in part by the ideological precept that the free market can only function optimally within a society governed by law and order. However, insofar as these functions also lend legitimacy to the state, it is in the interest of the state to maintain a social climate in which crime can flourish. This climate includes the normalization of gun ownership and gun violence, which breed legitimate fear, paranoia, and hate, as well as the criminal justice and penal systems, which not only fail to prevent or reduce crime but in fact reproduce the conditions that are hospitable to crime and locking more people up: poverty, unemployability, homelessness, and exclusion from communities, social networks, and the spaces where political activity occurs.

These manufactured conditions are used to promote the idea that society requires an ongoing war on crime, the infrastructure for which includes, as Gilmore describes, "the continued proliferation of laws, courts, judges, bailiffs, law enforcement personnel, technologies of surveillance, helicopters, and . . . prisons."[37] But they are also used to position employers, schools, and businesses as instrumental partners in the project of maintaining law and order. Both on and off the job, Elizabeth Anderson observes, American workers are subject to authoritarian control exercised "irregularly, arbitrarily, and without warning." Employers "have the legal authority to regulate workers' off-hour lives as well [as their working lives]—their political activities, speech, choice of sexual partner, use of recreational drugs, alcohol, smoking, and exercise." If these kinds of restrictions were imposed by the government, she continues, "we would rightly protest that our constitutional rights were being violated. But American workers have no such rights against their bosses. Even speaking out against such constraints can get them fired. So most keep silent."[38]

Constitutional rights are predicated on limiting the power of the government to interfere with the exercise of individuals' freedom—not with limiting the power of private interests to interfere with the exercise of those freedoms. The Constitution is concerned with what happens in public life—in the courts, on public property, and within public institutions. It is not so much that the Constitution secures the right to political speech and assembly as that it guarantees the government will not interfere with speech or assembly in public. Such rights are not guaranteed in the privately-owned spaces of the corporate workplace, but neither are they guaranteed in the local sports stadium, the private hospital system, the Facebook news feed, or our own cars and homes—if we're members of "communities" like Airbnb or "sharing" our vehicles using platforms like Uber. Thus, it is not only in the workplace that people in the United States are subject to authoritarian control by corporations, which are increasingly figured as quasi-public bodies where rights, laws, responsibilities, and social norms are defined and negotiated.

The neoliberal state, moreover, now frequently mandates the private adjudication of legal rights, especially those enshrined in antidiscrimination law. As recent feminist scholarship has confronted, individuals adjudged and sanctioned by Title VII and Title IX offices, which are responsible for ensuring compliance with antidiscrimination laws, are almost always bound by non-disclosure agreements, making adjudicative processes, sanctions, and the violations themselves opaque or invisible. Writing about Title IX in higher education, Laura Kipnis argues that this opacity secures and strengthens administrative power: "As more of us get charged with newly invented crimes, more administrators get hired to adjudicate them, administrators whose powers blossom the more malfeasance they can invent to ferret out." This is not to deny the existence of sexual violence either on campus or in the workplace. Rather, for Kipnis, Title IX offices operate with little or no public scrutiny or oversight, and their success in combatting discrimination "is measured in increased accusations"—much like the success of the criminal justice system is measured in increased convictions. Ultimately, Title IX offices, like the prison, require more and more bad actors in order to sustain themselves, such that the "professoriate has been transformed into a sexually suspicious class—would-be harassers all, sexual predators in waiting."[39] These processes—which frame all individuals as potential criminals, but without the right to due process or access to the rules of criminal or civil procedure—not only have a chilling effect on discourse, as when discussing sexuality in the classroom can result in Title IX investigations, but fundamentally alter individuals' relationship to the state. They curtail the rights of individuals accused of illegality and crime, making it difficult or impossible for them to assert their rights or seek recourse from the state when their rights are violated.

Kipnis attributes these transformations to longstanding forms of sexual paranoia coupled with recent demands by the federal government, tied to funding, to adjudicate all instances of sexual misconduct. But what she calls the "vast, unprecedented transfer of power into the hands of the institution"[40] is also part of a longer-standing project that strips individuals of their rights in order to shore up the administrative power of individual disciplinary institutions. The prison disciplinary hearing, which, beginning in the 1960s, became the standard for adjudicating prisoner misconduct, likewise removes from public view not only institutional infractions, such as not standing for count or ripping a bedsheet, but what in other contexts would be considered crimes ranging from assault to rape and, less often, murder. Prison disciplinary hearings, like Title IX hearings, do not feature due process, and the standard of proof is a preponderance of the evidence—as determined by the administrator or administrators adjudicating each case.

The reduction of rights for both victim and accused, and the removal of crimes from the public sphere, make it a matter of course for institutions—whether prisons, universities, airlines, sports teams, or workplaces—to determine the scope of acceptable behavior and the punishment for unacceptable behavior. The form of punishment may be one reason that misconduct, illegality, and criminality are so easily conflated in these settings. Administrators cannot levy fines, order a perpetrator to pay restitution, or sentence someone to a prison term. The most severe penalty is severance from the community (through termination in the workplace, expulsion from the university, or doing a stint in solitary confinement in the prison). This is no punishment for forcible rape, but if forcible rape is reduced to misconduct, it may appear perfectly acceptable. Like the administrative adjudication of Title IX claims in higher education, which can conflate sexual harassment with sexual battery, assault, and rape, the corporate adjudication of misconduct conflates serious crimes like assault with misconduct and unruly behavior. These processes not only transform the professor with wandering eyes into a potential (or actual) rapist, as Kipnis fears, but can also transform the rapist into a professor with wandering eyes and, as seen in this book's opening vignette, the assaulter into an unruly passenger.

The transfer of quasi-judicial authority in the realm of civil rights also contributes to a reframing of the private institution as an appropriate body for policing and adjudicating all manner of behavior, including some criminal behavior, that takes place on the job and at school, in retail establishments, restaurants, sports stadiums, and airplanes. By framing potentially all behavior as institutional misconduct, institutions of all kinds are poised to act like governments—to punish bad actors, develop policies that function as law, and determine the scope of individuals' rights.

While private companies have no legal obligation to guarantee rights, they have been implicitly and explicitly authorized to promote and restrict political speech and behavior and to dictate the terms of political discourse.[41] In their recent exposé of Facebook's internal policy machinations, *New York Times* journalists Sheera Frenkel and Cecilia Kang highlight founder and CEO Mark Zuckerberg's obsession with the company's role in defining and administering legal rights like free speech. In the wake of Russia's 2016 election interference, Zuckerberg fashioned himself as a "wartime CEO" in much the same way American heads of state fashion themselves as wartime presidents, and the office space reserved for employees on the election interference team as the "War Room."[42] One company insider suggested, in Frenkel and Kang's words, that "Zuckerberg felt his company had more potential to change history than any country—with [its then] 1.7 billion users, it was now in reality larger than any country." But at the same time, one of Zuckerberg's repeated mantras was "company over country."[43] Zuckerberg's view, in other words, seems to be that Facebook should not be bound by the laws of any particular country but rather should be able to exercise the kind of sovereignty typically reserved for states.

Nor are companies like Facebook content simply to shape political speech and behavior. They rather have designs on becoming quasi-governmental bodies. In 2019, in a bid to develop its own cryptocurrency, Facebook, in partnership with a number of other private firms, created Libra Association. In its white paper, Libra Association articulates its plans to develop a "global financial infrastructure" that is "designed and governed as a public good."[44] While rhetorically framing itself as a public institution—indeed as a new form of decentralized government—Libra Association exclusively comprises private firms in payments (PayU); technology and marketplaces (Facebook/Calibra, Farfetch, Lyft, Spotify AB, Uber Technologies, Tagomi); telecommunications (Iliad); blockchain (Anchorage, Bison Trails, Coinbase, Xapo Holdings); and venture capital (Andreessen Horowitz, Breakthrough Initiatives, Rabbit Capital, Thrive Capital, Union Square Ventures). A single category for nonprofit and multilateral organizations and academic units involved in the project includes participation by Creative Destruction Lab, Kiva, Mercy Corps, and Women's World Banking.[45] This putatively new vision of a decentralized government is profit-driven, constituted by private firms that traffic in the rhetoric of labor rights while exploiting their workers' labor power, restricting their ability to participate in political activity, and managing their minute, everyday behaviors. These restrictions on political activity and degradations of legal personhood are in part how corporations can fashion themselves as legal persons, as the public, and as quasi-governmental bodies—those best positioned to respond to social, political, and economic problems.

Some aspects of the global neoliberal *economic* order may be on the wane, as historian Gary Gerstle has recently argued. The white working-class backlash against free trade, migration, and cosmopolitan values that characterized the Trump era, Gerstle suggests, was a "phenomenal wrecking force on American politics, on the Republican Party, and on the neoliberal order."[46] In recent years, conservative officials have indeed asserted their political power, including against large corporations. Florida Governor Ron DeSantis, for example, has taken steps to dismantle Disney's private government, which operates much like an autonomous municipality. Tellingly, these moves, which respond to the company's refusal to fall in line with DeSantis's anti-LGBTQ agenda, have been decried by progressives as state overreach. Like NPR media commentators who look to Nike and Apple to stand up to China, Democratic Party–style neoliberals view companies like Disney as partners in governance, and as the best hope for withstanding authoritarianism. Neoliberalism, then, is not just a right-wing movement, nor is it exclusively an economic order characterized by open markets and free trade.

Neoliberalism is also, in part, a moral project that is not incompatible with Trump-style ethnonationalism. As Wendy Brown has written, neoliberalism "aims to protect traditional hierarchies by negating the very idea of the social and radically restricting the reach of democratic political power in nation-states." From *Citizens United* to *Masterpiece Cakeshop* to *Burwell v. Hobby Lobby Stores*, the Supreme Court has ruled consistently in favor of businesses acting in accordance with their own moral agendas, framing them as the public and expanding their expressive and religious liberties and political power at the expense of legal and political rights for racial minorities, immigrants, women, and LGBTQ people.[47] Here, too, it is not only conservative jurists who hold such views. Florida state representative Anna Eskamani, a progressive Democrat, arguing in reference to DeSantis's Disney legislation that "government should not be weaponized to cancel one company because they expressed freedom of speech," endorses the view that corporations are entitled to constitutional rights on par with individuals, framing them as the public.[48] These expanded liberties are part and parcel of the policy-and-order society, which authorizes and mandates businesses to impose their own moral judgments and penalties on individuals deemed, in Milton Friedman's words, "not responsible."

From the Courtroom to the Boardroom addresses this interplay between the state and the corporation as they co-produce subjectivities compatible with the neoliberal social contract. The criminal conviction restricts the formal rights and obligations of citizenship, such as the ability to vote, hold public office, or serve on juries or in the military. It also restricts less formal, though no less important, activities of citizenship such as civic participation, the attainment of social and symbolic capital, and the ability to make claims on the state.[49] At the same time, the consumer background report industry, with a mandate from law, transforms the criminal record into a commodity to be traded on the open market. The perpetual criminal is through this process transformed into a product that can be circulated within the knowledge and service industries—among and between halfway houses, community corrections centers, job training programs, drug treatment facilities, and behavioral health clinics.[50] The circulation of criminal offenders as capital within these industries can be considered a "twin form," to use Foucault's framework, of the objectification and monetization of consumers in the digital economy. No longer clients or customers, users of Facebook and Google are its *products*, which they sell to advertisers. These two forms of productification are central to constructing and maintaining a social and political climate that is hostile to legal rights like due process and to democratic processes like making claims on the state.

Although this book draws on a number of intellectual traditions, including political and legal theory, critical race studies, prison studies, and criminology, it is primarily a work of cultural studies that examines how power is created, exercised, and articulated across institutions and discourses. This approach can "read" the law—a key site in which power is created, exercised, and articulated—as one aspect of culture, where culture is defined as the circulation of meaning and power. In this book, the law and impoverishments of the law under neoliberalism are understood to shape a shared cultural understanding about how society is and ought to be. While attentive to theories and theoretical treatments of neoliberalism, *From the Courtroom to the Boardroom* is concerned above all with culture as a site of shared meaning. It observes concrete manifestations of neoliberal rationality in public institutions, industry, and popular culture, and also how these cultures intervene in and transform law and public policy. I read a number of cultural texts—including laws, legal opinions, and prison handbooks and policies, but also corporate policies, the rhetoric of trade groups and professional organizations, and media and other popular discourses—to examine how public and private institutions craft a regime of neoliberal legality and securitization that shapes the way individuals define crime, justice, and citizenship, and how they participate in the process of justice.

Chapter 1 traces the trajectory of an increasingly privatized political landscape, showing how the criminal justice system was mobilized to craft the contemporary American state as a public-private partnership. Chapter 2 observes how, in addition to the criminal justice system broadly speaking, the administrative adjudication of criminal acts by prison administrators diminishes the legal rights and personhood of both perpetrator and victim, transforming the prisoner into a commodity to be circulated within the knowledge and service economies.

Chapter 3 addresses how the consumer background report industry exploits the ubiquity of the criminal conviction to traffic in the ideology of risk, crafting increasingly more people as perpetually threatening. Capitalizing on this ideology, employers and landlords, and their trade groups and professional organizations, frame themselves as quasi-judicial bodies not only capable of securing institutional and social security but also of determining the scope of individuals' rights. In chapter 4, Airbnb's criminal ban is used as a case study to examine how the sharing economy capitalizes on the production of risk and impoverishments of legal and political personhood effected through the combination of public and private technologies described in the first three chapters. The company's banishment policy is an example of how corporate entities are increasingly vested with the authority to determine things like the seriousness or severity of crimes and crime types and the post-sentence sanctions that people with criminal convictions should face, removing key political issues from the public sphere and shoring up the power of the boardroom to define the terms of the neoliberal social contract. Chapter 5 turns outward from the boardroom to public debates about the transgression of social norms and their punishment. By reading more traditional "culture wars" events alongside the ubiquitous use of home surveillance and the practices of web sleuths who conduct murder investigations from their home computers, it defines "cancel culture" as an aspect of neoliberal post-juridicalism —a way of imagining and pursuing justice by, for, and against the individual, but always in concert with those who have the power to impose sentence. Finally, a postscript reflects on how these new post-juridical techniques for adjudicating bad acts and punishing bad actors, in attempting to overcome the perceived deficiencies of the liberal state, actually rearticulate the failures of the state to secure justice.

1. An American Neoliberal Revolution

Journalist and activist Naomi Klein argues in her influential 2007 book *The Shock Doctrine* that since the 1970s disaster has been the catalyst for neoliberal restructuring across the developing world, and particularly in Latin America, beginning with Chile. As an economic advisor to Pinochet in the aftermath of his violent coup, Milton Friedman led the "Chicago School Revolution" in Chile, a "rapid-fire transformation of the economy—tax cuts, free trade, privatized services, cuts to social spending and deregulation."[1] This "experiment" was an unmitigated disaster for Chileans, who were already reeling from a coup and massive hyperinflation. It sent millions of people into even more extreme poverty and was a resounding success for American corporations, which extracted vast sums of wealth and natural resources from the country before abandoning it. The Chile experiment served as a model for restructuring Latin America—and ultimately Eastern Europe, Russia, and much of Asia—according to the principles of neoliberalism in the wake of political, economic, and natural disasters.

The 9/11 attacks would be the impetus for expanding the disaster capitalism model to the Middle East. The neoliberal restructuring of Iraq included dismantling and privatizing state-owned enterprises, as well as its agricultural sector. As Wendy Brown puts it, the bombing of seed banks Iraqi farmers relied on, a crisis manufactured by war, precipitated the entry of Western agribusiness. The introduction of Monsanto seed would lead to the same kinds of dependency, exploitation, and eventual land appropriation that can be seen across the developing world: "The US government handout of genetically modified seed in 2004 was like offering heroin to a desperate single mother out of a job, facing eviction, and despairing of the future. Not only did it promise relief, but the first bag was free. It permanently attached the recipient to the supplier, and the addiction was deadly—to sustainable Iraqi farming, Iraqi self-sufficiency, and even the farmers themselves."[2] For the United States, the war in Iraq was an opportunity to outsource military labor to private mercenaries and rebuilding to a network of private subcontractors.³ The result was a vast extraction of wealth from the Iraqi people, which was redistributed to multinational corporations with immediate ties to Vice President Dick Cheney and Secretary of Defense Donald Rumsfeld, among others with influential posts in government.

While 9/11 served as the impetus for war—a manufactured shock that would lead to the economic restructuring of Iraq in service of American business—it also presented the United States with a new opportunity to privatize and profit from its own military industrial complex. For Klein, 9/11 represented a state of emergency akin to those that had been exploited across Latin America, Eastern Europe, and Asia. As Americans reeled from the shock of disaster, they, too, would be more amenable to privatizing the military, public services, and disaster relief. The new class of political-corporate elites borne of the war in Iraq would apply the principles they learned there to New Orleans in the wake of Hurricane Katrina. A complementary web of private contractors and subcontractors would extract the wealth of New Orleanians, paying local workers pennies on the dollar of government contracts for disaster relief. In addition to privatizing disaster response, 9/11 was an opportunity to impose laws and policies giving the federal government broad powers to police and surveil its residents and to pursue new forms of imperialism and domination, both domestically and abroad.

Journalist Chris Hedges similarly argues that 9/11 led to the emergence of a surveillance state that would significantly reduce Americans' rights. In his interview with former attorney Lynn Stewart, Hedges describes "the collapse of the American court system and the rise of the post-constitutional era, in which the courts are used to revoke the constitutional rights of citizens by judicial fiat." Stewart was sentenced to ten years in prison for conveying a press release issued by her client, a Muslim cleric convicted of conspiracy in an aborted New York City bombing in the mid-1990s. Hedges describes the sentence of Stewart's client to life plus sixty-three years as a "judicial assault" that would form a trend in the treatment of Muslims by the courts after 9/11. Hedges and Stewart also suggest that in subsequent years this trend would spill over into the more general functioning of the criminal justice system.⁴ Post 9/11, "the federal government's heavy-handed orchestration of fear," especially in its prosecution of criminal cases, "has cowed the nation." Stewart "no longer believes the working class has the ability or consciousness to revolt."[5]

For Hedges, the American surveillance state began in earnest with the USA PATRIOT Act of 2001, which eliminated some of the most important remaining legal structures of liberal democracy: "The courts were perhaps the last institution that liberal reformers had faith in before they too fell victim to the demands of corporate power. There are no institutions left that provide the citizen with a voice."[6] This formulation provides a useful starting point for understanding the relationship between the state and the corporation under neoliberalism: the state is not dismantled but rather plays a central role in governing in the interests of capital, in accordance with the demands of the market, and many times in partnership with private interests, for example to collect data and conduct surveillance operations.[7] In fact, this is one of the primary functions of the neoliberal state: to manage the population through surveillance, policing, and detention. While promising to shrink, in Ruth Gilmore's formulation, the state extends its power significantly—but also selectively.[8] Where the state relinquishes its power, businesses and a privatized civil society are called on to manage society in their own interests.

A SLOWER-MOVING REVOLUTION

While Hedges and Klein are of the view that American neoliberalism is largely a feature of the post-9/11 landscape, there are more correspondences between the Chicago School Revolution in Chile and the somewhat slower-moving neoliberal revolution that gained traction in the United States in the 1970s. While the crises of neoliberalism and the justice system grew as the wars in Iraq and Afghanistan progressed, the wars on drugs, poverty, and crime that dominated the 1970s played a significant role in the transfer of political and economic power from the people and the state to corporations in subsequent decades. These wars, which were key drivers of mass incarceration, are often seen as a backlash to the rights and legal protections realized by

Black Americans during the civil rights era. Historian Julilly Kohler-Hausmann notes that criminal justice policy became a "key [site] in the ongoing renegotiation of the social contract raging in the post–civil rights era," while Elizabeth Hinton argues that "the expansion of the carceral state should be understood as the federal government's response to the demographic transformation of the nation at mid-century, the gains of the African American civil rights movement, and the persistent threat of urban rebellion."[9] Those who view carceralization through the lens of the economy likewise underscore how the various wars on drugs and poverty were wars on Black people and communities of color, and consider them antecedents to mass incarceration. They identify the bleak economic conditions of the mid-1970s—especially in urban manufacturing centers—as a chief catalyst for the prison's exponential expansion throughout the 1980s and 1990s. In this view, early prison expansion was driven by the need to contain and manage the large pool of newly unemployed laborers displaced from the manufacturing sector and was a major driver of what would become the American project of mass incarceration.[10]

The practices of the mid-1970s—militarization of local police forces, vast surveillance nets in urban centers, including within social welfare programs and agencies, and increasingly draconian criminal sentencing guidelines—were akin, though not identical, to the methods deployed in places like Chile during the Chicago School Revolution. While perhaps not designed for such a revolution, the American state's deployment of surveillance, terror, and the threat of real and social death debilitated people, stripping them of social, political, and economic capital and reducing their rights and obligations as citizens. The veritable police state that would come to organize America's large urban centers beginning in the 1970s produced fear, anxiety, and paranoia. It also exacerbated longstanding distrust of law enforcement among communities of color, reproducing and further entrenching well-established forms of both imposed segregation and self-isolation.[11] These transformations in policing and criminal justice did limit the rights of Black Americans and were undoubtedly part of a backlash against civil rights gains. However, the wars on drugs, poverty, and crime, and the system of mass incarceration that they undergirded in subsequent decades, would contribute to the consolidation of the neoliberal agenda and way of life. This process initially expropriated social, political, and economic capital from Black individuals, families, businesses, social institutions, and communities. Criminalization, but also other forms of racial subjugation, such as the neglect of public services and institutions in predominantly Black communities, effectively reduced the legal and political personhood of millions of people. It was not just, or even principally, the right to vote that the law-and-order state sought to diminish, but the conditions under which political speech and activity are made possible. These methods were palatable because they targeted Black and Brown populations and seemed to leave intact the political and economic power of whites.

The Chile experiment was therefore in some ways an extension or co-experiment of the experiment taking place in the United States, where the precipitating shocks were the social transformations borne of the civil rights era, ongoing Cold War conflicts, including the devastating effects of the American War in Vietnam, and the oil and manufacturing crises, which led to a period of deep economic contraction. Like Chileans in 1973, Americans in the early and mid-1970s were dealing with the shock of cultural and economic crises when the dismantling of America's social welfare system, mass criminalization, the privatization of many public institutions, and the ultra-liberalization of markets began taking place. However, the neoliberal transformation of a liberal democratic system of government and Keynesian economic system did not require fully dismantling either the state or the economy, as it did in socialist or communist countries whose economies were dominated by state-owned enterprises. Rather, the neoliberalism that emerged in the United States proceeded from the political and economic liberalism on which the country was founded. It was informed by and shared qualities with German ordoliberalism, a movement whose express purpose was to counter the type of authoritarianism that the nationalist socialism of the Nazi party represented. In Foucault's account, drawn in large part from the writing of F. A. Hayek, ordoliberals viewed Nazism almost exclusively through the lens of the economy, such that the fascist state was presented as an outgrowth of an attempt to maintain a planned economy. They suggested that because any planned economy would always encounter "basic economic errors," economic planning would always be fundamentally irrational. As a result, any state that attempted to maintain such an economy would "only be able to make up for the intrinsic error or irrationality of planning by the suppression of basic freedoms."[12] While Foucault maintains that American neoliberalism is endogenous to the United States, he suggests that, like German ordoliberalism, it developed in response to crisis, albeit of a different nature—namely to a crisis of political credibility beginning with the New Deal and extending into the Johnson, Nixon, and Carter administrations.[13]

Because liberalism was not adopted by the United States but rather served as its founding principle, the entire American political tradition is grounded in placing limitations on the state. Thus, the state "phobia" that characterized early ordo- and neoliberal theories—a phobia that initially congealed around expressions of authoritarianism such as Nazism—expressed a historical truth about American liberalism. However, against the backdrop of German ordoliberalism and its emergence in response to the planned economy of Nazi Germany, Foucault rarely mentions the relationship of American neoliberalism to the Cold War. He does address how ordo- and neoliberal state phobias intersect at planned economies, including that of the Soviet Union, but concerns about Soviet communism play a limited role in his discussion of a specifically American neoliberalism, where he places an almost exclusive emphasis on its proponents' relationship to Keynesianism and the historical trajectory of classical liberalism in the United States. While the 1970s do not mark a U-turn towards neoliberalism, the period's continuity with the post–World War II era is constituted not only by weak social democratic institutions that excluded or subordinated women and racial minorities but also by a significant bloc of pro-business, small-government, and expressly anticommunist conservatives.[14] The express goal of the neoliberalism exported to Chile from the United States—and eventually to many other South American and Asian countries—was to counter the socialist or communist planned economies of those countries. Anticommunist sentiment in the United States during the Cold War was one of the reasons that political and economic interventionism in the Global South was palatable to many Americans.

Anticommunist sentiment was also a significant reason that the early wars on drugs, poverty, and crime were palatable to many Americans. In conjunction with the foreign or external threat of destruction—either actual destruction by bombs or the destruction of an American way of life through invasion—the state crafted an internal communist threat beginning in the immediate aftermath of World War II through racialized propaganda that presented a correspondence between Blackness, drug addiction, poverty, and criminality. American anticommunist rhetoric as early as the 1950s began to shift away from the external threat of military attack and towards the threat of ideological invasion from within.[15] Even in the early twentieth century, "drugs attracted spiraling social and cultural anxieties about proper gender, sexual, racial, and class boundaries, since drug users and their incipient subcultures seemed to promiscuously cross borders of respectability, and became major signifiers of unstable identities and unrepressed social spaces."[16] By framing drug manufacturing and use as a foreign problem, "[early] narcotics restrictionists had tapped into deep nativistic undercurrents in the American tradition and justified punitive legislation."[17] During the Cold War, these anxieties were remobilized. Harry Anslinger, who led the Federal Bureau of Narcotics from its inception in 1930 until 1962, played a central role in targeting ostensibly foreign sources of narcotics within the United States. As the Cold War intensified, he took aim at the Italian American "mafia," which he asserted trafficked in drugs for communist enemies such as China and Korea.[18] Later, he focused on drugs ostensibly imported into the United States from communist Cuba, and on drug users who were racial and ethnic minorities and whose status as Americans was therefore already in question. The identities of drug users and what many conservative twentieth-century politicians considered "hyphenated Americans" were doubly unstable, supposedly making them susceptible to communist ideology.[19] In this way, drug addiction was a disease not in the medical sense but in the sense that the instability and susceptibility to communism that drug addiction signified could, if left unchecked, spread through the entire social body.

The vilification of drug users as those who transgress borders—and the rhetorical collapsing of drug use, criminality, communism, and

Blackness—was intimately tied to US foreign policy in Latin America. Among the complaints of Latin American officials during the 1980s was the United States' insistence on maintaining policies that foregrounded the supply side of the drug economy.[20] This insistence meant that the United States could wage various wars in Latin America in the name of limiting the supply of drugs entering the country, even if another, more central, purpose of these wars was to displace socialist or communist governments. According to the chain of logic that connected communism with drugs and drug addiction, these two purposes were in fact identical. Thus, the United States waged its drug wars on multiple fronts, both foreign and domestic, but always in the name of abolishing communism, among whose primary expressions were drug production, trafficking, and addiction.

On one hand, the neoliberal revolution that took place in Latin America, whose express purpose was to eliminate communism, was also deeply tied to American domestic policies that aimed to criminalize racial and ethnic minorities through a rhetorical joining together of drug addiction, communism, and non-white/non-American identities. On the other, American neoliberalism, as an evolving set of discourses and technologies, did not emerge purely as an organic response to a crisis of political credibility beginning with the New Deal. Instead, the New Deal was crafted as a political crisis by conservative politicians who attacked it "as the forerunner of American bolshevism."[21] American conservatives viewed the redistribution of wealth represented by New Deal policies as anathema to the American way of life—constituted by the private accumulation of wealth and risk mitigation—and as a precursor to the putative authoritarianism of communism. In order to avoid the redistribution of wealth, federal regulation of banks and securities, and worker protections that it defined as authoritarian, conservative politicians, many of whom were business owners and other wealthy elites, unironically subscribed to the authoritarianism of McCarthyism to root out communist ideology from the white, domestic, elite sphere—an authoritarianism that Milton Friedman, incidentally, decries, even though, he argues, targets of McCarthyism were protected by "the existence of a private-market economy in which they could earn a living."[22] At the same time, they enacted punitive, authoritarian legislation against drug addiction to control the ostensible spread of communist ideology among the domestic underclasses.

While these forms of authoritarianism waxed and waned throughout the Cold War, the expressly socialist politics of Black power movements in the 1960s provided additional impetus for punitive state action against Black people and communities. Beginning in the late 1960s, the prison increasingly came to be used to control popular rebellions and urban insurrections. For Jordan Camp, the "organic crisis of Jim Crow capitalism" gave rise to "structural unemployment, concentrated urban poverty, mass unemployment, and mass homelessness," all of which coincided with a dramatic increase in the US prison population.[23] Policing the crisis, however, in the classic formulation by Stuart Hall and colleagues, was not without historical precedent.[24] Angela Davis has examined how Blackness was policed in the immediate aftermath of the Civil War, noting how "southern states hastened to develop a criminal justice system that could legally restrict the possibilities of freedom for newly released slaves." The transition from the forced labor of slavery to the forced labor of convict leasing in the post–Civil War era was accomplished in part through the manufacture of moral panics about the criminality of Black people and in part through the criminalization of everyday behaviors transformed into indolence, vagrancy, and loitering.[25] As Alex Lichtenstein observes, convict leasing was an integral part of the postbellum agricultural industry as well as its emerging industrial economy: "In the South's coal and iron mines, railroad camps, brickyards, sawmills and turpentine camps, capitalists often relied on the forced labor of convicts as a spur towards industrial development."[26] For Michelle Alexander, the prison industrial complex of the 1980s and beyond is a direct descendent of slavery, the convict lease system, and Jim Crow, and the most recent iteration of social, political, and economic policies aimed at subordinating Black people.[27] While moral panics about crime and disorder have been key features of law-and-order discourses throughout American history, they were "the primary legitimating discourse for the expanded use of policing, prisons, and urban securitization in the state's management of social and economic crises" during the 1970s.[28] For Bruce Western and Katherine

Beckett, incarcerating the urban unemployed was one part of the solution to the economic contraction, loss of manufacturing jobs, and
high inflation that resulted from the oil and steel crises of the early and
mid-1970s insofar as it would remove a significant number of people—
namely Black people—from the workforce, consequently tightening
the labor market and increasing wages, especially for whites.[29] Thus,
from the perspective of policing and prisons, the governing rationality
of the US economy is not capitalism but racial capitalism.[30]

In her classic study of mass incarceration in California, Ruth Gilmore argues that the prison was one of the tools used to manage the
surplus labor pool that emerged in the wake of the 1970s financial crisis.[31] Incarceration served to tighten the labor market and remove the
surplus labor pool from unemployment numbers,[32] but a side effect
of this initial management was economic growth: prison building and
administration created jobs and, when successful, revived small-town
economies.[33] This side effect soon transformed into a "pattern of using carceral growth to resolve issues of political economic crisis and
resulting surpluses of land, as well as replacing lost industry and jobs."[34]
In the wake of these transformations, the prison industrial complex,
which is "bound up in matters of finance, electoral politics, land use,
racial ordering, labor deregulation, citizenship, gender governance,
and urban restructuring," has come to play a central role in the maintenance and reproduction of the capitalist economy.[35]

By 2013, Black people accounted for 13 percent of the overall population and 37 percent of the US prison population, and the imprisonment rate for Black women was twice that of white women.[36] While
3 percent of the American population has been to prison, 15 percent of
the Black adult male population has been to prison, and by 2010, one
in three Black men in the United States had a felony conviction.[37] Loïc
Wacquant has drawn attention to the paradoxical relationship between
neoliberal discourse promising small government and the staggering
bureaucratization that emerges alongside it, especially in policing and
criminal justice.[38] Others likewise argue that the expenditures required
to maintain a carceral state run contrary to neoliberal theory, "as does
the extraordinary level of state intervention into the lives of individuals that has occurred in many neoliberal countries in recent years."[39]

However, this is not strictly true, since, for neoliberals, one of the most important roles of government in capitalist societies is to maintain law and order in the service of an optimally functioning market. Moreover, the reduction of rights and the degradations of legal and political subjectivity that this increasing state intervention achieves are in part what makes neoliberal reforms and the maintenance of a neoliberal state and society possible.

The American prison is a project of racialized containment and wealth extraction, but it is also a project of terror. The post-9/11, Patriot Act–era surveillance state no longer denies that "we can be tortured or assassinated or locked up indefinitely by the military, be denied due process, and be spied upon without warrants."[40] But while post-9/11 legislation has formalized these processes in new ways, the criminal justice and penal systems have been used similarly as tools of terror—especially within communities of color—for much longer. In Gilmore's estimation, by the late twentieth century, "crime [had become] firmly established as a permanent problem, for which the solution is the continued proliferation of laws, courts, judges, bailiffs, law enforcement personnel, technologies of surveillance, helicopters, and other means of *domestic warfare*, including, of course, prisons."[41] By 2010, as many as 19 million Americans were living with a felony conviction,[42] and by 2012, the number of police records across American states and jurisdictions exceeded 110 million, or 44 percent of adults.[43] While this number likely includes some individuals with more than one police record, just over 91 million Americans were included in the Interstate Identification Index in 2016.[44] Nationwide, 10–11 million people are arrested each year, and in 2016, there were more than 6.5 million people under some form of criminal justice supervision.[45]

The state project of mass criminalization—not just incarceration—in the United States is a project of terror that appears to target a handful of unmanageable, racialized criminals while actually creating a national climate that is hostile to both social and political activity.[46] As Bernard Harcourt explains, also in reference to the post-9/11 era, state violence is not really "aimed . . . against a rebel minority—since none really exists in the United States—but instead it creates the illusion of an active minority which it can then deploy to target particular groups and communities, and to govern the entire population on the basis of a counterinsurgency warfare model."[47] This project, however, was also central to American neoliberal reforms. Neoliberalism is a process that required "[undermining] the institutions and rights which the working-class movement succeeded in establishing from the late nineteenth century onwards."[48] Post-1960s policing and penal policies were used to undermine those institutions and rights, "degrading the civic standing of those convicted of crimes, imposing limitations on their access to state benefits, employment opportunities, and civil and political rights."[49] Ultimately, a significant portion of these people would be transformed not into productive workers but into commodities to be traded within the knowledge economy. As Gilmore explains, "The expansion of prison constitutes a geographical solution to socioeconomic problems, politically organized by the state which is itself in the process of radically restructuring."[50]

NEOLIBERAL GOVERNANCE AND DISCIPLINE

As Foucault describes it, placing limits on the state is a central tenet of neoliberalism, but the reasons for these limitations differ substantially from the ones defined by classical liberalism. In classical liberalism, limitations must be placed on the state because individuals are thought to have rights that the state must respect. A similar principle operates with regard to the market: Within classical liberalism, the state is called on to respect the form and operations of the market, into which it is expected not to intervene. But within neoliberalism, the state's orientation towards the market transforms. The reason it must not intervene is because it cannot possibly apprehend the full scope of market relations. David Graeber puts it this way in relation to contemporary financial capitalism: the market, comprising "ultrasophisticated financial innovations [like] credit and commodity derivatives, collateralized mortgage obligation derivatives, hybrid securities, debt swaps, and so on," is "so incredibly sophisticated, that—according to one persistent story—a prominent investment house had to employ astrophysicists to run trading programs so complex that even the financiers couldn't begin to understand them."[51] In this myth, any state intervention into such a complicated system would surely have unintended, and disastrous, consequences. Instead, the state *must* intervene in any aspect of society that may prevent the market from functioning optimally.[52] For Foucault, neoliberalism posits a shift in causality regarding the economic issues that classical liberalism sought to resolve through market interventions, namely competition. Whereas classical liberalism viewed monopoly as an effect of the competition inherent to the market that as such required regulation, neoliberals try "to demonstrate that . . . the monopolistic tendency is not in fact part of the economic and historical logic of competition," but that it arises *because* of market interventions. In the German institutional framework of the 1950s, Foucault argues, this view resulted in a vast body of legislation, "the function of which is not at all to intervene in the economic field to prevent the economy itself from producing a monopoly, but whose function is to prevent external processes from intervening in and creating monopolistic phenomena."[53] American neoliberals agree: Friedman writes that "in practice, monopoly frequently, if not generally, arises from government support or from collusive individuals," rather than from the general structure of the capitalist economy.[54] The state's role, then, is not to manage the economy but to manage any aspect of society that might interfere with the optimal functioning of the market while never intervening directly in the market itself.

A similar principle operates with regard to individuals, who "become the correlate of a governmentality which will act on the environment and systematically modify its variables."[55] The new type of subject that social policy aims to promote is *homo oeconomicus*, which Foucault describes as "the subject or object of laissez-faire"—the subject who, like the market, must be left alone.[56] In contrast to the legal subject of right that formed the basis of the Anglo-American juridical order of the eighteenth and nineteenth centuries, the economic subject in the form of *homo oeconomicus* is not constituted by his relationship to rights. *Homo oeconomicus* is a subject of interest within a general framework that suggests "not only may each pursue their own interest, they *must* pursue their own interest, and they must pursue it through and through by pushing it to the utmost, and then, at that point, you will find the elements on the basis of which not only will the interest of others be preserved, but will thereby be increased."[57] The subject of interest, Foucault insists, is irreducible to the subject of right. Whereas the subject of right respects the (social) contract because he is obligated to, the subject of interest respects the contract because it is in his own interest. If a subject of interest existed as early as Hume, as Foucault suggests, it was subjecting this subject to empirical economic analysis—thereby defining him as someone whose action, spurred by his own interest, "has a multiplying and beneficial value through the intensification of interest"—that transformed him into *homo oeconomicus*.[58] Like the market itself, *homo oeconomicus* exists within a field of infinite, unknowable, and uncontrollable events and phenomena. For this reason, *homo oeconomicus* must be left alone to pursue his own interest. While the state should avoid intervening at the level of the individual subject, it must manage or govern society in a way that promotes competition among individuals and their pure pursuit of self-interest.

As a technique of government, neoliberalism promotes the view that "the population's wellbeing [is] intimately tied to individuals' ability to make market principles the guiding values of their lives, to see themselves as products to create, sell, and optimize."[59] In this way, some social theorists critical of neoliberalism have asserted that in contrast to the top-down penal discipline of the nineteenth and twentieth centuries, neoliberal discipline is adopted freely and willingly. Individuals removed from the realm of collective identity assert their individuality as a matter of self-branding as they become self-contained units of growth, competition, and enterprise.[60] Pierre Dardot and Christian Laval maintain that neoliberalism "enjoins everyone to live in a world of generalized competition; it calls upon wage-earning classes and populations to engage in economic struggle against one another; it aligns social relations with the model of the market; it promotes the justification of ever greater inequalities; it even transforms the individual, now called on to conduct him- or herself as an enterprise."[61] Because the logic of competition has imposed itself on every aspect of life, individuals-competitors are motivated by efficiency and productivity, which are the keys to success in the ultra-competitive marketplace. In order to be the most efficient and productive unit of individual enterprise one can be, in order to build and maintain a personal brand that can compete in an ever more competitive marketplace, individuals elect to *optimize* or *marketize* every aspect of their lives—from their health and their relationships to their aesthetic tastes and political beliefs. Optimization theorists, as they might be called, do not always contend that there is no coercion involved in individuals' choices about how to market themselves. On the contrary, coercion that begins with the market is no less coercive than coercion that begins with the state. But this form of neoliberal power, according to Byung-Chul Han, *appears* as freedom: The neoliberal subject chooses its subjugation and disciplines itself through "self-management workshops, motivational retreats and seminars on personality or mental training [that] promise boundless self-optimization and heightened efficiency."[62] As units of individual enterprise, we adopt strategies of optimization in order to succeed; for example, we elect to become fit because fitness is a trait that employers or clients value, and fitness will make us more desirable to employers or clients and more competitive in the marketplace.

A propensity to underscore the seemingly autonomous nature of subjective transformation corresponds to what some consider to be a dominant paradigm among critics of neoliberalism: to take for granted that one of its most salient features is a shrunken, increasingly impotent, and hands-off state, one that has been superseded by the private market and the free actors who operate within it. Others argue to the contrary that using an "analytical lens that mirrors a neoliberal logic of a market-dominated world misses the ways in which the restructuring of the state sets in motion a set of state practices and interventions that are not reducible to market actors."[63] Instead, the neoliberal state imposes its logics of competition, self-branding, managerialism, and efficiency, and it enforces the reduction of political participation in order to diminish the rights of individuals and guarantee the supremacy of a small class of wealthy elites.[64] People are "encouraged, educated, and hounded into using their autonomy in ways that bind them to the market."[65] Of course, many people may *elect* to optimize, to become fit in order to gain a competitive advantage, or they may strive to hit their step goal because their employer will reduce their health insurance rates or allow them to earn points that can be redeemed for Amazon gift cards or a new Fitbit. But if everyone "chose" optimization to gain a competitive advantage, there would be no need for health insurance providers to maintain expensive pricing schemes for smokers and those they deem overweight. Likewise, many people elect to optimize their credit score because financial literacy is a valuable and marketable commodity. But if everyone optimized their credit scores, banks would not need to punish those with lower scores by charging them higher interest rates on credit cards, car loans, and home mortgages, and landlords would not need to increase security deposits for so-called high-risk renters. However, where the private sector fails to incentivize optimization—acting in one's own interest—by either carrot or stick, the state is called on to intervene. For the most part, it should not do so at the level of the individual or his interests but only at the level of those fields of activity that might affect his ability or desire to act in his own best interest.

Gary Becker's theory of human capital provides a framework for this field of environmentalist intervention. For Becker, human beings are a form of capital whose difference from other forms of capital is that it cannot change states. Because the economic value of human capital is located within the body, human beings cannot move or sell off their assets, as it were, cannot divorce or separate (all or part of) their economic value from its persistent material state.[66] Becker proposes that government invest in human capital in the same way it invests in other forms of capital—namely by investing in infrastructure that supports its reproduction. In *Human Capital*, education is the most critical aspect of this infrastructure. Education produces a significant return on investment since, on average, those who are more educated earn more money. The wide adoption of Becker's theory of human capital in public policy has played a significant role in the transformation of educational institutions into labor market institutions. Whereas a liberal arts education was once thought to promote well-rounded citizenship in preparation for participation in civic life, since the 1970s and 1980s, the purpose of education increasingly has been to prepare students to earn as much money as possible in the capitalist marketplace so as to grow the national economy—to produce a return on the state's investment.[67]

Thus, much like Milton Friedman's government, which sells products and services to consumers, Becker's state is a shareholder in a corporation constituted by bodies-as-capital who are expected to increase the state-as-shareholder's wealth.[68]

It stands to reason that where investment in human capital through infrastructure fails to produce a return on investment, the state must also provide negative incentives, including criminalization. Laws may be enacted to criminalize certain forms of non-optimized behavior and incentive more optimized behavior. However, for Becker, the primary concern for governments in deciding which laws to enforce and punish, and to what extent, ought to be financial. Thus, states must conduct a cost-benefit analysis, the result of which will always be an optimal level of crime—one at which the financial costs of enforcement outweigh the financial costs of harm.[69] In theory, as Bernard Harcourt contends, Becker's model implies that all non-optimized behavior should be criminalized, so long as it is economically feasible:

> Any human behavior that can be efficiently regulated by means of the criminal sanction—by means of punishment properly applied—should be criminalized. If [Becker] had done that, of course, *all* domains of economic, social, political life would have been subjected to potential regulation. It opens all human activity to state sanction, including, well, anything. We can draw the list: infidelity, impoliteness, sexism, political protest, financial contributions to political parties—in sum, any activity could be subjected to the kind of analysis that [Becker is] proposing, and we would then know what should be criminal: that which you can efficiently regulate by means of the criminal law and punishment.[70]

Becker, however, counters that he is a "small government person," not because small government is necessarily better from an economic standpoint but because large government risks "overregulating society."[71] Although he proffers little defense against Harcourt's accusation that this assessment is ideological rather than economic, his ideology is consistent in two ways. First, many non-optimized behaviors, especially those that constitute manners or customs, are managed within the private sector through both positive and negative reinforcements. As Friedman puts it,

The widespread use of the market reduces the strain on the social fabric by rendering conformity unnecessary with respect to any activities it encompasses. The wider the range of activities covered by the market, the fewer are the issues on which explicitly political decisions are required and hence on which it is necessary to achieve agreement. In turn, the fewer the issues on which agreement is necessary, the greater is the likelihood of getting agreement while maintaining a free society.[72]

It is patently false, of course, to say that conformity is rendered unnecessary. In this formulation, conformity is obviously rendered through coercion, but it is rendered by the market rather than by the state. If it is not necessary to achieve agreement about political issues, this is not because political decisions are "covered" by the market but are made, determined by it. In this view, it is only by reducing the scope of politics —essentially transforming all political activity into either market-based behavior or corporate decision-making—that social cohesion is possible. In other words, an economic theory aimed at evaluating the costs and benefits of the state management and sanctioning of behaviors that fall outside the scope of the law is unnecessary because it is abundantly clear that in capitalist societies the population can be and is managed by market forces. Moreover, the market can and ought to manage not only behavior but political ideals, attitudes, and aspirations, reducing or eliminating the need for the public negotiation of complex political issues. Second, since society has been reduced to an assemblage of human capitals—essentially units of individual enterprise—overregulating society is tantamount to regulating the market, which is antithetical to the pursuit of self-interest. Because the state is blind to the totality of economic processes that drive the behavior of individuals-as-capital, it should only intervene in the general field in which their decisions are made.

Workfare policies act within this field, ideologically if not practically, by providing incentives for those who fail to act in their own best interest by mandating participation in job training or rehabilitation schemes that ostensibly make them more desirable on the job market. These can be seen as environmental interventions because participants are ostensibly "free" to opt out—even though the cost of opting out, such as the loss of welfare benefits, may be so high as to make it no choice at all. On the other hand, however, the non-optimized class and the public and private schemes developed to govern and manage them are also, importantly, profit-generating. Smokers and people labeled obese generate revenue for insurance companies and private hospitals, and so-called high-risk renters, home buyers, or vehicle owners generate revenues for lenders in excess of their optimized counterparts. The job training and rehabilitation schemes that constitute workfare are often owned and operated by private enterprises or nonprofit organizations whose executive employees are paid sometimes exorbitant salaries. Because individuals and companies stand to profit from the management of the non-optimized classes, "full optimization" in the ultra-free marketplace, like full unemployment in the national economy, has in fact proven to be less than economically ideal.

Management of the non-optimized represents a particular type of profit-generating governmentality under neoliberalism. For Foucault, *homo oeconomicus* not only corresponds to neoliberal economic principles but "[enables] an art of government to be determined according to the principle of the economy, both in the sense of political economy and in the sense of restriction, self-limitation, and frugality of government."[73] Because the state is blind to the totality of the market, and because *homo oeconomicus* is blind to the effects of his actions, "the collective good must not be an objective" for either, since "it cannot be calculated, at least, not within an economic strategy."[74] For the state, this means that aims such as economic equality based on race or gender are not appropriate. This is not to say that neoliberal economists promote racial or gender discrimination as a matter of policy. In fact, they may consider these suboptimal insofar as they reduce human capital accumulation.[75] Nevertheless, as Foucault describes it, the state's role for neoliberals is not to allocate resources to those disadvantaged *because* of racial and gender discrimination. This would be an overstepping of the state's role: Since it ostensibly cannot know the causes of inequality, it cannot intervene in that cause to provide solutions. Instead, a free marketplace of individuals pursuing their own interests is the corrective since the market should determine the optimal distribution of resources. Indeed, as Becker concludes in *The Economics of Discrimination*, more competitive markets tend to be less discriminatory, and thus one solution to the suboptimal effects of racial and gender discrimination is freer, more competitive markets. Of course, for capitalists more generally, economic (if not racial or gender) inequality is not a bug but a feature of the capitalist economy, and the downward transfer of wealth should only be considered in matters of bare survival. This, for Foucault, "is not a matter of maintaining purchasing power but merely of ensuring a vital minimum for those who, either permanently or temporarily, would not be able to ensure their own existence."[76]

In place of a state that ensures a certain level of subsistence, what emerges within the capitalist marketplace is a series of organizations—including philanthropic and nonprofit organizations, but also for-profit enterprises—that ostensibly seek to produce this same effect. Foucault calls this form of social organization civil society, which is a governmental technology that responds to "the heterogeneity of the economic and the juridical," a solution to the problem of governing when "the juridical structure (*économie juridique*) of governmentality is pegged to the economic structure (*économie économique*)."[77] Foucault explains that civil society under neoliberalism is not the same civil society that existed in the eighteenth and nineteenth centuries—namely "a society characterized by a juridical-political structure."[78] Rather, under neoliberalism, the economic "[lodges] itself" within civil society, and civil society comes to "[serve] as the medium of the economic bond."[79] As Miguel Vatter explains, "By deregulating civil society, neoliberalism seeks to further unleash its 'natural' dynamics in the name of the liberty of enterprise."[80] If neoliberalism is "a technology of government whose objective is its own self-limitation insofar as it is pegged to the specificity of economic processes," then civil society is a transactional reality correlate to this technology.[81] "Civil society," according to Foucault, "is the concrete ensemble within which these ideal points, economic men, must be placed so that they can be appropriately managed. So, *homo oeconomicus* and civil society belong to the same ensemble of the technology of liberal governmentality."[82]

PRISONS, PROFITS, AND
PUBLIC-PRIVATE PARTNERSHIPS

Under neoliberalism, the purpose and function of the criminal justice system and the prison begin to transform to suit—and to facilitate—these transforming modes of civil society. The modernist prison, the one described by Foucault in *Discipline and Punish* and in his lectures on the punitive society at the Collège de France in 1972–73, is intimately bound to the consolidation of the capitalist form. Because the employer has purchased the worker's labor power with wages, that employer comes to consider the worker's body to be his property, over which he has authority. Beginning in the nineteenth century, "it is always the worker's body in its relationship to wealth, to profit, to the law, that constitutes the major stake around which the penal system will be organized."[83] This conflation of the worker's labor power with his body, and the need to control that body, necessitates an "apparatus that is sufficiently discriminating and far-reaching to affect . . . the worker's body, desire, need."[84] The penal system was such an apparatus designed to discipline the body, desire, and need in ways that conformed to contemporary modes of capitalist production. The neoliberal prison transforms such that it is no longer committed to disciplining criminals into productive workers but rather to removing them from the ranks of the working class and transforming them into objects to be managed by new profit-generating industries in the knowledge and service economies.[85]

Prison expansion during the 1980s resulted in economic revitalization for some towns, as Gilmore argues, but as carceral growth emerged as an express goal for local, state, and federal jurisdictions, massive prison expansion became the basis for another economic growth sector, what Douglas Thompkins calls the prisoner reentry industry—a series of nonprofits and private companies providing services to the formerly incarcerated.[86] While Craig Willse's focus is on homelessness rather than incarceration per se, he shows how a whole range of corporate, philanthropic, and nonprofit enterprises have emerged to profit from the management of a permanent underclass manufactured through processes like mass incarceration and criminalization, but

also through housing courts, whose purpose, he argues, is "to desta-
bilize and destroy the lives of poor tenants and to protect the wealth
and immunity of landlords and developers."[87] The formerly incarcerated, people with substance use disorders, poor people, and people experiencing housing insecurity are "served" by job training programs,
homeless shelters, drug treatment facilities, community corrections
facilities, and halfway houses, all of whom profit from the exclusions
manufactured by mass incarceration.[88] Even when nonprofits or the
public sector provide these services, both private contractors and employees profit from the revenues generated by the industry, and the
public sector extracts wealth from this class of people through public-
private partnerships. The "services" provided by the organizations that
aim to put so-called chronically underemployed people, ex-offenders,
and people experiencing homeless "back to work" are often job training
schemes that require so-called clients to gain "work experience." The
public-private partnership in job training sometimes includes putting
people to work in the public sector—for example in trash collection—
where the local government pays the service provider rather than the
worker, in this case the job training "client," extracting the labor of the
worker and the wealth of taxpayers at the same time.[89]

If neoliberalism enjoins (normative) individuals to optimize or
marketize themselves, it also transforms "every human need or desire into a profitable enterprise, from college admissions preparation
to human organ transplants, from baby adoptions to pollution rights,
from avoiding lines to securing legroom on an airplane."[90] Moreover,
neoliberalized states "substitute individually debt-financed education
for public higher education, personal savings and interminable employment for social security, individually purchased services for public
services of all kinds, privately sponsored research for public research
and knowledge,"[91] and private sector philanthropy and public-private
partnerships for public welfare. For entrenched social problems like
poverty, homelessness, crime, and drug addiction, the efficiency of
corporations driven by profit and unrestrained by health and safety
standards, worker protections, and other regulations are proffered as
market-based solutions grounded in private sector best practices.

Brown argues that "best practices stand for value-free technical knowledge validated by experience and consensus, where the alternative is not only tradition or mandate, but partisanship and contestation over purposes, values, and ends." Best practices not only respond to the neoliberal demand to eschew politics but also create one of the conditions under which political problems can be subsumed under the rubric of corporate expertise: They "connote both expertise and neutrality; they emerge from and cite research, as well as frame it. Their authority and legitimacy is corroborated through replacing rigid rules and top-down commands with organically gestated procedures validated by experience and success." The result is not merely that best practices are apolitical, as they claim to be, but that they "constitute an antipolitics and thereby construct a particular image of the political."[92] Indeed, "it is through carrying market values while claiming only to be [technical or neutral] techniques that best practices promulgate certain norms and foreclose arguments about norms and ends."[93] Best practices for responding to homelessness, for example, which often include mandated drug and alcohol treatment, psychological counseling, and job training or work acquisition, are grounded in implicit normative claims about the causes of homelessness and the social, political, and economic value of people experiencing homelessness. Yet, as best practices, they foreclose the possibility of assessing the historical, social, economic, and political bases for those norms.

Corporate philanthropy and public-private partnerships give the appearance of public projects being funded with private wealth (even though corporate contributions may be much less than what they advertise). But when private companies are deemed responsible for responding to homelessness, poverty, or public health crises, public debate and negotiation about such issues can be reduced and replaced by corporate decision-making. The public-private partnership not only shifts the burden of financing public projects to the private sector; it also shifts the burden of designing and implementing these projects, subjecting them to the same kinds of ostensibly neutral expertise and algorithmic logic developed in the corporate boardroom—expertise and logic used to surveil, mine data, sell products, and modify consumer behavior—and reframing the boardroom as the public and as the site where political activity is best exercised.

From the perspective of the neoliberal worldview—one inspired by neoliberal theories although not necessarily contained within those theories themselves—the state has failed to secure the conditions for a functioning society, and neither government, nonprofits, nor other non-governmental organizations have the resources to respond to structural challenges like crime, homelessness, poverty, or the opioid crisis: "Nation-state sovereignty has been undercut . . . by neoliberal rationality, which recognizes no sovereign apart from entrepreneurial decision makers (large and small), which displaces the legal and political principles (especially liberal commitments to universal inclusion, equality, liberty, and the rule of law) with market criteria, and which demotes the political sovereign to managerial status."[94] As a result, corporations are fashioned (by themselves, as well as in hegemonic popular and policy discourses) as the only remaining entities thought to possess the resources and expertise necessary to respond to the structural issues they have manufactured. The political sovereign, in its managerial function, is tasked mainly with ensuring that these corporations continue to operate unimpeded by regulation or the burden of taxation.

Beyond the simple fact of prioritizing corporate wealth over public interests, the redistribution of wealth from American taxpayers to private defense contractors and Fortune 500 companies is one reason that the state lacks the resources to respond to a range of social problems, from public health crises to homelessness. One notable exception to this prioritization occurred in Salt Lake City, which in the mid-2010s was regularly making national headlines for reducing homelessness by more than 90 percent. In 2005, Utah had adopted its "Housing First" policy, which, simply put, provided homes to people experiencing homelessness—regardless of whether they worked, used drugs, or had a disability. The initiative—which ignored neoliberal best practices such as forcing people into work or ejecting them from public housing for using drugs—by most accounts, was working. Because the program faced funding cuts, its implementation has slowed, and homelessness has been on the rise again since 2018. This manufactured lack of funding, despite public projects that succeed by ignoring the best practices, is one reason for the popularity and acceptance of the public-private partnership.

In the San Francisco Bay Area, the housing crisis—partly caused by the massive economic growth of the technology sector and rising wages of tech workers—has flummoxed local and state governments. The cost of living in the Bay Area has skyrocketed over the last twenty years, and both government officials and nonprofits have been at a loss about how to respond to the poverty and homelessness accompanying that growth. Between 2012 and 2017, employment in San Francisco grew by 373,000 jobs while only 58,000 permits were issued for new housing units. Governor Gavin Newsom in 2019 proposed building 3.5 million new housing units by 2025. With California averaging 80,000 new units annually, his proposal would require the state to increase its output almost nine-fold. Early in the same year, Google presented its own plan to spend $1 billion to build 20,000 affordable homes in the Bay Area. If Facebook's revenue in 2018 was a mere $56 billion, Google's $136 billion matched that of the state of California, while Apple's revenue was nearly twice that. The tech companies that proliferate in the Bay Area take credit for job growth and rising wages but are less keen to take responsibility for uneven economic development, vast income inequality, and the housing crisis. Nonetheless, given the manufactured impotence and financial straits of local municipalities, these companies have positioned themselves as the best hope for solving social problems. After all, "these are companies—they're hugely powerful. They're hugely popular. If they can't [do it], who can?"[95] Rather than pay taxes, which under ideal circumstances might provide the basis for a public response to the housing crisis, companies like Google seek to replace their tax burden with philanthropic activity. The $1 billion Google committed to spending on affordable housing sounds in press releases like a number worthy of praise while representing far less than its tax burden should be. But Google did not spend $1 billion. By November, it had donated $850,000 to the nonprofit group Hamilton Families, which runs an emergency shelter and helps place families in permanent housing.

In the same way that the Bay Area housing crisis was instigated by the exponential growth of the technology industry, the American opioid crisis is a public health disaster instigated by big pharma and the profit-driven medical industrial complex. Executives of Purdue Pharma first pleaded guilty to misleading regulators in 2008, since which time its owners, members of the Sackler family, have withdrawn almost $11 billion from the company—much of which has been moved offshore. In 2020, the company pleaded guilty to three federal felonies related to how it marketed and distributed OxyContin and admitted to defrauding officials and paying kickbacks to doctors to boost sales.[96] Despite evidence that members of the Sackler family, as well as other employees of the company, were involved in this criminal misconduct, no individuals were implicated in the 2020 ruling. Thus, the company itself is framed as a legal person while the legal personhood of the individuals who own and manage it is nullified. And when corporations are fashioned as the public—in all its senses—they are poised to intervene to ameliorate the social devastation they have caused, using the same ostensible neutral and technical expertise they deploy to increase profits.

In negotiations with the Justice Department, Purdue capitalized on this framing, proposing to transform itself into a quasi-public organization whose profits—which would continue to come from opioid sales—would be used to ameliorate the opioid crisis. Amid the massive opioid litigation against pharmaceutical companies like Purdue beginning in the 2010s, evidence has also come to light that government regulators and the Drug Enforcement Agency did little to stem the tide of overprescribing that began in the mid-1990s. The lack of political will to regulate or place limits on the power of the pharmaceutical industry would later be combined with a lack of resources and expertise among state and federal governments to combat the public health crisis that resulted from it. As a result, it is left to the private medical industrial complex and public-private partnerships to deploy their own expertise to treat the symptoms of an underlying structural problem they continue to profit from.

While the opioid crisis has cost the public billions of dollars, it has generated billions of dollars for the private healthcare industry, and especially for the addiction treatment sector. Acadia Healthcare, for instance, is, according to its website, "the largest provider of behavioral healthcare services in the world," "[owning and operating] treatment facilities in nearly 600 cities throughout the United States, Puerto Rico, and the United Kingdom." Acadia runs more than one hundred methadone clinics, which it purchased in 2014 from Bain Capital, the private equity firm and brainchild of Mitt Romney. As with military contracts, past, present, and future government officials make and profit from the financial and business decisions of banks, private equity firms, and profit-driven medicine—at the same time they are writing and enacting legislation that ensures their profitability. Acadia's annual revenue grew from $49 million in 2009 to $3.1 billion in 2019, partly because of legislation requiring health insurance companies to provide coverage for behavioral health, including addiction, on par with its coverage for physical health. While this kind of parity is the least bad option in a profit-driven healthcare system, it created the opportunity for companies like Acadia to exploit addiction.

The near total medicalization of addiction treatment during the same period essentially destroyed alternative treatment paradigms that don't conform to the best practices of neoliberalized medicine, which is constituted almost exclusively by medication assisted treatment (MAT), which consists of prescribing opioids to opioid addicts in a clinical setting. This ostensible cure for addiction is explicitly lifelong, since MAT drugs—like methadone, buprenorphine, and Suboxone —can be significantly harder to kick than heroin. MAT does not stem the tide of addiction because it isn't meant to. It is designed to keep addicts addicted to opioids—ones that the medical industrial complex can sell to them. All the better if the payment for this addiction treatment can be extracted from taxpayers at inflated prices under a private, profit-driven health care system. Within the medical model of addiction, it seems not to matter whether addicts, whom executives at one major opioid distributor have referred to as "pillbillies,"[97] are addicted to Oxycontin, fentanyl, Suboxone, or methadone—only that their use of heroin doesn't interfere with their use of profit-generating pharmaceuticals.

Housing insecurity and drug addiction are overlapping crises affecting the same populations, which provide sustenance for both the penal system and the knowledge and service economies. The American jail has long been a means of managing members of the underclass—the "disreputables," "petty hustlers," "derelicts," "junkies," "outlaws," and "crazies," to name a few.[98] Beginning in the 1950s and 1960s, jails increasingly came to serve a variety of functions that were previously served, and would be best be served, by other public institutions: "as a drunk tank, short-term mental ward, truant hall, and holding facility for people who cannot be placed elsewhere."[99] From the perspective of profit, the criminal justice system's ability to destroy the livelihood, legal personhood, political will, and economic value of those it incarcerates, keeping them locked in cycles of addiction and homelessness, is part of the economic lifeblood of the private medical industrial complex. And the medical industrial complex, which correspondingly medicalizes the social and subjective suffering resulting from incarceration and wealth expropriation constitutive of carceral capitalism, closes the circle—ensuring that the poor and drug addicted remain addicted and continue to cycle through the criminal justice system and service providers in the adjacent knowledge economy. As Micol Seigel describes it, the "state and the market are so deeply intertwined as to be in practice and in essence inextricable."[100]

If the criminal justice system broadly speaking serves to degrade the civic standing of people convicted of crimes in order consolidate the wealth and political power of corporations and corporate elites, the prison itself also crafts a particular kind of degraded legal and political personhood. Once in prison, most of an inmate's existence is subject to and dictated by little more than administrative policy. Individual prisons' policies dictate what she can purchase and consume, how her speech and behaviors are monitored and policed, whom she can visit and speak to on the phone, and what services she is entitled or conscripted to, such as parenting classes or drug and alcohol treatment. More, these policies also dictate how guilt and innocence are adjudicated and punished, both for institutional and, in many cases, criminal infractions. In the prison, guilt and innocence are determined by administrative rather than legal procedure, outside the purview of the courts and out of public view.

The next chapter draws a historical and geographical line between the legal gray zones of post-9/11 terrorist detention at Guantánamo Bay and other colonial jurisdictions to examine the role of the domestic prison disciplinary procedure in reducing legal and political personhood within the United States. The administrative adjudication of criminal acts by prison administrators diminishes the legal rights of both perpetrator and victim, shaping them both into partial citizens compatible with the neoliberal economy. Moreover, determinations about what constitutes criminal behavior, criminal liability, normative behavior, and legal personhood are an index of public values. When administrative reasoning and judgment replace judicial reasoning and judgment, ostensibly public values are shaped by prison administrators whose interest is not to uphold the law but to maintain an institutional status quo. These trends—removing individuals from the public and effecting reductions in their legal and political personhood—contribute significantly to reframing the corporation as the best site to respond to social, political, and economic problems.

2. Adjudicating Guilt, Innocence, and Citizenship in the Neoliberal Prison

In the 1972 case of *Haines v. Kerner*, the petitioner, Francis Haines, a prisoner at Illinois State Penitentiary at Menard, claimed that his due process rights were violated when he was placed in solitary confinement after assaulting another inmate with a shovel.[1] The Supreme Court in *Haines* echoed the district court's previous finding that "only under exceptional circumstances should courts inquire into the internal operations of state penitentiaries," and the appeals court's finding that "prison officials are vested with 'wide discretion' in disciplinary matters." In fact, the only reason the Supreme Court heard the case at all was because the lower courts had failed to allow Mr. Haines to present evidence about the injuries he claimed he sustained while in solitary confinement.

In 1974, Robert O. McDonnell, an inmate of what was then the Nebraska Penal and Correctional Center, filed a class action lawsuit claiming that the institution's disciplinary proceedings violated prisoners' due process rights. Among the disciplinary measures the prison had taken was to reduce the good-time credits inmates had earned, which would have entitled them to early release. The Supreme Court agreed with McDonnell that the state of Nebraska violated the Fourteenth Amendment but held that prisoners are not entitled to full due process protections: "A prisoner is not wholly stripped of constitutional protections, and though prison disciplinary proceedings do not implicate the full panoply of rights due a defendant in a criminal prosecution, such proceedings must be governed by a mutual accommodation between institutional needs and generally applicable constitutional requirements."[2] In the Court's opinion, inmates should be allowed to call witnesses and present evidence, as long as doing so does not impinge on institutional safety or correctional goals. Because prison administrators are the sole arbiters of what constitute institutional safety and correctional goals, the Court's ruling, while upholding prisoners' partial rights to due process in the abstract, all but eliminated them in practice. Justice Thurgood Marshall dissented, claiming that the constitutional protections of presenting evidence and calling witnesses are absolute. Justice William Douglas agreed that due process protections are especially urgent for prisoners, who are already substantially deprived of liberty.

The partial rights established by the Supreme Court in *Wolff v. McDonnell* were a vast improvement over the Thirteenth Amendment, which abolished slavery, except for criminals: "Neither slavery nor involuntary servitude, except as a punishment for crime whereof the party shall have been duly convicted, shall exist within the United States, or any place subject to their jurisdiction." And they were also a vast improvement over the Virginia Supreme Court's ruling of 1871 in *Ruffin v. Commonwealth*, which established that a prisoner, "as a consequence of his crime, not only forfeited his liberty, but all his personal rights except those which the law in its humanity accords him. He is for the time being a slave of the state."[3] Due to prisoners' historical status as slaves or objects of property, due process and other constitutional rights have been the object of considerable attention among legal and prison studies scholars. Academic and popular discourse has tended to center on the right of prisoners to be free from cruel and unusual punishment administered by the state, and analyses of due process protections have centered on the rights of inmates to bring civil lawsuits and defend themselves during criminal trials. Except in the case of sexual assault, the legal rights of prisoners who are victims of crime have often been neglected, in part because so few infractions are charged as crimes. This is in stark contrast to the criminal courts, where victims' rights are both privileged and codified in law.

This chapter examines how the administrative adjudication of criminal acts by prison administrators diminishes the legal rights of both perpetrator and victim, fashioning them as quasi-citizens destined to become clients in the knowledge economy. It frames this practice as part of a longer tradition in American law in which some people are relegated to legal gray zones: geographies where the courts cede their jurisdiction and the law does not apply in full. The prison, therefore, and its adjudicative processes in particular, can be seen as an antecedent and significant contributor to the neoliberal policy-and-order society.

CARCERAL-LEGAL GRAY ZONES

In early January of 2002, twenty suspected 9/11 conspirators arrived at the US naval base at Guantánamo Bay, Cuba. Guantánamo Bay was not designed as a prison camp, and the early detainees were housed in open-air cages. Less than four months later, Camp Delta had been erected. Modeled after high-security prisons in the United States, the facility would eventually consist of nineteen cellblocks, each of which contained forty-eight cells. In the twenty years that the naval base has been used as a prison for suspected terrorist conspirators, more than eight hundred people have been detained there. The abuse and torture of prisoners at Guantánamo were made possible in part because of its location. The Bush administration claimed that because the base was situated in Cuba, the United States lacked formal sovereignty, and as such, the laws of the United States were not applicable to the prisoners being held there. Donald Rumsfeld notably argued that they also did "not have any rights under the Geneva Convention."[4] By relinquishing its sovereignty, the Bush administration could claim that "it can do whatever it wants there, and the military can act with impunity to brutally control every aspect of prisoners' lives."[5]

Amy Kaplan situates the rhetorical and legal positioning of Guantánamo's exceptionality and its geography as a kind of legal black site as part of a long history of American empire building. She argues that the Supreme Court's "legal decisions [in the 2004 case of *Rasul v. Bush*] respond to the changing demands of empire by creating new persons before the law that extend far beyond Guantánamo Bay" itself.[6] The United States began exercising imperial control over Cuba in the late nineteenth century. After occupying Cuba for three years in the wake of Spanish defeat, the United States finally agreed to withdraw troops from the island—but only on the condition, formalized in the new nation's constitution in the form of the Platt Amendment, that it could exercise the right to intervene in the island's military, economic, and foreign policy affairs. As Kaplan explains, "Cuba's independence [was] dependent on the US right to violate its autonomy." The US leasing of Guantánamo Bay was also a part of the Platt Amendment, and though the Amendment was nullified in 1934, the Guantánamo Bay lease was extended in perpetuity.[7]

Cuban independence from Spain was predicated on its military occupation by the United States, such that Cuba never exercised sovereignty over Guantánamo Bay. As Kaplan explains, the language of the 1903 lease agreement "[renders] Cuban sovereignty of Guantánamo Bay contingent on the acknowledgement of the United States, in exchange for which Cuba agrees to cede sovereignty over part of the territory it never controlled."[8] While Cuba today views the United States as an occupying force, the United States continues to pay for the lease on the naval base under the terms of the 1934 agreement, and under the legal reasoning that it is neither an occupying force nor a sovereign. "Thus," Kaplan writes, "as a territory held by the United States in perpetuity, over which sovereignty is indefinitely deferred, the temporal dimensions of Guantánamo's location make it a chillingly appropriate place for the indefinite detention of unnamed enemies in what the [Bush] administration calls a perpetual war against terror."[9]

The historical and geographical specificity of Guantánamo Bay is, for Kaplan, central to understanding how the naval base is embedded within a larger project of American imperialism. This imperial history and geography, in turn, make possible the erasure of legal personhood from those persons deemed "enemy combatants," a term that is itself a kind of legal fiction situating the accused 9/11 conspirators within but also outside the jurisdiction of the United States. While the prisoners at Guantánamo are ostensibly outside the reach of US law, they also remain outside the reach of international law: "In establishing Guantánamo as a space removed from the reach of US domestic law, the [Bush] administration has concomitantly created the category of 'enemy combatants' to deny the prisoners the protections and rights of international law and the Geneva conventions, which they would have as prisoners of war."[10]

Guantánamo did not become a legal black hole after 9/11, however. It may be more accurate to think of Guantánamo as a perpetual legal black hole (at least since 1903) mostly, though by no means completely, sitting idle until the late twentieth century. Prior to becoming the detention facility for accused 9/11 conspirators, the US naval base at Guantánamo Bay was used as an immigration detention facility, especially for Haitians fleeing to the United States. "Legally," writes Kaplan, "the justification for detaining Haitians and Cubans without constitutional or international rights at Guantánamo was the same one used by the government today, involving the absence of US sovereignty."[11]

The legal status of the naval base at Guantánamo accords with and is informed by the United States' broader position on the legal status of its territories—a position that was developed over a series of Supreme Court cases during the early twentieth century.[12] These *Insular Cases*, as they came to be known, dealt with a number of procedural issues between the United States and the territories it acquired from Spain in 1898 at the conclusion of the Spanish-American War. In the first two *Insular Cases*, *DeLima v. Bidwell* and *Downes v. Bidwell*, the Court established the difference between incorporated and unincorporated territories and defined the Philippine Islands, Puerto Rico, and Guam and unincorporated territories—ones not bound for US statehood.[13] While the matters under consideration in *DeLima* and *Downes* were procedural, the Court's findings had far-reaching implications for the legal status of both the territories and their residents. The Court determined that the full panoply of rights and protections afforded to US citizens would not apply to the residents of unincorporated territories.

The case law governing constitutional protections for Puerto Ricans, for example, "is riddled with inconsistencies, inaccuracies, and plain misinformation."[14] While the Jones-Shafroth Act of 1917 granted Puerto Ricans US citizenship, the Supreme Court held that constitutional protections within the territory were partial: the *Insular Cases* "legalized the full extension of United States sovereignty to overseas territories without requiring the full extension of constitutional rights."[15] Writing in 2013, Juan Torruella notes that *Balzac v. Porto Rico*, a criminal libel case, is one example of how constitutional law can be perverted to maintain colonial supremacy. In *Balzac*, the Court denied the petitioner his right to a jury trial, reasoning that while the constitution extended to US citizens of Puerto Rico, it did not extend

to the territory itself. While the Court affirmed the fundamental constitutional rights of Puerto Ricans, it did not define what those rights
were and explicitly excluded the Sixth Amendment right to a trial by
jury: "The idea that the constitutional rights of US citizens against their
government vary depending on what US jurisdiction those citizens are
standing in is not only absurd on its face, but has also been rejected
by the Supreme Court in cases where the extraterritorial extension of
rights concerns citizens that reside in States rather than territories."
Nevertheless, *Balzac* is still considered "good" law and continues to be
cited by the Court as precedent.[16]

The *Insular Cases* are considered by many legal scholars to provide the legal basis for US colonialism, albeit by a different name:
"*Downes* . . . is commonly conceived as the defining moment in the
construction of American colonialism overseas, while *Balzac* . . . is
understood to be the crucial instance in the definition of colonial citizenship."[17] Torruella cites the *Balzac* opinion as a titular example of the
way US colonial supremacy is maintained across the decades through
the racialized understandings of the colonial subject living in "compact
and ancient communities" incompatible with Anglo-American legal
traditions.[18] For Kaplan, "the designation of territory [in *Downes*] as
neither quite foreign nor domestic was inseparable from a view of its
inhabitants as neither capable of self-government nor civilized enough
for US citizenship."[19] Indeed, it was precisely because of Puerto Rico's
status as a territory per *Downes* that its residents could be defined as
partial, colonial citizens in *Balzac*.[20]

Even as *Downes* was decided, the legal liminality of Puerto Rico was
understood by some to be inconsistent with the ideals of the American
Constitution. In his dissent in that case, Chief Justice Melville Weston
Fuller suggested that the legal status of Puerto Rico was "like a disembodied shade in an intermediate state of ambiguous existence for
an indefinite period."[21] For Kaplan, this liminality echoes through the
twentieth century to its natural conclusion in the Guantánamo Bay naval base and detention camp. Like the Puerto Rico of *Downes*, Guantánamo Bay is also a kind of disembodied shade in an intermedia state of
ambiguous existence for an indefinite period. And the prisoners there
are also relegated to an intermediate state of ambiguous existence in

which they are neither prisoners nor prisoners of war—both of which are entitled to at least some legal protections under domestic and international law—and in which they are neither on nor off US soil. In this intermediate state, detainees are stripped of their legal status and figured as outside the jurisdiction of US law.

Alexa Koenig frames the experience of Guantánamo detainees as one of social, not civil, death, in the sense described by Orlando Patterson.[22] Koenig highlights the particularly liminal dimensions of indefinite detention at Guantánamo and its social aftermath while downplaying their legal foundations: the detainees' experience of these dual forms of social death, she writes, "has led to Guantánamo *feeling* like a particularly punitive experience in [detainees'] lives—despite the fact that their detention was technically not punishment, since they were never found guilty of any crime."[23] Moreover, because "none of [her] interviewees were convicted of a crime," Koenig explains easily, "the phenomenon of legal or civil death triggered by conviction is irrelevant."[24] If civil death is irrelevant in the strictly legal sense, this is only because these detainees were not granted the right to a trial and, as such, could not be convicted, and nor could any court- or state-imposed penalties be imposed. While social death is a useful analytic for understanding the range of detrimental effects facing the Guantánamo detainees, when used in isolation, it ignores the way these detainees were relegated by the state to an extrajudicial site precisely in order to effect the erasure of the legal personhood, which is what constitutes civil death, a penalty that in any case no longer is formally imposed in the United States.

There is a direct parallel between Guantánamo and the US penal system. The creation and maintenance of quasi- or non-legal subjects—individuals afforded partial rights and relegated to spaces where the law does not apply in full as a matter of jurisdictional concerns— is not the sole domain of Guantánamo or other American possessions. American prisoners are entitled to some constitutional rights, but they are also denied by law access to the courts to pursue those rights, are routinely denied the right to trial and punished extrajudicially for crimes committed while in prison, and are denied the rights as crime victims that other citizens are entitled to. The reasoning that undergirds prisoners' status as quasi-citizens resembles the reasoning that undergirds colonial subjects' legal status under American law. The limited rights and protections afforded to Puerto Ricans in the *Insular Cases* were framed as a "natural" consequence of the inapplicability of the Constitution outside of the mainland United States—even if this reasoning rested squarely on a racialized view of Puerto Rican people as less suited to participation in Anglo-American political life. Within the state's borders, criminals, people of color, but Black, post-slavery subjects in particular, historically have been framed as uncivilized and therefore unsuited to participation in the Anglo-American legal and political tradition. As such, they are subject to selective policing and prosecution, characterized as a result as having broken the terms of the social contract, and then relegated to prisons where law enforcement agencies and the criminal courts cede their jurisdiction to prison administrators.

While prisoners in the United States historically have been treated as partial subjects under the law, the bureaucratization of prisons beginning in the 1960s systematized a new set of processes by which their status as quasi-citizens could be formalized. By formalizing the nullification of their standing not only as criminal defendants but as victims, the prison disciplinary procedure played a crucial role in shaping and upholding a new neoliberal paradigm that relied on ideas about victimhood to promote a degraded version of citizenship divorced from political activity. This procedure not only prepares inmates to become client-commodities in the knowledge economy but also contributes to transformations in the way justice is imagined. When crime is adjudicated and punished administratively rather than judicially—as it is in both Guantánamo and in US prisons—the criminal justice system becomes less relevant as an institution where democratic norms and rights can be negotiated.

CITIZEN VICTIMS AND NON-CITIZEN CRIMINALS

The standardized adjudication of criminal acts in the prison disciplinary hearing was borne in part of bureaucratic reforms instigated by judicial activism beginning in the 1960s that sought to standardize the care, custody, and control of inmates. Grievance and disciplinary procedures were largely homogenized to ensure inmates' protection from the gross injustices that were especially prevalent in the Southern plantation model of corrections. These same mechanisms, however, did little to bring prisoners into the sphere of legal, judicial, and, more broadly, public oversight. The failure to prosecute crimes committed inside the prison functions to diminish the legal and political standing of both criminal and victim. This is not to say that more prisoners should be arrested and prosecuted. However, in handling crime as an extrajudicial matter, adjudicated by prison administrators, the prisoner-criminal and prisoner-victim are crafted as quasi-legal subjects, bearing neither the rights nor responsibilities of citizenship.

While the standardization of prison administration had begun in the 1960s, especially in the aftermath of large-scale closures of state mental hospitals,[25] it was in the 1970s, according to Malcolm Feeley and Van Swearingen, that a series of "superintending judges self-consciously sought institutionalized reforms by strengthening the organizational capacities of correctional systems through increased bureaucratization."[26] From their perspective, the judicial system began acting not on precedent but in line with social trends that had come to view the prison as regressive, cruel, and excessively punitive. However, as Feeley and Swearingen also note, judicial activism in prison conditions cases was also motivated by other factors.

> Despite the language of individual rights that gives rise to and shapes so much constitutional litigation, prison conditions cases were about institution building; clarification of basic mission, insistence on tight and responsible administration, development of written policies, cajoling legislatures to increase funding, and garnering public support for change. These goals were not explicitly articulated by prisoners' counsel or judges in these cases, but they were loosely and intuitively embraced by both. The unarticulated reason: in the "organization society," the protection of individual rights requires competent and constrained administration. Bureaucracy fosters rules, supervision, and accountability, and in so doing substitutes the rule of law for the will of the ruler.[27]

This institution building systematized the treatment of prisoners for the express purpose of decreasing the incidence of arbitrary and ad hoc violence, but it also helped to shape a series of sometimes disparate institutions into a well-organized bureaucracy—one prepared to respond to the economic crises of the 1970s. Mass incarceration, in other words, was anticipated to some extent by the bureaucratization of the penal system.

This bureaucratization was due in part to the reliance of activist and policy-making judges on expert witnesses, largely comprising prison administrators themselves: "Nowhere did judges—or prisoners' rights lawyers—attempt to innovate on their own. Nowhere did judges offer a new or novel approach to penology. Nowhere did any judge strike out boldly to promote new alternatives."[28] Thus, while these judges wished to improve the lot of America's incarcerated population, they could see no alternative to incarceration, nor envision a different kind of justice system. Judicial reforms saw the emergence of any number of bureaucratic instruments meant to standardize the care, custody, and control of inmates, and prison conditions did improve in many cases, especially in relation to the plantation model. As a result, the well-organized, bureaucratic penal system would also become a "model" institution for the management of life that was both authorized and legitimated by the courts.

The bureaucratization of prisons into a system of mass incarceration coincided with neoliberal reforms of the 1970s and 1980s. Among the most important of these reforms beginning in the 1970s was the elimination of welfare as an entitlement and its replacement with right-to-work policies: "Welfare reform was designed to compel people to think of themselves as individuals, not as members of society."[29] Welfare commonly has been referred to as the "social safety net," and those members of society who rely on it are quintessentially social creatures, both part of and reliant on the broader social body for survival. Welfare reform relies on and reinscribes the capitalist logic that the individual and the family, and not society, are the foundational units of social and economic reproduction: "Reagan argued that welfare recipients needed to be liberated from . . . societal bonds by entering the workforce and getting off welfare, subjecting themselves to capitalist relations."[30] The criminalization of poverty and drug addiction in the early 1970s was compounded by the Reaganite and, later, Clintonite dismantling of the welfare system, subjecting increasingly broader swaths of the population to the criminal justice system. Beginning in the 1970s, and increasing through the 1980s, 1990s, and beyond, the life being managed by the reformed prison system was the life of the welfare recipient, the drug addict, the "petty hustler"—figures whose lives may have been managed in previous eras by the drunk tank, short-term mental ward, or rehabilitation clinic.[31]

In Raphael Ginsburg's estimation, victims' rights activism and advocacy also arose alongside and within the neoliberal project, "emerging in the 1970s, gaining strength in the 1980s, triumphing in the 1990s and maintaining their predominance in the 2000s and beyond."[32] Ginsburg also observes that many of the same actors who were central to promoting neoliberal policies like workfare also played a crucial role in codifying victims' rights. Both projects, he contends, undermine and deny society in favor of the individual.[33] Ultimately, the wish of victims for peace of mind, and even retribution (especially in death penalty cases), trumps the goals of a more just and equitable society. In concert with policies such as welfare reform that foreground individual responsibility over social relations, victims' rights legislation has contributed to the success of the neoliberal project more broadly: "Victims' rights denial of society is consistent with neoliberalism's economic project and has been advocated for by neoliberalism's champions, functioning as an integral element of its articulation."[34] Where victims' rights discourse has continued unabated since the 1980s, prisoners' rights discourse became increasingly narrow, focused almost exclusively on conditions and due process rights in the originating criminal cases. But prisoners who are victims of crime face substantial reductions to their legal rights and legal personhood compared to their counterparts on the outside.

In 2001, Human Rights Watch (HRW) published a lengthy report highlighting the pervasiveness of rape in men's prisons in the United States. Among its many recommendations is that rape should be reported to the police by Department of Corrections (DOC) officials and prosecuted to the fullest extent of the law.[35] Like other crimes committed in prison, rape is more frequently than not treated as an internal disciplinary matter, subject to neither criminal investigation nor legal proceedings. HRW finds that prison rape is in many cases ignored by corrections staff, and in these cases, is not even subject to internal disciplinary hearings.

While rape is a serious and pervasive problem in men's prisons, it is not the only crime that goes unprosecuted. The relatively few cases of prisoner-on-prisoner murder also sometimes go unprosecuted, especially when the perpetrator is already serving a life sentence. Whether prosecuted or not, committing murder in prison usually results in multiple years of, or indefinite, solitary confinement. Very serious assaults, which under other circumstances would be prosecuted, are in prison either ignored or subject only to internal disciplinary procedures. Even very violent assaults may be chalked up to "fighting," such that the question of who the victim and perpetrator are is never considered. Criminologists Kimmett Edgar and Ian O'Donnell write that "in the aftermath of a fight between two prisoners of comparable strength, labels of aggressor and victim are ill-suited to describe the roles of those who took part."[36] However careful these authors are to avoid the label of victim blaming, they nonetheless assert that prison fights—at least between two equally matched opponents—cannot be categorized as assault. Since both parties are equally responsible, and in their reading, equally willing to participate in the fight, there is no victim, and therefore no crime. Importantly, however, there is no procedure to determine the willingness of each participant or the extent to which the "match" was even. The disciplinary procedure for fights typically determines only whether a fight has occurred and what type of punishment is suitable for disciplining the parties. The disciplinary procedure reflects the attitude of Edgar and O'Donnell insofar as it, too, implies that a fight between inmates can have no victim. Both parties to a fight are typically disciplined in the same manner.

The normalized, routinized violence of the prison, in conjunction with the quasi-judicial disciplinary proceedings that respond to and govern it, subordinates the crime victim. Francis Haines, for example, whose assault of a fellow inmate with a shovel landed him in solitary confinement for fifteen days, sued the State of Illinois for violating his due process rights. Haines's guilt or innocence in the assault was not at issue in the constitutional case. What was at issue were his protections under the Fifth and Fourteenth Amendments. However, federal courts have been reluctant to intervene in matters of prison discipline, since the prison, according to the *Haines* reasoning, is "vested with 'wide discretion' in disciplinary matters."[37] The prison may do what it wishes with its criminals, whether their crimes were committed before being incarcerated or after. Constitutional due process clauses recognize the right to procedural due process in civil and criminal matters, but internal disciplinary hearings are neither civil nor criminal matters but administrative ones. Prisons have been granted the authority to settle disputes internally, and this is as true for disputes pertaining to the institution as it is for disputes among inmates.[38]

Illinois's sentencing guidelines afford the courts wide discretion in punishing assault crimes. Assault with a deadly weapon—such as a shovel—constitutes felony assault regardless of the injuries caused to the victim. Francis Haines, by admission, committed such a crime, and if he had been tried in court, he might have faced a substantial prison sentence. Administrative punishment for violent assault often consists of a multiple-year or indefinite commitment to solitary confinement. It is not at all obvious what punishment—for example a fifteen-day stint in solitary confinement—corresponds to a yearlong or a fifty-year-long prison sentence. But this case was never adjudicated in court. No one will know the details of the assault or what Francis Haines's intentions were. No one will know what the subjective effects of the assault were on his victim or his victim's family. Haines was punished, but he was punished without the benefit of being heard by a judge or jury. Whether or not his victim found any comfort in Haines's punishment, it is certain that this victim was denied the benefit of testifying to the truth of what happened to him and to his damages, of being heard, of appealing to a court for justice, and of being recognized before the law. In handling this assault as a disciplinary matter, rather than as a matter of public interest, both the crime and its victim were effaced.

Crime victims are entitled to certain rights under the Crime Victims' Rights Act of 2004 (CVRA), including the right to be reasonably protected from the accused; to timely notice of court or parole proceedings and to be heard at those proceedings; to confer with prosecutors handling the case; to full and timely restitution provided by law; and to be treated with fairness, respect, dignity, and privacy.[39] These are not simply administrative or technical rights. The right to be treated with fairness, dignity, and respect is akin to the right to be recognized as a subject and citizen with standing before the law, the community, and the polis. The instruments associated with the CVRA—preliminary hearings, court proceedings, prosecutor investigations, and parole hearings—are absent from prison disciplinary proceedings. When a crime is adjudicated administratively, as it is for many that are committed in the prison, the victims of these crimes are denied such rights. Both perpetrator and victim are denied certain legal rights, but they are also denied the truth as it is constructed, authorized, and legitimated by the courts.

The CVRA is not without problems. First, while the law highlights victims' right to be treated with fairness, respect, dignity, and privacy, victims' rights advocacy has more often focused on participation rights and sentencing laws. Ginsburg notes that beginning in the early 1980s, victims' rights groups began to conflate several of their often-overlapping goals: victims' services, such as mental health counseling and support groups; victim participation in judicial proceedings; and tough-on-crime policies and legislation. "A logical chain developed in which victims' services were equated with victim participation, victim participation was equated with punishment and conviction, and, accordingly, victims' services were equated with conviction and punishment. This chain worked to solidify the most questionable element of victims' rights, the contention that punishment and conviction . . . themselves are a victim's right, not the things designed to achieve societal goals, as previously conceived."[40] Since victims' rights advocates never faced significant barriers, their major goal—achieving participation rights— had been enshrined in most state constitutions by the mid-1980s and was later protected as a matter of federal law under the CVRA. Thus "having achieved victim participation rights, victims' rights groups today primarily focus on making life worse for prisoners and harshening sentences and post-release conditions, all in the name of victims."[41]

Second, this focus on participation rights and harsher sentencing— over the right, for example, to be treated with dignity and respect—is indicative of who warrants the status of rights bearer. As Ginsburg points out, victims' rights advocacy never faced opposition. It was largely taken for granted from the movement's earliest instantiation, by the courts and by legislators, that crime victims should be entitled to the rights they sought. Indeed, the history of victims' rights advocacy appears as the history of formalizing or codifying rights that seem already to have existed. This may be due at least in part to the racial and class makeup of victims and victims' rights advocates. The way that victims' rights were taken up as a matter of commonsense suggests who may be counted as a victim: those who have done no victimizing of their own.

Critical criminologists have demonstrated convincingly that most prisoners and ex-offenders have at some point been the victims of crime. Some studies suggest a majority of women convicted of crimes have been crime victims at some point prior to their incarceration.[42] In her study of women offenders, Kathleen Ferraro argues that the "social evaluation of victims and offenders draws upon narratives of good and bad people that are also mutually constituting."[43] For Ferraro, these narratives, particularly when applied to women, are deeply tied to issues of race, class, sexuality, and work. The extent to which a woman adheres to or deviates from the norms of respectable white womanhood affects the extent to which she might be considered either a victim or an offender.

White, middle-class victims of violent or property crimes are legible as victims, whereas people of color, poor people, gender-nonconforming people, and especially criminals are not. The dignity and respect putatively offered by the CVRA and state laws are available to those who are legible as victims. Ginsburg points out that many of the harsh sentencing laws enacted as a result of victims' rights advocacy have been named for certain types of victims.

> There are demographic similarities among the victims for which [these] bills are named. All of the victims are white, and most are children. Of these children, most were girls victimized by strangers. The particular horror of the crimes that catalyze vigorous legislative responses derives from the victim's socio-economic location. Most of these victims belonged to

socio-economic classes typically insulated from everyday criminal victim-ization. They were not homeless or addicted to drugs, did not live in high-crime areas, were not a member of a racial minority, were not involved in criminal activity themselves and did not possess any other socio-economic or behavioral factors that predict one's vulnerability to victimization. The absence of socio-economic risk factors enhanced the unique innocence of the victims these bills were named after. It was not their societal location that placed these victims at risk, but the evil of offenders.[44]

While members of the white middle class are much less likely to risk victimization than poor people, racial minorities, people experienc-ing homelessness, and gender-nonconforming people, they are much more likely to be viewed as members of the victim class. Correspond-ingly, poor people, people of color, people experiencing homelessness, and gender-nonconforming people, even when they are crime victims, are much less likely to be counted among this victim class. Ginsburg's critique illustrates how this focus on white, middle-class victims and their unique innocence actually perpetuates violence by failing to ac-count for the systemic, socioeconomic causes of crime.

At the same time, however, victimization has become a hegemonic narrative and marker of identity for white, middle-class society. For Stuart Hall, Reagan-Thatcher neoliberal discourse of the 1980s was characterized by the libertarian fantasy of the private citizen who needed to be protected from what conservatives would come to call "big government."[45] Government interference in personal decision-making was framed as the predominant threat to liberal freedoms, and the primary responsibility of Reaganite governance, rhetorically, was to protect so-called individual liberties. The definition of individual liberties also grew increasingly narrow, eventually coming to be char-acterized almost exclusively by consumption: the private citizen could watch, purchase, eat, wear, or drive whatever he wished. The period was characterized by a return to, or increased focus on, the individual and the family as the primary site of social bonds and economic repro-duction, creating a disparity between the Reaganite rhetoric of individ-ual freedoms and the reality of the culture wars during the 1980s, when sexual behavior and morality were policed vociferously.[46] The family, especially vis-à-vis the figure of childhood innocence, was framed as the future of the nation, and the individual citizen was tasked with ensuring that the family unit remained intact, protected from immorality and other dangerous pollutants threatening the American way of life. By framing the family as the site of political action, the site from within which the nation would be produced and reproduced, the citizen's duties and obligations could center exclusively on the home and work. Reaganite discourse presented the government as a threat to the privacy and sanctity of the family, and criminality, sexual deviancy, and ethnic or other cultural difference as threats to the sealed-off and self-contained morality of the white, middle-class home. The fear of urban decay and degeneracy, which drove white flight from urban centers beginning in the 1950s and 1960s, would be reactivated by Reagan-Thatcher discourse highlighting the vulnerability of the American family to the threat of any influence coming from outside the home.

In *The Queen of America Goes to Washington City*, Lauren Berlant traces this shifting landscape of American citizenship, grounding her analysis in a "privatized, intimate core of national culture" that precludes a public sphere.[47] The true legal and political subject, the citizen, is someone whose social and political value and values are always being negotiated within and produced by a broad array of institutions—family and work, certainly, but also schools, political parties, and governmental and nongovernmental agencies and organizations. "Downsizing citizenship," on the other hand, "to a mode of voluntarism and privacy has radically changed the ways national identity is imagined, experienced, and governed in political and mass-media spheres and in everyday life."[48] Within this shifting landscape, the American Dream continues to produce a certain kind of citizenship: "A popular form of optimism, it fuses private fortune with that of the nation: it promises that if you invest your energies in work and family-making, the nation will secure the broader social and economic conditions in which your labor can gain value and your life can be lived with dignity."[49] Citizenship generally, and not just for women, comes to be measured against one's value as a worker and as a family member; political action is directed inward rather than outward.

Berlant locates this shift as one that begins in the 1970s and gains momentum as part of the Reaganite cultural agenda, an agenda constructed around and maintained by images of dangerous and threatening others: "In the cartoon version of the shaken nation, a citizen is defined as a person traumatized by some aspect of life in the United States. Portraits and stories of citizen-victims—pathological, poignant, heroic, and grotesque—now permeate the political public sphere, putting on display a mass experience of economic insecurity, racial discord, class conflict, and sexual unease."[50] It is this victimization, perhaps more than anything else, that comes to define citizenship in the Reagan and post-Reagan eras. While Berlant does not expressly take up the question of criminality, focusing instead on national imaginary dangers mostly related to sexual immorality, her position aligns with those who contend that national and social identities are constructed in opposition to the dangerous and threatening criminal.[51] Against these citizen-victims are those who threaten them and their national way of life, their American Dream.

The criminal in his heroic dimensions—the dimensions of Butch Cassidy and Billy the Kid—is someone who refuses to be taken in or co-opted by infantile citizenship, to buy into the fantasy that the nation is capable of fulfilling its promise of securing the conditions under which its citizens might thrive. But this image of the criminal rebel rejecting social and cultural norms, constraints, and beliefs is itself a fantasy of the outlaw—one that has been central to the enduring appeal of the hugely popular American true crime genre.[52] These two narratives—one in which the criminal is a dangerous and polluting other, and one in which he represents the fantasy of American freedom and independence—strip the criminal of social ties and exclude them from the legal and political institutions that historically have shaped civic life. The outlaw's status and value are imagined to be produced through something like the code or law of the street. The convict's status and value are predetermined—first by the criminal code and later by the unambiguous set of institutions to which he is relegated: the criminal courtroom, the prison, and the probation or parole office. Where the convict is sometimes stripped of what is often considered the most important of citizenship rights—franchise—the perhaps more damaging consequence of a criminal conviction is the de facto exclusion from the institutions in and by which legal and political subjectivities are produced and negotiated. Thus, both versions of criminality represent a model of (non) citizenship stripped of its social and political dimensions and constituted exclusively by a narrow set of rules, regulations, and codes. While the neoliberal imaginary opposes the citizen-victim to the noncitizen-criminal (who therefore is excluded from becoming a citizen-victim himself), both are formulated, albeit in sometimes different ways, as "pathological, poignant, heroic, and grotesque,"[53] and both are relegated to increasingly insulated, privatized spheres controlled and administered by putatively neutral and technical expertise.

SHIFTING THE BURDEN OF POLICING AND PROSECUTION

Prisoners are not the only victims of crime who are illegible as victims or whose perpetrators go unprosecuted. Rather, the non-prosecution of crimes in everyday life implicitly disavows the social value and legal standing of some victims, whereas the prison systematizes and codifies this disavowal. It does so through a series of formal mechanisms, including the disciplinary procedure, grievance procedures, and other institutional policies, that not only make the courts inaccessible to prisoners but also produce a reality in which crime—and therefore its victims—do not exist.

Prisons and jails usually produce inmate handbooks outlining facility rules and regulations. But these handbooks, especially in large county jails with frequently rotating populations, are often not actually distributed to inmates. They may also be misleading, especially when it comes to conveying to prisoners what their rights and responsibilities are. For example, according to Pennsylvania DC-ADM 004, and as outlined in the Pennsylvania DOC Inmate Handbook, "If any act constituting a crime in Pennsylvania is committed against [an inmate] by anyone, [an inmate] may press charges against that individual. If such an act occurs, it is [the inmate's] duty to notify the staff so that they may take appropriate action."[54] Placing the onus of responsibility on the crime victim for bringing charges against her perpetrator—making this her duty—not only shifts the burden of responsibility to the individual for pursuing justice but also mitigates the prison's responsibility for providing a safe, secure, and well-surveilled facility. Here, it is not the prison's duty but the inmate's to police the activity of its prisoners.

In the criminal justice system, charges are brought by the state. It is not the prerogative of a victim to press charges or not, as bringing charges is within the purview of the state. In certain cases, the state may opt not to prosecute a crime it knows to have taken place, for example in cases where the victim may be unwilling to testify against a perpetrator or cooperate with the state in its prosecution. If the prosecution does not have sufficient evidence to prosecute a case, it will not bring charges. (Since the police are almost never invited into prisons to investigate crimes, these crimes have little chance of being referred to prosecutors.) However, the state may opt to bring charges whether or not it has any cooperating witnesses, and whether or not a victim wishes for his perpetrator to be prosecuted; the state would be unlikely to opt not to pursue serious felony charges, for example, if the victim of an armed robbery resulting in serious injury were unwilling to "press charges." Taken to its extreme, one might speculate how often the state fails to prosecute a murder because the victim was unwilling to cooperate.

Individuals "pressing charges" is something that happens in television crime dramas. This language often simply shifts the burden of responsibility onto the victim for pursuing justice in cases in which the state is disinclined to bring charges, either because it does not have sufficient evidence or because the case, perhaps a misdemeanor, does not, in its opinion, warrant the financial resources necessary for prosecution. Most often, the language of victims pressing charges is used in cases of sexual assault. Sexual assault is substantially underreported outside of prisons for a number of reasons, not least of which are the historical construction of women as liars and the propensity in court proceedings to question the credibility of women victims of sexual assault.[55] It is estimated that some two-thirds of sexual assaults go unreported,[56] and once a sexual assault is reported to police, police—and then prosecutors—have broad discretion to determine whether a crime has occurred.[57] So while women may choose or not to report sexual assault, they have very little to do with whether they are believed as witnesses to their own assault, or the extent to which police will make an arrest or prosecutors will bring charges. But in most cases, should a victim decide not to cooperate in an investigation or trial for these or other reasons, for example out of fear of retaliation or further victimization, the rhetoric of police and prosecutors will suggest that she was in near total control of investigatory and prosecutorial decision-making.

Whether justice is to be pursued by the individual or as a matter of public interest often hinges on race, class, and gender. Historically, justice is pursued as a matter of public interest when the victim is a white, heterosexual man (or, especially in cases of sexual assault, when a white woman is the alleged victim of a Black man). For women and racial and sexual minorities, especially when they are victims of white, heterosexual men, the burden of pursuing justice shifts rhetorically and oftentimes practically to the individual. Citizenship in the liberal imagination is a set of rights and obligations historically applicable only to those considered fully autonomous subjects—those who are either entirely self-supporting through waged work or "independently" wealthy. The un- and underemployed, those who choose not to work, and the working poor are considered, like women, to be dependents, especially but not solely when they rely on public benefits. People assumed to be poor are subject to increased surveillance in both public and private spaces, and their choices—especially the choices they make about what to purchase and consume—are subject to strict scrutiny.[58] They are suspect, and they are less likely to trust the police when they have been victims of crime because they are assumed to be on the "wrong side" of the law.[59] They are the population from which the citizen class requires protection.

Most inmates held in US jails and prisons hail from these classes of partial citizens. Once they arrive in jail or prison, their status as dependents or wards of the state is confirmed and formalized. As the Supreme Court held in *Wolff*, "a prisoner is not *wholly* stripped of constitutional protections,"[60] although she clearly is stripped of some. Prisoners do not have the right to speech or expression, although they do maintain the right to practice the religion of their choosing.[61] Prisoners have some due process rights in the prison disciplinary hearing, but only insofar as these do not impinge on the safety of the institution or its correctional mandate, both of which the prison has broad discretion to determine. Prisoners do not exercise freedom of movement or assembly, nor can they communicate privately via mail or telephone, excepting privileged communications with legal counsel. Finally, as the class from which the citizen class needs protection, they are assumed not to need or want access to law enforcement. If this last right is not strictly a constitutional protection, it is an assumed and at least semiformal right of American citizens to be served and protected by police.[62]

Prisoners' access to law enforcement is, in addition, mediated by the institution. A prisoner may inform a corrections officer or other staff member that she has been victimized, or she may file an internal grievance. A prisoner cannot simply call the police, but neither does the prison function as a law enforcement agency. While its mandate is the care, custody, and control of its inmates, the prison has a vested interest in shielding itself from the public scrutiny that might emerge from the regular prosecution of crimes committed within its walls. Instead, the internal grievance procedure is the primary method of communication between inmate and institution. It is an all-purpose procedure for lodging complaints, requesting access to medical care, and reporting criminal or other misconduct. It is the primary mechanism by which inmates are denied access to the courts, and it also governs the process by which infractions and crimes are reported and investigated.

Prisoners' ability to respond to and communicate with the courts is also limited. Despite some constitutionally guaranteed access to courts, prisoners' actual access to courts is restricted in several different ways.[63] First, while prisons are required to maintain legal resources so that inmates may conduct legal research, most prisoners lack the kinds of financial and other resources necessary for successful litigation. Second, under the Prison Litigation Reform Act (PLRA) enacted in 1996, inmates must exhaust internal, administrative grievance procedures before filing any suit related to prison conditions; prison officials have broad discretion to determine what constitutes the exhaustion of grievance procedures, and inmates who grieve staff members are routinely targeted for intimidation and retaliation.[64] Furthermore, inmates themselves may be unaware of the grievance process or the extent to which this process is or is not the only mechanism by which their grievances may be addressed.

Among the problems associated with internal grievance processes is that individual institutions determine, internally, the rules and procedures that must be followed by inmates in order for the grievance to be considered legitimate. Many institutions have restrictive time limits such that, in some cases, grievances must be filed within several days of an instigating event. Other times, grievances are returned because an inmate has written on the reverse side of the form or filled out information on incorrect lines or boxes. The most significant barrier, however, is that "prisons and correctional departments have a set of priorities that is so at odds with prisoners' interests that a neutral body might more effectively resolve inmate grievances."[65] The adjudication of inmate grievances, which are largely directed towards the institution itself as opposed to other inmates, results in a process by which the prison is the sole arbiter of its own conduct and policies: "By having in place elaborate internal procedures guaranteeing multiple levels of review, prisons may signal compliance with judicially-imposed standards when, in fact, their grievance procedures do not actually protect constitutionally defined rights."[66]

Grievance procedures, which emerged as part of the bureaucratization of prisons during the 1960s, are how prisons resolve inmate complaints internally, and thus "tend to keep . . . [disputes] within the prison's walls and out of the public sphere."[67] In other words, unlike the rhetorical and practical effect of shifting the burden of responsibility from the state to the private individual for bringing criminal charges, the PLRA and concomitant administrative rules within the prison actually have the legal effect of eliminating the state's burden to act within the confines of the Constitution. That prisoners' access to the courts is mediated by the administrative grievance procedure means that inmates are frequently unable "to address serious, even life-threatening grievances."[68] The kinds of inmate grievances routinely dealt with in prisoner rights cases include access to medical care, freedom of religion, and prison conditions. Concerns about the right not to endure physical abuse are typically directed towards the institution and its agents, and grievances are initiated by inmates against officers. Much more rarely does prisoner rights discourse highlight inmates' right to be free from victimization or abuse by other inmates.

While most state and federal inmates receive inmate handbooks outlining the basics of grievance and other procedures, inmates of county jails frequently do not. In neither case do inmate handbooks offer anything nearing the kind of detail necessary to understand the complex administrative rules governing the institution, or the relationship between those rules and legal rights.[69] To take one example, the Inmate Information Handbook for the Cook County Jail in Chicago outlines the types of complaints that may be addressed by inmates through the grievance process. These include violations of constitutional rights, breaking of law or institutional rules by Cook County Department of Corrections staff, threats to safety or well-being, unsafe or unclean living areas, mishandling of money or property, lack of access to court-ordered programming, and not receiving necessary medical attention. Departmental policies and decisions by the disciplinary board cannot be grieved.[70]

THE NEUTRAL, TECHNICAL EXPERTISE OF NEOLIBERAL PRISON DISCIPLINE

Especially since the 1980s, criminal courts have become progressively automated: in the name of race and gender neutrality, sentencing guidelines have left judges in many cases unable to exercise the kind of discretion (including leniency) they once had in determining appropriate disciplinary measures,[71] and prosecutors and judges are increasingly reliant on standardized instruments and algorithms that purport to gauge offenders' danger to society and their chances of reoffending in the future.[72] Robert Ferguson writes that these transformations move the criminal justice system towards becoming a punishment regime—one in which "punishment will [eventually] trump every other concern, including the meaning of crime, procedural integrity, verification of guilt, the rights of the punished, proportionality in punishment, and the mental balance of the punisher."[73] In a punishment regime, these other concerns eventually become negligible, and punishment is carried out solely by way of bureaucratized administrative expertise.

Despite these similarities between the administration of justice in the courts and in the prison disciplinary hearing, the courts are subject to public scrutiny and oversight, and are therefore subject, at least to some extent, to reform. While trials are vanishingly rare in the criminal courts—having been supplanted by plea agreements—criminal procedure provides a framework for protecting the rights of the accused, adjudicating guilt and innocence according to public law, and installing judges and prosecutors elected or otherwise authorized by the public. The prison disciplinary procedure not only serves as a kind of model for how to transform justice into an administrative enterprise; it degrades the civic standing and legal consciousness of perpetrators and victims, depoliticizing for both inmates and the public the processes that traditionally constitute justice.

Other forms of discipline deployed in the prison also contribute to degrading the legal consciousness of prisoners and framing the criminal justice system as just one among many neoliberal labor market institutions. The ostensibly neutral and technical expertise of prison discipline begins with psychological and behavioral testing. Many prisons and parole boards continue to use the Criminal Sentiment Scale—Modified (CSS) to determine new intakes' and potential parolees' propensity for future crime. The CSS is a generally accepted measurement of what social scientists call prosocial attitudes.[74] The scale is divided into three sections: Attitudes towards the Law, Courts, and Police (LCP); Tolerance for Law Violations (TLV); and Identification with Criminal Others (ICO). The LCP portion of the test evaluates respect for the law and criminal justice system as they are envisioned by these same institutions. The scale generally calls for blind trust in the criminal justice system, and any response that is critical of this system results in a lower score. Some of the statements with which examinees are meant to agree include: pretty well all laws deserve our respect; it is our duty to obey all laws; all laws should be obeyed just because they are laws; the law is good; lawyers are honest; judges are honest and kind; court decisions are pretty well always fair; a judge is a good person; the police are honest; a cop is a friend to people in need. Some of the statements with which examinees are meant to disagree include: the law does not help the average person; the law makes slaves out of most people for a few people on the top; you cannot get justice in court; the prosecution often produces fake witnesses; the police are as crooked as the people they arrest.

This scale and others like it determine the course of behavioral and psychological treatment and adjustment to which inmates will be assigned in prison, contribute to their classification status, which determines their security level and the type of facility they will be sent to, and may impact the parole board's decision to release them once the minimum sentence has been completed. The decision to use, and how to use, these instruments is at the discretion of prison administrators. Social scientists have continued to validate the effectiveness of the CSS in evaluating prosocial attitudes and behaviors. Here, however, prosocial attitudes and behaviors are figured as pure and abiding faith in the law, law enforcement, courts, and judges. These are the (only) apparatuses comprising society and "the social." Deviation from this norm of abiding faith in the legal and criminal justice system, including any acknowledgment of structural racism or gender discrimination within these institutions, or the role of the law in shoring up the power of corporations and elites, constitutes an antisocial attitude, which in turn requires continued incarceration and additional programming. Unlike the normative neoliberal subject whose social and political life is meant to congeal around the family and the workplace, the prisoner-subject is assumed to be perpetually in need of services that can be provided by the criminal justice system and the justice system–adjacent knowledge economy—such as job training programs, drug and alcohol treatment, behavioral health treatment, and parenting classes. At the same time, the criminal justice system is reduced from a public institution where democratic rights and obligations can be negotiated into a profit-based system of commodified services.

A prosocial attitude—blind trust in the law and criminal justice system—is figured, and made explicit in the intake process, as the condition for parole. In concert with the disciplinary hearing, which is used to effect reductions in legal personhood, coercive ideological conditioning attempts to interpellate the criminal as a docile subject prepared for reentry not into the social and political world but into a limited set of institutions that are opposed to social and political activity. Under threat of continued incarceration or reincarceration, the prison prepares inmates to enter a community corrections facility upon release, obey a parole officer, and participate in drug treatment and workfare programs—in other words, to enter into the system of institutions that can profit from her transformation from a legal subject into a "client" in the knowledge and service economies.

The American prisoner has consistently been figured as abject and external to the social body. The removal of his crimes from the realm of judicial opinion is longstanding. In the early modern through mid-twentieth century prison, administrators employed whatever internal disciplinary techniques were at their disposal to punish institutional infractions and new crimes committed by their charges. Often, these techniques included precisely those that the disciplinary hearing was designed to replace—namely techniques of corporal punishment or harsh work assignments. Criminal acts committed within the prison were rarely brought to the attention of law enforcement or judicial authorities. Thus, the bureaucratization of prison discipline did not achieve a new way to remove the criminal and his punishment from public view. It rather systematized and codified what had previously been an ad hoc practice that could vary widely from institution to institution. The prison disciplinary hearing would become the default, apolitical, and systematic mechanism of exclusion that formalized the improvisatory mechanisms preceding it.

The prison disciplinary procedure is framed as a neutral, quasi-judicial hearing, its boards made up of impartial and disinterested legal professionals. But these boards comprise prison administrators rather than legal professionals who are invested not in pursuing justice but in maintaining the institutional status quo. This status quo includes safety and security, but it also includes the objectification of prisoners—the production and maintenance of their status as objects or property that belong to the state and, eventually, to the profit-generating industries that serve them upon release. This objectification, effected through systematic, mechanized, and bureaucratic procedures, aims to reduce the legal personhood of the masses that are incarcerated. By effecting these reductions on the inside—restricting prisoners' access to the courts, nullifying their status as victims entitled to certain rights, pathologizing critical attitudes towards the law and law enforcement—they craft individuals as objects, clients who, on the outside, require services from the knowledge and service economies that have partially replaced the mid-century manufacturing economy.

Should ex-offenders attempt to remove themselves from the narrow set of institutions that profit from their status as clients, an elaborate system of public and private technologies has emerged to make it incredibly difficult for people with criminal records to reenter social and political life. The next chapter addresses how the consumer background report industry works in concert with the state's system of collateral consequences to ensure the long-term, often permanent, subjugation of the criminal class. This long-term subjugation serves as the basis for certain knowledge economy industries and contributes to the transfer of capital, political power, and legal personhood from individuals to businesses. At the same time, the private "wing" of this system—the consumer background report industry—casts a much wider net, ultimately crafting all individuals as a potential risk to employers, lenders, and rental agents, but also to each other. This industry plays a significant role in shaping a regime of lateral surveillance in which each individual is responsible for monitoring and policing their neighbors, romantic partners, casual acquaintances, and social media contacts—much like prisoners are vested by administrators with the duty to police each other. Chapter 3 points out the historical and contemporary gaps in those state apparatuses such as policing and prosecution that purport to ensure public security. It examines how private entities historically have filled in those gaps and how the consumer background report industry serves to craft a specifically neoliberal security regime.

3. Consumer Background Reports and the Making of Neoliberal Cops and Robbers

Alessandro De Giorgi has written that "masses of marginalized young men and women are dumped on a daily basis into the segregated neighborhoods of urban containment from which they were forcefully removed months, years, or decades earlier." He notes that "a few 'successful' [ex-offenders] will be channeled into the secondary labor market of minimum-wage, insecure, and degraded work, where they will serve alternatively as a hyper-exploited labor force or as a disposable reserve army of labor." The vast majority of returning prisoners, however—averaging seventeen hundred per day from state and federal prisons and many more from the rotating population of the nation's eleven million jail inmates—are "caught between the daily realities of poverty, homelessness, illness, addiction, and the looming threat of reincarceration," and "most of them will scramble to survive as chronically unemployed recyclers, panhandlers, hustlers, and backsliders."[1]

In the "segregated neighborhoods of urban containment" that De Giorgi describes, the solution to the mass exclusion of former prisoners from social institutions has been to erect what he calls the "service ghetto": "a self-contained space, bordered on all sides by gentrifying uptown neighborhoods, which local authorities have designated as the ideal location for homeless shelters, transitional houses, community clinics, women's shelters, halfway houses, SRO hotels, and rehabilitation programs"—in other words, the institutions that comprise Douglas Thompkins's "prisoner reentry industry."[2] In his ethnographic study of one neighborhood in Oakland, California, De Giorgi describes how many of these so-called service providers exploit the labor of and expropriate funds from former prisoners by offering them low-paying jobs and housing at a cost that is only slightly less than their wages. Excluded as they are from normative models of work and housing,

ex-offenders may have no alternatives to the service ghetto—a knowledge economy prison outside the prison.

Ex-offenders are on one hand relegated by default to this arrangement of criminal justice system adjacent institutions, since the criminal record leaves a great number of them unemployable. On the other,
most ex-offenders will be subject to some sort of state supervision in
the form of probation or parole. Some of the terms of probation and
parole may be set by judges, but many are set by state parole boards or
by individual probation and parole officers. Standard features of supervision include mandatory reporting, mandatory drug testing, and
mandatory employment, job seeking, or enrollment in a job training
program. Many people on probation and parole will be mandated to
inpatient or outpatient drug or alcohol treatment, behavioral health
treatment, or parenting classes. For those fortunate enough to have a
home to return to, these standard features of probation and parole can
be pursued from home, although they will also likely be subjected to
a curfew, at least for some period of time. For those who do not have
a stable home to return to, as defined by the state, the most likely alternative will be a community corrections center or halfway house. In
this way, the criminal justice system mandates that ex-offenders exist
as products to be exchanged within the prisoner reentry industry. At
the same time, the terms of probation and parole are difficult to abide
by, and any technical violation—such as missing a parenting class, failing a drug test, being in the presence of other people with criminal
records, going to a bar or restaurant that serves alcohol, being out past
curfew, or leaving a halfway house—can, at the discretion of a probation or parole officer, lead to reincarceration. A single failed drug test
might result in recommitment for anywhere between several months
and several years, at which point the cycle of reentering and failing out
of the reentry industry begins anew.

The permanent or semi-permanent state of objectification or productification within the reentry industry is further supplemented by
a vast set of collateral consequences codified in state and federal laws
that limits the civil rights and political standing of those convicted
of crimes. Across all jurisdictions, there are approximately forty-five

thousand collateral consequences codified in US law. Many of these sanctions serve to degrade the legal, political, and civic standing of those convicted of crimes, ensuring that they remain bound to the terms of their status as clients in the knowledge economy. However, while the aims of the criminal justice and penal systems have transformed in concert with shifting political and economic agendas—and even at times have driven those shifts—other disciplinary technologies have emerged from non-state actors. One of the technologies that has been central to promoting a subject compatible with the neoliberal agenda is the commercial or consumer background report. The consumer background report makes possible a system in which private entities—like employers and landlords—are responsible for designing and imposing their own collateral consequences. Privately imposed collateral consequences may restrict the everyday freedoms of people convicted of crimes even more than those imposed by the state. Because discriminating against people with convictions is completely legal, ex-offenders can be and often are denied housing and employment to the extent that they have few alternatives but to exist as products within the knowledge economy.

While the population marked as criminal by arrest and conviction records has increased steadily over the past forty years, the consumer background report industry has become a growth sector because it has been able to craft risk as a ubiquitous and normal part of everyday life. It traffics in a popular discourse about the perpetual threat posed by convicted criminals while also framing every individual as a potential threat to the safety and security of other individuals and private institutions. As a number of scholars working in fields such as security and media studies have argued, consumer background report companies cultivate and capitalize on the idea that friends, family members, social media contacts, current or potential romantic partners, and neighbors all pose a significant safety risk.[3] In so doing, they craft a society dominated by lateral surveillance, in which each individual is thought to be responsible for identifying and managing the threats posed by their social contacts. Background reports, however, while increasingly used by individuals to manage risk in their personal lives, are overwhelmingly used by employers and landlords. The rhetoric of ubiquitous risk and the normalization of lateral surveillance reduce the burden of the state to ensure public safety and security.[4] They place the onus of responsibility for securing these conditions on private entities such as universities, employers, and landlords. This form of neoliberal securitization, which frames employers and landlords as quasi-law enforcement authorities—and all individuals as potential criminals—is one of the ways in which both wealth and political power are transferred from the public to the private sector.

COLLATERAL CONSEQUENCES FOR SOCIAL ENEMIES

People convicted of crimes face a variety of post-conviction consequences that exceed the punishments set out in their sentences. As a legal concept, collateral consequences are those consequences imposed by the state alongside or in addition to traditional punishments, such as terms of imprisonment or probation, fines, and restitution. These range from the revocation of driver's licenses and proscriptions on the attainment of professional licenses to the prohibition on suing for wrongful imprisonment and mandatory household registration for sex offenders to disenfranchisement. Gabriel Chin notes that "while the particulars of the regime of collateral consequences change from time to time, by 1960 (or perhaps earlier), it was clear that the State could deprive convicted persons of civil rights, public benefits, occupational licenses, and employment in regulated industries, subject only to minimal judicial review. It was also clear that deprivations could be imposed retroactively as well as prospectively."[5] Chin argues that this regime of collateral consequences was not a result of a "rational, systematic, careful policy." Instead, it emerged piecemeal, out of a process of increasing government regulation and bureaucracy in the mid-twentieth century and beyond.[6] "For decades," moreover, "the legal system largely ignored collateral consequences. For the most part, legislatures generated them on an ad hoc basis, courts treated them as outside the criminal justice system, and the organized bar paid them little attention."[7]

Taken in isolation, courts have ruled rather consistently that collateral consequences fall outside the definition of punishment, and are therefore "exempt from the protections against bills of attainder, double jeopardy, cruel and unusual punishment, . . . excessive fines," and ex post facto clauses.[8] Joshua Kaiser calls the so-called collateral consequences rule, which separates collateral consequences from criminal law processes, a "formalistic fiction."[9] The collateral consequences rule maintains that criminal defendants must be informed prior to entering a guilty plea only what the direct consequences of such a plea will be, such as court costs, fines, restitution, and terms of prison or probation. In an early case addressing this issue, *United States v. Parrino*, the Second Circuit Court failed to define what collateral consequences were, "except by contrasting the 'sentence directly flowing from the judgment' with examples of civil forfeiture, loss of employment or civil rights, ineligibility for military service, and deportation."[10]

In the seventy years since *Parrino*, the courts have done little to actually define what collateral consequences are. Kaiser identifies a number of circular arguments made by the courts in an effort to respond to the challenges brought by criminal defendants regarding the imposition of collateral consequences. The courts have ruled extensively on the distinction between punishment and remediation, between punishment and regulatory action, and between punishment and consequences that serve the purpose of promoting public safety. Ultimately, these distinctions almost always rely on tautology: a punishment is a punishment when it is intended as a punishment.[11] In practical application, "only the criminal fines and tenure of prison, jail, or probation constitute 'direct' consequences of the sentence; anything else is (probably) 'collateral.'"[12]

Apart from a few Supreme Court cases, notably *Weems v. United States* and *Trop v. Dulles*, the courts have sought to define collateral consequences in opposition to punishments. In these two cases, the Court did find that some collateral consequences represented cruel and unusual punishment consistent with Eighth Amendment definitions. Chin suggests that "the Court's cases . . . simultaneously suggest that individual collateral consequences are not punishment, but that systematic loss of legal status in the form of actual or potential subjection to an interlocking system of collateral consequences is punishment."[13]

Thus, Chin explains, it is mostly when considering collateral conse-quences in isolation that the Supreme Court has been unwilling to define them as punishment. On the other hand, "the same Court has understood civil death and other systematic loss of status as punish-ment and has used the existence of collateral consequences to shape important criminal procedure doctrines, such as the rights to counsel and to jury trial."[14]

These confusions and ambiguities in the law regarding the treat-ment of offenders and ex-offenders shape how private institutions impose their own penalties on people convicted of crimes. Especially since the 1990s, when the use of consumer background reports was becoming pervasive, it has been within private institutions that people convicted of crimes face some of the most severe consequences of hav-ing a criminal record. It is not the courts, for example, that determine whether people with criminal convictions can occupy rental units in the private housing market or whether they can be employed within various industries—from meat processing to retail to fast food. In-dividual realtors and employers make these decisions, and with little or no oversight from the courts or any other legal or administrative body. These institutions, however, deploy a similar logic to the courts when making decisions about whether to exclude people convicted of crimes: they consider the denial of housing and employment to be preventive rather than punitive, to promote public safety and security rather than to punish.

There are several reasons that employers and landlords have been tasked with playing the role of the state in determining and impos-ing collateral consequences. As a result of the twentieth-century wars on crime, drugs, and poverty, according to Ruth Gilmore, crime has become "firmly established as a permanent problem, for which the solution is the continued proliferation of laws, courts, judges, bailiffs, law enforcement personnel, technologies of surveillance, helicopters, and other means of domestic warfare, including, of course, prisons."[15] But other responses to the permanent problem of crime also emerged alongside the proliferation of these state-based "solutions." Especially since the 1980s, according to Barbara Glesner, "one response has been to distribute the burden of fighting crime among the citizenry. From drug testing in the work place to *America's Most Wanted* on television, American citizens have become an integral part of the process of investigating and apprehending criminals."[16]

This view is a central one to neoliberal theories of law enforcement. As Chicago School economist George J. Stigler writes, "All prescriptions of behavior for individuals require enforcement."[17] What is at issue for the state, as the title of his 1970 essay suggests, is the optimum enforcement of laws. Although most people elect to conform to socially prescribed behavior as a matter of course, Stigler argues, those behaviors that are mandated unilaterally, from above, are matters of regulation or law that require enforcement. The major reason that the state can enforce only some of these prescriptions is that enforcement is a financial burden on the state. However, built into Stigler's analysis is the assumption that "there is a division of labor between the state and the citizen in the prevention of virtually every offense." For those with means, the policing of property may be an almost exclusively private affair: "The owner of large properties is required to do much of his direct policing: there are surely more watchmen and guards than policemen in a typical city," and "devices such as nonnegotiability and custody of funds" are used to protect the monetary assets of those who own them. Because the wealthy essentially employ a private police force, public enforcement and "punishments for crimes against property do not increase in proportion to the value of the property." Moreover, all individuals are "required to protect [themselves] from minor offenses or at least to detect their occurrence and assume a large part of the burden of prosecution (for example, shoplifting, insults, simple trespass)."[18]

Stigler's is a descriptive rather than normative argument, and it is a description that reflects the central role that private policing has played especially but not exclusively in the protection of property across American history. Since the late 1960s, however, there has been what some have called a "quiet revolution" in private policing, with thousands of new security firms coming into existence.[19] Especially in the digital age, however, it is not only the wealthy that are tasked with providing for their own risk mitigation. The ready availability of consumer background reports among the general public, which can be purchased online for anywhere between twenty and a few hundred dollars, has prompted a wave of lateral surveillance in which private individuals are encouraged to monitor the behavior of their friends, neighbors, and other social contacts. Nora Draper frames the background report industry as one "that capitalizes on contemporary anxieties . . . to normalize lateral surveillance and self-monitoring as essential parts of everyday life, thereby pressing ordinary people into the role of digital detectives."[20] She notes that the management of risk by individuals is part of a broader trend in which "responsibilities for safety traditionally assigned to state actors have been pushed onto ordinary citizens."[21] This, in turn, further legitimates the private enforcement of law across other institutions. In other words, at the same time that state-based criminal justice and criminal justice adjacent institutions were growing and bureaucratizing at alarming rates, the burden of surveilling and policing criminal behaviors was also being shifted onto private individuals and institutions.

It is not only the availability of consumer background reports, however, that transforms the historical practice of private policing into a form of neoliberal securitization. Rather, a central feature of the contemporary moment is the state's role not only in deciding what the optimal level of law enforcement should be but in mandating the privatization of security for businesses of every income bracket and size. This mandate normalizes private security and lateral surveillance for individuals, but more importantly, manufactures an entire market-based infrastructure in which businesses *must* purchase on the open market the services that might otherwise be provided by public infrastructure.

The 1970 case of *Kline v. 1500 Massachusetts Avenue Apartment Corp.* represented a significant transformation in the landlord-tenant relationship.[22] The plaintiff in *Kline* sued her landlord for injuries sustained by a third party during a robbery in a common hallway of the property. While landlords historically have had some legal liability to provide for the safety and security of tenants—for example by ensuring the structural integrity of the premises—*Kline* placed legal liability on landlords for the behavior of third parties, including other tenants. Over time, the legal standards established in *Kline* "have evolved from narrow exceptions, to a general rule of immunity, to a broad duty of care. This evolution signifies a dramatic shift in the landlord's common law tort liability and provides the foundation for reconceptualizing the landlord's overall responsibility for criminal activities on leased premises."[23] The principles that undergird the *Kline* decision also apply to workplaces. Under the theories of negligent hiring and negligent retention, employers can be held liable for employees' criminal behavior on, and sometimes off, the clock.

Since *Kline*, courts have ruled on the liability of landlords to protect tenants against criminal activity, and some have taken issue with characterizing the presence of criminals as a "defective condition." Moreover, "assuming that an actionable defect can be proven, courts will still not impose liability unless the criminal activity has taken place in a common area; that is, in an area over which the landlord retains a superior ability to control."[24] In employment, some states, such as Texas, have enacted laws that limit the legal liability of employers for negligent hiring and retention.[25] Despite a patchwork of limitations on landlord and employer liability, most landlords and almost all employers avoid the risk of litigation by conducting criminal background screenings on all potential tenants and job candidates. The Society for Human Resources Management reports that by 2012, 69 percent of employers obtained criminal background checks for all potential hires, and 87 percent obtained them for at least some potential hires. The HR Research Institute, in a study sponsored by the Professional Background Screening Association, finds that by 2020, 94 percent of employers conducted background checks on some or all employees.[26] This trend reflects the success of the neoliberal agenda in crafting a vision of society in which normative citizens identify as victims who are always at risk of being victimized by criminals. This vision, however, is preceded by, and finds ready legitimacy in, an existing framework that understands the criminal as a social enemy.

In his lectures on the punitive society, Foucault describes the transformation of criminality during the eighteenth century from its status as a transgression against another individual to its more contemporary conceptualization as a transgression against the whole of society. "From the eighteenth century," Foucault writes, "we see the formulation of the idea that crime is not just an offense, the category of offenses involving injury to another person, but that crime is what harms society, that is to say an action by which the individual breaks the social pact binding him to others and goes to war against his own society."[27] According to this formulation, punishment for crime is not a matter of providing restitution to the injured party but of protecting the public. The ideal of justice under liberalism—including within the American criminal justice system—posits a correspondence between the punishment and the crime, such that punishments are relevant and proportional to their respective crimes. But under a system in which the criminal is considered an enemy of society, this ideal begins to degrade. Crime is not a matter of harm done to another individual that can be amended through restitution but calls for a range of sanctions that also serve a preventive function.

Rather than simply replacing one paradigm or ideal with another, however, the two exist alongside each other in sometimes conflicting ways. The law continues to espouse the traditional liberal view that the punishment for crime should be commensurate with the harm caused by that crime. But the coexisting paradigm that figures the criminal as a social enemy, and therefore figures certain sanctions as having a preventive or public safety function, leads to a variety of legal maneuverings aimed at avoiding the inherent contradiction between the two ways in which the criminal is figured—one in which she deserves punishment or rehabilitation fitting her crime, and one in which she is a perpetual threat to society and deserving of perpetual punishment. This maneuvering is perhaps most evident in the legal separation of collateral consequences from punishments. Whereas court-imposed sentences continue, at least to some extent, to work under the logic that particular crimes warrant particular and commensurate punishments that serve to make whole the victims of crime, collateral consequences work under the logic that all of society must be defended from criminals. Rather than punishing crime, collateral consequences assume that criminality is an aspect of an individual's character that must be continuously managed for the good of society. Using felon disenfranchisement as a titular example of this paradigm, Andrew Dilts writes that, "as disenfranchisement is practiced across the United States, it cannot reasonably be said to apply to a crime. It applies, rather, to the criminal. Individuals are disenfranchised with reference to their status as convicted felons or as currently incarcerated and not by virtue of their particular criminal transgressions."[28]

It is worth noting that the model of the social enemy is in many ways in conflict with the neoliberal project of undermining "society" in favor of a model that privileges individuals and families as the basic unit of political activity. Indeed, one of Gary Becker's proposals for improving the criminal justice system is to transform it almost exclusively into a tort system—into the kind of model of civil penalties that existed prior to the nineteenth century, in which fines and restitution would constitute payment for almost any harm. In this model, the only thing that would make a behavior criminal would be a defendant's inability to pay her mandated monetary damages, or "uncompensated harm." Defending against the counterargument that such a model would essentially entail putting a price on harmful behaviors, such that criminals could simply pay to be allowed to commit crimes, he notes that, in fact, this is precisely already the case—except that in the current system the price offenders must pay is quantified in time.[29] One likely reason that the model of the social enemy continues to thrive, despite the best efforts of neoliberalism to undermine society, is that it is extremely profitable for businesses to traffic in the rhetoric of perpetual risk. This conflict also demonstrates how two or more forms of social organization can exist alongside each other, even as both are subjected to the logic of the market and undergo subtle definitional shifts: The criminal on one hand is someone who harms the individual. In this role, the criminal pays a price (in time) in the form of a sentence, which, as evidenced through the discourses and policies of crime victims' rights, is now meant to make individual victims whole; at the same time, the individual who is at risk of harm must engage the services of private security. On the other hand, the criminal poses a risk to all of society. In this role, the criminal is subject to a range of state-based collateral consequences serving a preventive or public safety function. The society at risk, however, is now constituted in large part by private businesses, including employers and landlords, who must also impose their own collateral consequences in order to protect those segments of the population for whom they are thought to be responsible.

This shifting paradigm, as Dilts argues, is also reflective of another feature of neoliberalism: responsibilization. The liberal tradition of the eighteenth and nineteenth centuries crafted various figures of danger and monstrosity to explain and respond to crime. Under neoliberalism, "the monstrous individual, the criminally insane, the incorrigible offender, and the recidivist each persist as recognizable figures, yet they become fully responsible despite their 'known' condition of fundamental irresponsibility." Whereas penalties like disenfranchisement were once used to protect society from those who were fundamentally irresponsible, "by the late twentieth century, . . . the felon must be excluded purely as a collateral effect, as a public safety concern, and as a figure who remains dangerous but is fully responsible for that danger as a rational (and therefore predictable) actor."[30]

The figure of *homo oeconomicus* plays a significant role in the production of this perpetually dangerous but fully rational and responsible actor. "While the figure of *homo oeconomicus*," Dilts continues, "proclaims that there is no fundamental difference between the murderer and the traffic violator, neoliberalism still allows these differences to assert themselves, albeit in a different venue or on a different level." Dilts believes that the figure of the felon is one of the ways this difference asserts itself. The felon—as disenfranchised—marks a limit. Having lost his status as a citizen, the felon "carries the burden of the demands of both a punitive discourse and a membership discourse (specifically the terms of participatory US citizenship that developed through the mutually reinforcing terms of patriarchy, heteronormativity, ableism, and white supremacy)." He continues:

> The neoliberal proposal to radically reconceive the human subject as the rational actor represents . . . [an] attempt to reform and perfect the liberal ideal of an unencumbered, atomistic, and universal subject before the law. The only relevant difference between professor and murderer is to be found in their respective tastes, in their indifference curves and budget lines. Neoliberalism rejects the dangerous effects of discursive exchanges by insisting there are no such exchanges because there is only one discursive sphere: the market form. No specifically "criminological" figures are necessary to smooth over these tensions; no monsters really exist, as the only monstrosity out there is a tyrannical and inefficient legal system that

is ignorant of the universal character placed before the law: *homo oeco-nomicus.* As such, it is first and foremost on the level of the law that reform must take place, rationalizing, purifying, and simplifying it so that players might more readily know the "rules of the game."[31]

For Dilts, then, the law acts as one of the fields that is adjacent to the market that may prevent the market from functioning optimally. As Foucault describes it, the neoliberal state cannot intervene in the market, since it is ultimately incapable of apprehending the full scope of economic relations. Instead, however, it must intervene in any aspect of society which prevents the market from functioning optimally.[32] In order to transform the legal or political subject into *homo oeconomicus,* as a rational agent whose rationality is purely market-based,[33] the state cannot act directly on either the market or the subject, but can and must act on the law to clarify the terms of acceptable behavior according to the neoliberal social contract.[34] Rather than simplifying the law, however, these reforms actually have a similar effect to those Foucault describes in his analysis of the German ordoliberal institutional frameworks of the 1950s: a vast body of confusing and contradictory legislation avoids at all costs being associated with market interventions at the same time it is designed to promote a certain version of market relations and to clarify the relationship between the market and the state.[35] As Bernard Harcourt explains, "The rules and regulations surrounding our modern markets are intricate and often arcane, and they belie the simplistic idea that our markets are 'free.'"[36] Nevertheless, neoliberal rhetoric "naturalizes the market and thereby hides the massive distributions that take place there," as well as the intricate and arcane rules that regulate it.[37]

The abstract concepts of criminality and danger under neoliberalism are certainly simplified compared their nineteenth- and twentieth-century counterparts by reducing a range of concepts related to deviance, monstrosity, abnormality, and pathology to a simple, actuarial assessment of risk or danger.[38] As Malcolm Feeley and Jonathan Simon define it in the early 1990s, actuarial justice describes a transformation of the criminal justice system from a set of punishments designed to modify the convict, into a set of strategies designed to mitigate the risk of criminality at the level of the population.[39] This account of actuarial justice operates along the logics of population as expressed by Foucault in his lectures at the Collège de France in 1977–78, *Security, Territory, Population*: what is of concern for government at a certain point is not the welfare, management, or discipline of individuals but the management of society as a whole thought of as the population.

Under neoliberalism, the management of society, including the management of crime, becomes more and more closely tied to the operations of the market. Gary Becker was an early proponent of applying market principles to the criminal justice system, arguing in the late 1960s that there is an "optimal amount of enforcement," which "is shown to depend on, among other things, the cost of catching and convicting offenders, the nature of punishments—for example, whether they are fines or prison terms—and the responses of offenders to changes in enforcement." In his essay proposing an economic approach to the management of crime, he calls crime an "economically important activity or 'industry,'" that can be measured using the metric of harm.[40] While providing formulae for assessing the financial harm of criminal activity, Becker also notes that the values arrived at

> are important components of, but are not identical to, the net damages to society. For example, the cost of murder is measured by the loss in earnings of victims and excludes, among other things, the value placed by society on life itself; the cost of gambling excludes both the utility to those gambling and the "external" disutility to some clergy and others; the cost of "transfers" like burglary and embezzlement excludes social attitudes toward forced wealth redistributions and also the effects on capital accumulation of the possibility of theft. Consequently, the [financial estimates] for the cost of crime . . . [arrived at through economic analysis] may be a significant understatement of the net damages to society, not only because the costs of many white-collar crimes are omitted, but also because much of the damage is omitted even for the crimes covered.[41]

Nevertheless, Becker proposes that both crime and punishment can be reduced to what amounts to a cost-benefit analysis—especially when providing for the fact that people who commit crimes are essentially rational, market-based actors who, despite different levels of risk aversion, will also conduct a cost-benefit analysis in advance of committing crimes—and that harm can, to a significant degree, be quantified in monetary terms.[42] This means that the criminal justice system, in theory, can set the price, as it were, of criminal offenses and punishments in a way that produces a net gain for society.[43] As Dilts summarizes the basic contours of this line of reasoning,

> under neoliberalism, we are no longer concerned about the eradication of crime, nor are we concerned about individual criminals. The only relevant questions are those that operate at the general level of the population: the crime rate. Further, in drawing on the assumptions of neoliberal economic theory, the equilibrium point is determined by market conditions and never assumed to be equal to zero. As with other market phenomena (e.g., employment, inflation), there is some nonzero level of crime that can be called a "natural" rate.[44]

Feeley and Simon note that in the actuarial justice model, imprisonment—which is actually incapacitation—is not designed to promote rehabilitation but to "[rearrange] the distribution of offenders in society." Incarceration "can detain offenders for a time and thus delay the resumption of criminal activity in society."[45] A form of risk management, actuarial justice proposes that it can sort high-risk from low-risk offenders, maintaining long-term control over the former and shorter-term control over the latter.[46] Punishment is first detached from the crime and attached to the individual. For Harcourt, "the invention of actuarial methods at the dawn of the twentieth century and the steady rise in their use over the past fifty years fundamentally transformed what we punish in the twenty-first century—not just the act, but the character of the offender, who he is, his age, his schooling, his employment record, his marital history, his prior treatments and incarcerations."[47] In another respect, however, punishment is detached from the individual per se, and is tied instead to the way individuals' characteristics are indicative of their membership in a type, category, or population, since it is at the level of types, categories, and populations that risk can ostensibly be assessed. Feeley and Simon frame this form of biopower as an exercise of governmentality in the Foucauldian sense insofar as it acts on populations rather than individuals. As a result, individuals "increasingly . . . are grasped not as coherent subjects, whether understood as moral, psychological or economic agents, but as members of particular subpopulations and the intersection of various categorical indicators."[48] In other words, there is no need to identify the underlying causes of criminality (or other undesirable behavior) at the level of the individual offender—for example by examining his motivations or his mental state—but only to group and classify individual offenders into manageable populations (based on metrics such as age, level of education, employment record, marital history, and prior treatments and incarcerations).

Despite this particular form of simplification, legal reforms under neoliberalism, especially those that deal with sanctions for people convicted of crimes, rather than "rationalizing, purifying, and simplifying" the law, as Dilts describes it, have actually produced a complex web of collateral consequences, the rationality for which is a series of "formalistic fictions" in the law that separates punishments from other sanctions that serve preventive or public safety functions even though those sanctions carry the same punitive effects as punishment for those convicted of crimes.[49] Moreover, like the legislative frameworks that seek to simplify and clarify the relationship between the state and the market—such that market actors can be assured that the state will not intervene in their own rational behavior—at the same time that they actually obscure the relationship between the market and the law, the web of collateral consequences codified in state and federal law is obscure or incomprehensible even to those responsible for creating and administering them.[50]

In the actuarial model of justice, risk or danger under the law is simplified—reduced from deviance, monstrosity, and abnormality to an economic metric (where at its most fully realized, risk can be quantified according to a potentially limitless number of metrics such as family size, rental and eviction history, number of convictions, credit score, age, weight, and so on). But at the same time, the terms of the actual social contract are increasingly complex and opaque, since individuals can never be certain which metrics are being used to quantify them, or how or by whom such metrics will be used. This model finds an easy analogy in the reduction of all individual financial behavior to a single credit score, the algorithms for which are proprietary to each of the three credit bureaus. It is difficult or impossible to glean which financial behaviors are used to create this score, how each individual behavior is scored or combined with other scores, or why significant differences in scoring are possible between the three bureaus.

For Dilts, "what makes felons uniquely the subjects they are is that they can and must carry the burden of an excessive punishment on their physical bodies as well as on their abstract selves as members of a political community."[51] It is precisely this abstraction, however, that cannot be fathomed (either by the felon herself or by corporations, landlords, employers, or the public) when proprietary algorithms are tasked with delineating membership in the political community and defining the terms of the social contract. It is for this reason that exclusion from professional organizations, housing, and employment emerges less as an option than as an injunction in the form of a best practice. This best practice is sanctioned by the law insofar as it gives private companies the discretion to discriminate based on credit scores and criminal history. But it is also mandated by law insofar as these private actors can be held liable—to a greater or lesser extent, depending on individual jurisdictions and circumstances—for the behavior of third parties. However, while sanctioned and promoted by law, the consumer background report is what makes such exclusions possible.

PRIVATE RISK MITIGATION

Among Foucault's overarching concerns were the historical moments that gave rise to shifts in the circulation of power. One of the most important of these moments in modern history was the establishment and consolidation of the capitalist form during the eighteenth century. In the early 1970s—in his lectures on the punitive society in 1972–73 as well as in his published work, including *Discipline and Punish*—Foucault advanced a theory of the penitentiary that responded to transformations in the economy. He argued that the capitalist form in eighteenth-century England, and especially the increasing accumulation and concentration of goods, entailed new risks, which property owners sought to mitigate through new forms of social control.[52] These new forms of social control were focused less on behavior than they were during earlier periods, and more on morality and character. This moral training of the so-called lower classes—which were ultimately conflated with the working classes—was an exercise in what Foucault would later call governmentality, or the conduct of conduct: these "[populations'] manners must be reformed so as to reduce the risk to bourgeois wealth."[53] Controlling vice and immorality, but also the geographies where vice is exercised—such as gambling halls and brothels—was combined with social teaching about temperance, moderation, and virtue. For Foucault, the penitentiary model is an extension of this project, and as such is "situated on the borders of morality and penalty."[54] This coercive technology, as Foucault describes it, was "spontaneous" rather than rigorously planned or implemented from above. It was through the spontaneous social organization of the petite bourgeoisie to protect their own interests and mitigate the risks associated with new forms of producing and storing goods that the penitentiary as a system of moral-penal logic and techniques emerged. But importantly, the power to coerce was ultimately transferred from these spontaneous groups to the state—an aspect of the process Foucault would later call statification.[55]

Pursuits of justice and discipline were not always matters of public interest in the United States either. Through the mid-nineteenth century, policing was largely a non-professional activity, prosecutors often did their work on a volunteer or part-time basis as a supplement to their private legal practices, and criminal cases were often brought by private parties.[56] Alice Ristroph notes that it was "the perceived inefficiencies and arbitrariness of private prosecutions that led the United States to establish public prosecutors earlier and much more widely than other western democracies."[57] The professionalization of policing and prosecution and their transformation into activities of the state during the second half of the nineteenth century led to significant legal reforms, including the codification of an ever-expanding list of behaviors that qualified as criminal. As the power to bring charges moved from the private to the public realm, the prosecutor's office was endowed with increasing authority to determine which acts, and which people, the state would pursue as criminal. By 1940, Attorney General Robert Jackson would complain that "the prosecutor has more control over life, liberty, and reputation than any other person in America."[58] This control, in the form of prosecutorial discretion or selective prosecution, combined with targeted enforcement by a professionalized police force, both of which were historically racialized, has plagued the state-based criminal justice system since its inception—and provides both the political and historical foundations for the system of mass incarceration that emerges in the 1970s and 1980s.

Beginning in the 1970s, the increased use of criminalization and incarceration to manage entrenched social problems produced a population that could be ideologically delineated from the population of productive, normative citizens and workers. However, the public records that practically delineated this population were initially segregated and place-dependent, analogue, non-uniform, and difficult to access. Although it wouldn't find its fullest expression until decades later, the process of systematizing and streamlining criminal records began, James B. Jacobs argues, with the 1968 Gun Control Act, which disqualified felons, and later persons convicted of misdemeanor domestic violence charges, from owning or possessing firearms—a move, incidentally, that wedded criminality to the market and constitutional rights to ownership. The early days of the Act essentially worked on an honor system: while individuals were required to attest that they were eligible to purchase firearms, arms dealers had no way to verify this information. "In response," Jacobs continues, "gun control proponents lobbied for a law mandating that prospective purchasers be subject to a criminal record check by a designated state or county's chief law enforcement officer."[59] But it wasn't until 1993, with the passage of the Brady Handgun Violence Prevention Act, that the United States began in earnest to unify criminal records across all jurisdictions. The Brady Act mandated that the federal government develop the National Instant Criminal Background Check System (NICS), which would allow firearms dealers to verify customers' criminal history within three days. As a result, "the nationally integrated rap sheet system (Interstate Identification Index, or 'Triple I') made it possible for a police officer with access to a computer to find out practically instantly whether a suspect or arrestee had ever been arrested federally or in any state."[60]

While arrest and court records were instantly available to law enforcement agencies, they were initially less accessible to private companies and the general public, who still had to go through the courts to obtain public records. The consumer background report industry is a form of neoliberal destatification insofar as it promotes the transfer to businesses and individuals the power to police, surveil, and punish, and insofar as it transfers questions of policing, surveillance, and punishment from the political sphere to the technical one. This is unsurprising, given that the consumer background report emerged expressly to fill a technological gap—one that made it difficult for private parties to learn the criminal history of potential employees, clients, and renters, even though that information was now potentially available. By tapping into the state's upgraded records infrastructure, consumer background report agencies could compile their own private criminal history records, which could then be bought and sold on the open market.

As a profit-generating industry, the consumer background report industry would ultimately require an infinitely expanding number of high-risk individuals that its services might mitigate, but it would also require landlords, employers, and individuals to believe themselves at persistent risk of harm. Several decades of military-style policing, law-and-order rhetoric, and a criminal or quasi-criminal class that constituted a third of the population provided fertile soil for this venture. Moreover, in contrast to the state-based system of policing individuals that ostensibly pose a risk to public safety because they have already violated the law, the consumer background report industry conflates crime with bad credit, lack of insurance, eviction history, frequent moves, history of mental or behavioral health disorders, and even physical disease or disability. Criminals presumably represent a significant risk to the safety and security of individual institutions, but for the consumer background report industry, they are one among many types of risky consumer—consumer being the label attached to all individuals, as indicated in the name of the document called a consumer background report. In this way, the consumer background report industry represents one of the ways in which techniques and technologies of punishment continue to emerge spontaneously from the private sector to monitor, police, and punish the behavior of individuals in the service of consolidating its own financial and symbolic capital. While these technologies and techniques may emerge organically, however, the specifically neoliberal features of the consumer background report are evident in the manner in which they come to be regulated and then mandated by the state in ways that reduce the rights and political power of individuals and promote the consolidation of corporate power.

The main law that regulates and oversees the use of consumer background reports is the Fair Credit Reporting Act (FCRA). It gives consumer background report agencies wide discretion to collect private information and is essentially mute on how third parties can use that information. The purpose of the FCRA is "to require that consumer reporting agencies adopt reasonable procedures for meeting the needs of commerce for consumer credit, personnel, insurance, and other information in a manner which is fair and equitable to the consumer, with regard to the confidentiality, accuracy, relevancy, and proper utilization of such information in accordance with the requirements of this title."[61] As this language suggests, the law's primary stakeholder is "commerce," whereas protecting "consumers"—namely any individuals for whom a consumer background report has been created to meet the needs of commerce—is its subsidiary concern.

While the FCRA is overseen by the Federal Trade Commission and was initially concerned primarily with the accuracy of financial information, it now defines the consumer background report as

> any written, oral, or other communication of any information by a consumer reporting agency bearing on a consumer's credit worthiness, credit standing, credit capacity, character, general reputation, personal characteristics, or mode of living which is used or expected to be used or collected in whole or in part for the purpose of serving as a factor in establishing the consumer's eligibility for . . . credit or insurance to be used primarily for personal, family, or household purposes; . . . employment purposes; or . . . any other purpose authorized under section 604.[62]

Section 604 establishes that a consumer reporting agency may furnish a report to any person it *believes*

> intends to use the information in connection with a credit transaction involving the consumer on whom the information is to be furnished and involving the extension of credit to, or review or collection of an account of, the consumer; . . . intends to use the information for employment purposes; . . . intends to use the information in connection with the underwriting of insurance involving the consumer; . . . intends to use the information in connection with a determination of the consumer's eligibility for a license or other benefit granted by a governmental instrumentality required by law to consider an applicant's financial responsibility or status; . . . intends to use the information, as a potential investor or servicer, or current insurer, in connection with a valuation of, or an assessment of the credit or prepayment risks associated with, an existing credit obligation; . . . or otherwise has a legitimate business need for the information . . . [either] in connection with a business transaction . . . initiated by the consumer [or] to review an account to determine whether the consumer continues to meet the terms of the account.

Consumer background reporting agencies may also furnish reports to "executive departments and agencies in connection with the issuance of government-sponsored individually-billed travel charge cards," state and local child support enforcement agencies, to agencies setting child support awards, to the Federal Deposit Insurance Corporation (FDIC), or to the National Credit Union Administration. In other words, consumer background report agencies can furnish information about individuals' creditworthiness, credit standing, credit capacity, character, general reputation, personal characteristics, or mode of living to almost anyone. The FCRA places few limits on the types of information that consumer background report agencies can collect or distribute, or on the way third parties, such as lenders, landlords, or employers, can use that information.

Commercial or consumer background reports most often include information about an individual's credit history and criminal record. Some may contain information about social media activity, educational background, and citizenship status. Other "specialty" consumer background reports, as defined by the FCRA, may also include information about residential or tenant history, insurance claims, check writing history, and medical records and payments. The FCRA assumes that consumer background report agencies, employers, and landlords are capable of determining what constitutes things like "character," "reputation," and "mode of living," and that collecting and distributing any information whatsoever about individuals serves a legitimate, commercial purpose, at least in the context of the broad category of persons or entities listed in section 604. The FCRA does not legislate how the information in the report is used, for example what types of information contained in a report can or should be used to make which kinds of decisions. Such decisions remain fully within the purview of the employer or other entity in possession of the report.

Even though those in possession of a consumer background report—like employers and landlords—are granted wide discretion to use accurate information however they wish, the FCRA does offer protection to individuals regarding the accuracy of the information contained in their reports. It legislates that information contained in consumer background reports must be accurate, and it also requires that when an adverse action is taken as a result of information contained in a report, the affected person is notified, provided with the information in the report, and given an opportunity to correct any incorrect information. For this reason, employers and landlords are ill-advised to conduct their own background investigations. Reputable, commercial, for-profit, and FCRA-compliant agencies are a much safer alternative, since, in using them, the risk of non-compliance is transferred from the employer or landlord to the agency. However, the consumer background report industry is not strictly employer or landlord driven. There are thousands of consumer background report companies generating millions of dollars each year, and market research suggests that this is a substantial growth sector.[63] The consumer background report industry can sustain itself as a growth sector only by crafting the employment relation as inherently risky. It needs criminals to sustain that risk, and it needs them to be perceived as a persistent and perpetual danger.

Consumer background report agencies and trade groups for human resources professionals, such as the Society for Human Resources Management (SHRM), each traffic in the same rhetoric of risk. For consumer background report agencies, employers are a primary customer base, and marketing materials stress the dangers of not conducting thorough, FCRA-compliant screenings on all applicants. Their websites are often filled with worst-case scenarios and scandals about employees who were hired despite criminal records and who then committed new, and often violent, crimes. Though anecdotal and often outdated, these stories are frequently presented as evidence of a normal, everyday, and ubiquitous problem in US workplaces. The website of Pre-Employ, a major background screening vendor for US companies, features the story of a man convicted of murder, released on parole after twelve years, and hired by a state department of child welfare services twenty years after the event. Even though it does not appear that the employee committed any new crimes or endangered any clients or colleagues, the story is presented as a case in point against hiring people convicted of so-called serious crimes—and especially of hiring people without conducting a thorough, nationwide background check.[64]

The SHRM not only frames the criminal background check as a best practice, noting that the vast majority of employers conduct background checks on at least some of their potential hires, but underscores the dangers of not conducting them. The organization hosts a blog-style series of articles on its website, many of which are focused on the use of background checks, FCRA compliance, and the need for greater employer control over the hiring process. Among these articles are a number of anecdotes about people hired for jobs without having been properly vetted. Many of these are written by security professionals in other fields, or republished from other professional organizations focused on security, such as the American Society for Industrial Security and its online publication, *Security Management.* In one such article published in 2020 entitled "Do Organizations Rely on Background Checks Too Much?" the answer is a resounding no: "A cornerstone of a sound security program, preemployment screening is used almost universally by employers; the Professional Background Screening Association indicates that 96.1 percent of employers perform some sort of preemployment background screening."[65] Nonetheless, the article continues, there are gaps in this system, as well as "egregious examples of . . . abuse or poor oversight." These are not examples in which candidates were denied jobs because of incomplete or inaccurate information contained in background reports, or in which qualified candidates were denied jobs because their background reports contained minor crimes irrelevant to the positions for which they applied. Rather, they are examples in which, despite passing background checks, individuals nonetheless committed serious crimes. The authors note that "in more than 60,000 cases over the last 20 years alone, US security, intelligence, military and law enforcement personnel were charged with major felonies." While they neither cite any research nor provide any data on the number of those previously convicted, the authors contend that at least some of these crimes were made possible because the individuals in question falsified information, such as their names or social security numbers, or lied about their educational background, work experience, arrest history, or citizenship status. On the other hand, the authors contend, "passing a background investigation, even a properly conducted one, is no guarantee that the employee is law-abiding, psychologically sound or even who he or she claims to be. Nor does it ensure that he or she won't break [the law] in the future."

The primary target of these authors' blame is criminals themselves: "Criminals continually circumvent and outsmart the screening process." Despite a reality in which most people with a criminal record cannot find stable housing or employment, the authors cite two cases in which individuals falsified information to pass a background screening. Moreover, while framing criminal "guile" as a ubiquitous problem, their two cases are more than a decade old. The first features a Mexican citizen who had been arrested for "smuggling more than 100 illegal immigrants to the United States from Mexico," and who later falsified his birth certificate to get a job as a US Border Patrol agent. The authors do not provide any information about his performance or any criminal activity that took place on the job. However, their use of the terminology of "illegal immigrants" not only highlights the criminality of the agent in question but also constructs migrant workers or people who lack authorization to work in the United States as inherently criminal—reminding human resources professionals that the consumer background report can also mitigate the risk of hiring this form of criminal or illegal Other. The second ten-year-old case is of a man who falsified his date of birth and social security number to obtain a custodial job at a university. Later, he killed his supervisor, wounded another person, and killed himself. The authors note that, if not for having falsified his information, the university would have been privy to his five-year prison sentence. They do not mention that the man had been imprisoned for the non-violent crime of receiving stolen property,[66] or that guidance from the Equal Employment Opportunity Commission (EEOC) advises against using older convictions, non-violent convictions, or convictions unrelated to job performance to disqualify job applicants, since doing so has a disparate impact on people of color.

In addition to criminal "guile," another major problem with the employee background screening process, according to the authors, is the scope of checks: "Background checks don't go far enough."[67] They cite the case of a woman whom they suggest should have been denied a job as a paralegal in a US Attorney's Office because her sister was married to a member of a Mexican drug cartel.[68] The authors imply that one's own criminal history is insufficient to assess the potential for future law-breaking. In this case, had a background check revealed the job candidate's third-hand relationship, through marriage, to a cartel member, this should have been sufficient reason to deny her a job as a low-level paralegal. Taken to its extreme, the only acceptable job candidates seem to be those not only without any criminal history of their own, but without any friends or relatives, no matter how remote, who have a criminal or even suspected criminal history.[69] Given the vast number of people in the United States who have at least an arrest record, very few people—and perhaps no one—would be able to pass the kind of background screening these authors promote.

Consumer background report agencies and professional organizations such as the SHRM deploy legal concepts while espousing views that are in direct opposition to them. For example, they both frequently cite the need to maintain compliance with the accuracy standards of the FCRA while framing this compliance as a hindrance to employers' autonomy. Moreover, state laws that limit the availability of criminal records to a certain time period are seen as anathema to employers' ability to determine and control their own workforce. Industry-produced marketing materials and advice produced by professional organizations each stress the need to work towards loosening the legal restrictions placed on employers by the FCRA, which are framed as overly burdensome, even as they give employers wide discretion to use information about job candidates however they wish.

Beyond the FCRA, employers and landlords are both required to comply with civil rights law, which bars discrimination in employment and housing based on race, color, religion, sex, national origin, familial status, and disability. Even though it is legal to discriminate against people with criminal records, guidance from the EEOC and the US Department of Housing and Urban Development (HUD) stresses the disparate impact on people of color of imposing blanket bans on people with criminal convictions.[70] This guidance is in direct conflict with the goals of the consumer background report industry, which frames all people convicted of crimes—and even their family members and associates—as a persistent threat to the safety and security of workplaces and residential properties. Thus, at the same time the industry urges employers to adopt EEOC and HUD guidance to evaluate each individual on his or her own merits, for example by considering the amount of time that has elapsed since a conviction and the relevance of the conviction to the job being sought, it contends both implicitly and explicitly through the use of anecdotal evidence that anyone with a criminal conviction should be considered suspect—and therefore unemployable and unsuited to living in the private housing market. As a consequence, employers and landlords are urged to understand EEOC and HUD guidance as misguided, a hindrance to maintaining their institutional status quo, and as something that can be circumvented.

CIRCUMVENTING CIVIL RIGHTS

During the Clinton administration, the US Department of Housing and Urban Development released the *One Strike Guide*, a policy aimed at removing people with criminal records from public housing and barring them from obtaining public housing in the future. Congress transformed this policy into law when it passed the Quality Housing and Work Responsibility Act (QHWRA) in 1998.

> The Act encouraged [public housing authorities (PHAs)] to deny public housing to applicants if, during a "reasonable time" preceding their admission, a household member engaged in any drug-related or violent criminal activity, or any other criminal activity "which would adversely affect the health, safety, or right to peaceful enjoyment of the premises by other residents." The Act did not define "reasonable time," leaving it to individual PHAs' discretion to determine how recent a conviction must be to qualify as a basis for denying housing.[71]

The QHWRA was an integral part of the Clintonite War on Drugs. Aside from people subject to lifetime sex offender registration, all of the illegal activities requiring banishment from public housing in the Act were of a drug-related nature. Beyond these, public housing authorities were offered wide discretion to determine who should be evicted. Furthermore, "under HUD's implementing regulations, neither the filing of criminal charges nor a resulting conviction are required prior to eviction—a mere accusation of criminal activity or drug-related activity can trigger an eviction."[72] The same guidance applied to applicants for public housing, and not just to those who were already residents: "Many housing authorities interpreted the various one-strike rules to indicate HUD's support for broad bans on applicants with any type of criminal history, regardless of whether the conviction was recent or whether the crime alleged is predictive of potential lease violation or behavior that would endanger other tenants."[73] The exclusion from public housing of both criminal offenders and suspected criminals was one of the strategies, along with the criminalization of drug use and drug addiction, that allowed mass incarceration to flourish.

Large, inner-city housing projects have been paradigmatic of state control over Black people's bodies, behaviors, and movements, and their disproportionate policing by law enforcement has been one method for carrying out the mass displacement of Black communities into prisons. Robin D. G. Kelley has explained how housing projects were a key site of police repression during the mid- to late-1980s. In Los Angeles,

> Black working class communities . . . were turned into war zones. . . . Police helicopters, complex electronic surveillance, even small tanks armed with battering rams became part of this increasingly militarized urban landscape. Housing projects, such as Imperial Courts, were renovated along the lines of minimum security prisons and equipped with fortified fencing and a Los Angeles Police Department Substation. Imperial Courts residents were suddenly required to carry identity cards and visitors were routinely searched.[74]

The techniques endemic to the administration of public housing disrupt the spatial and temporal conditions that typically delimit the prison. Public housing is a literal and symbolic prison insofar as it is constituted through its relationship to surveillance and control and fueled by paranoia and anxiety—of both existing in and being expelled from. This is true not only for convicted or suspected criminals and people who use drugs but for the individuals and families who have relationships with them. Everyone who inhabits the public housing space is both suspect and subject to surveillance and arbitrary eviction. Seen through the lens of public housing, carceral space is not only constituted by confinement, surveillance, and control; here, carcerality is a set of spaces and practices that produce fear, insecurity, precarity, exclusion, and criminalization, independent of criminal activity or even suspected criminal activity.

The private rental market followed in the footsteps of public housing authorities, in full accordance with the law. Private landlords may legally discriminate against people with criminal convictions, as well as against those with only an arrest record. Many local jurisdictions have implemented programs aimed at creating so-called crime-free neighborhoods that actually encourage the use of blanket bans to deny housing to those with arrests or convictions.[75] Due in part to the easy availability of commercial criminal background checks, "private landlords . . . may be permitted to deny housing to as much as one quarter of the US population, the majority of whom are people of color, due to a past criminal record."[76]

There are substantial housing inequities for people of color even when a wide range of factors is controlled for, and discrimination against people of color in policing and the criminal justice system reinforces and exacerbates the existing impact of racial discrimination in housing.[77] While it is difficult, and often impossible, to prove overt racial discrimination in court, paired testing is a research methodology widely used to measure discrimination in both housing and employment contexts. In paired testing, two equally qualified subjects apply for the same job, the same rental unit, or the same mortgage loan, and the differences in treatment and outcomes of white candidates and candidates of color are compared. Research conducted by HUD in 2012 used paired testing to measure discrimination against Black, Hispanic, and Asian renters. In their study, all races were treated approximately the same during the initial telephone inquiry. Minor disparities begin to occur during the first in-person meeting, when Black, Hispanic, and Asian renters were all told less information about available rental units than their white counterparts. Disparities grew at the viewing stage, when Black renters were shown one fewer unit for every twenty-five visits, Hispanic renters were shown one fewer unit for every fourteen visits, and Asian renters were shown one fewer unit for every thirteen visits. The cumulative data showed that Black renters learned about 11.4 percent fewer available units and were shown 4.2 percent fewer units than white renters, while Hispanic renters learned about 12.5 percent fewer available units and were shown 7.5 percent fewer units than white renters, and Asian renters learned about 9.8 percent fewer available units and were shown 6.6 percent fewer units than white renters.[78] While this HUD study did not address the compounding effects of a criminal record, Devah Pager's paired testing studies in employment contexts documents that not only are people of color disproportionately arrested, convicted, and sentenced for crimes that tend to be committed equally across races, but they are also disproportionately affected by the stigma associated with a criminal record. In her study, Black men with no criminal record are not only less likely to receive positive responses from potential employers than white men without felony convictions, they are also less likely to receive a positive response than white men *with* felony convictions.[79] Put simply, the widespread use of blanket bans denying employment and housing to people with criminal records is one of the ways that racial discrimination continues to take place in a quasi-covert manner.

In April of 2016, the Office of the General Counsel of HUD acknowledged this fact when it published guidance meant to alleviate some of the effects of race-based housing discrimination. This guidance suggests that where blanket policies denying housing to people with criminal records "has a disparate impact on individuals of a particular race, national origin, or other protected class, such policy or practice is unlawful under the Fair Housing Act if it is not necessary to serve a substantial, legitimate, nondiscriminatory interest of the housing provider or if such interest could be served by another practice that has a less discriminatory effect."[80] This guidance works under the theory of disparate impact, which addresses the systemic or institutional nature of discrimination rather than the overt and intentional racism that ostensibly preceded it. Under disparate impact theory, housing advocates can challenge the legality of housing practices without having to identify specific discriminatory actors or prove discriminatory intent by those actors. Instead, they need only to identify that members of a protected class are disproportionately affected by institutional policies, practices, or behaviors.

The Supreme Court in *Griggs v. Duke Power Co.*, an equal employment case, recognized disparate impact as a form of discrimination under Title VII of the Civil Rights Act of 1964: "Under the Act, practices, procedures, or tests neutral on their face, and even neutral in terms of intent, cannot be maintained if they operate to 'freeze' the status quo of prior discriminatory employment practices."[81] Disparate impact theory, however, largely "has been a failure for housing advocates. It is overly complicated, infrequently used, and seldom leads to plaintiff success."[82] Furthermore, "the standards applied to determine liability under the substantive antidiscrimination provisions of the Fair Housing Act of 1968 . . . remain inchoate,"[83] and "outside of the original context in which the theory arose, namely written employment texts, the disparate impact theory has produced no substantial change and there is no reason to think that extending the theory to other contexts would have produced meaningful reform."[84] In fact, despite the *Griggs* reasoning, courts have continued to require proof of discriminatory intent when deciding equal protection cases.[85] These trends reflect, for one legal scholar, that the Supreme Court's discrimination doctrine "largely [mirrors] American society in its desire to wish away racial injustice," and that the Court has been "restrained by little more than its own normative vision."[86] The 2016 HUD guidance, therefore, while a significant piece of public policy that acknowledges racial discrimination in both the criminal justice system and in the private rental market, was never likely to lead to substantive reform.

Another reason that public policy is unlikely to lead to substantive reform is the entrenched set of beliefs about criminal offenders that is continually invoked by consumer background report agencies and professional organizations for landlords, such as the National Association for Independent Landlords. While employers are one primary target market for consumer background report agencies, landlords represent another significant market. In fact, in housing, the line between trade groups or professional organizations and consumer background report agencies is often opaque or non-existent. One trade group, the American Apartment Owners Association (AAOA), is also a consumer background report agency. On the home page of its website, the AAOA lists the services it offers in several different places, each time placing tenant screening services at the top of the list. Like consumer background report agencies whose target market is employers, the AAOA uses almost every page of its website to promote tenant screening services, and hosts dozens of stories and hypothetical scenarios framing the background report as the only way to mitigate the risk of renting to undesirable tenants. While highlighting the perpetual danger posed by people with criminal records, consumer background report agencies targeting landlords, along with trade or professional organizations for landlords and property managers, traffic in a rhetoric of risk that is much broader than criminality.

A tenant background check provides a comprehensive look at the applicant, including everything from rental history to criminal records. Landlords can screen prospective tenants with a renter background check, often along with a credit report, in order to verify and choose the best renter for the property. If you do not perform a background check on tenants, you are putting the safety and security of your rental property, and any other tenants who share that property, at risk.[87]

In fact, among consumer background report agencies and professional organizations, the risk to landlords of so-called bad tenants primarily focuses not on their prior criminality but on their propensity to destroy property and evade paying rent. The website of the National Association for Independent Landlords, which also offers criminal, eviction, and credit reports, hosts a page of "Landlord Horror Stories," none of which feature stories about people convicted of crimes. They focus instead on instances in which renters stole or destroyed property and avoided paying rent. For this organization, the main justification for the use of criminal background checks specifically is simply that "you don't want a criminal in your home."[88] In other words, while trade groups and consumer background report agencies acknowledge the legal dangers of discriminating against or appearing to discriminate against people on the basis of their membership in legally protected groups, they implicitly and explicitly endorse practices like blanket bans that have a disparate impact on people who are members of these groups.

For landlords and property management companies, professional and trade groups, and consumer background report agencies, the rhetoric of criminality is conflated with other forms of risk to produce a figure of perpetual danger. The state, as Dilts argues, may no longer need to produce the figures of "the monstrous individual, the criminally insane, the incorrigible offender, and the recidivist" in order to realize its vision of actuarial justice.[89] But these other non-state actors—landlords, employers, and the professional organizations that provide them with practical and legal guidance—have transformed the management of the incorrigible offender into a best practice. As the state before them did, these entities use the (raced and classed) figure of the perpetual criminal to banish or exclude those they believe pose a risk to their institutional status quo. This status quo includes, at its most fundamental level, extracting symbolic, financial, and political capital from the poor within a marketplace where wealth is more and more difficult to amass, since it is increasingly concentrated in the hands of a few wealthy elites who are shielded from tax liability and other forms of wealth redistribution. This is one form of destatification, then, in which employers, landlords, and consumer background report agencies spontaneously organize themselves to craft a certain figure of perpetual danger—one that allows them, like the petite bourgeoisie of the eighteenth century, to protect their own interests and mitigate the risks associated with operating in the neoliberal marketplace. At the same time, what makes this political-economic arrangement a specifically neoliberal one is the fact that it is mandated by the state. This mandate reduces the political and economic power of large swaths of the population while consolidating the political and economic power of property owners, limited liability companies, and large corporations.

State-based institutional disciplinary and grievance procedures, such as those used in prisons, and the use of the commercial background report, were both forms of bureaucratization and institution building—one emerging from the public sector of the courtroom and the penal system, and one emerging from the private sector. Each formalized and systematized a series of often inconsistent and ad hoc practices that proceeded them. The prison disciplinary procedure replaced older, more arbitrary methods of adjudicating or simply punishing prisoners' infractions. The disciplinary board functions as a quasi-judicial body—a body that is treated as a judicial body—that respects due process, even though due process can only be realized in the courtroom. While the disciplinary procedure represented an improvement over the ad hoc imposition of corporal punishment, for example, it also formalized or institutionalized the removal of prisoners from courtrooms as both perpetrators and victims, diminishing their legal personhood. Similarly, the consumer background report did not create marginalization or exclusion for ex-offenders, which have always existed in some form. It did, however, formalize or institutionalize their exclusion, transforming inconsistent and ad hoc practices into a series of consistent, formal, and systematic best practices.[90]

Chapter 2 of this book argued that guilt, innocence, and the type and severity of criminal sanctions are an index of public values, and that the adjudication and punishment of criminal behavior by administrators rather than judges or juries erodes the ability of the public to engage in discourse about and negotiate its shared values. This chapter examined how the consumer background report industry not only makes the criminal record a permanent mark of persistent risk but also conflates criminality and other forms of risk, promoting the view that risk is a normal and ubiquitous part of everyday life to be managed and mitigated not by the state but by private interests, like landlords and employers. The next chapter turns to Airbnb's 2018 criminal ban as a case study to examine how tech platforms capitalize on this cultural production of risk to readjudicate criminal behavior and to impose post-sentence sanctions—collateral consequences—on people convicted of crimes. Institutional exclusion effected through algorithmic and putatively neutral and technical expertise has become a best practice that, as such, falls largely outside the realm of political debate. At the same, Airbnb does not limit itself to adjudicating and imposing sanctions for criminal behavior. It relies on commonsense and depoliticized ideas about criminals and other individuals considered high-risk to install itself as an ostensibly innocuous and disinterested quasi-governmental body as it legislates the terms of social belonging.

4. Readjudicating Crimes and Imposing Sanctions in Airbnb's Neoliberal "Community"

Airbnb hosts six million listings in more than one hundred thousand cities across the world. In the fifteen years since its founding, more than a half billion people have stayed in lodgings listed on Airbnb, and on an average day, two million people will stay at an Airbnb listing.[1] While the company's image is tied to ideas about leisure and tourism, Airbnb has created a vast short-term rental market often relied upon by those who are excluded from the traditional rental market, and a professional class that manages and operates that market. In this market, hosts are subject to the exploitative and discriminatory practices of the gig economy, and guests are subject to the exploitative and discriminatory conditions of the private rental market. It is in part by fashioning its members as part of a post-national and globalized "community" that Airbnb promotes a neoliberal, post-wage vision of life, labor, and economic participation. The company goads its members into adopting identities that are compatible with neoliberalism—into crafting themselves as units of individual enterprise that are nonetheless reliant on the company to promote their brand.

While Airbnb frames itself as an apolitical and disinterested platform for the free exchange of services and ideas, it relies on raced and classed exclusions to craft its community, achieve market dominance, and attain political power. In the summer of 2018, Airbnb implemented a policy banning certain criminals from its site. The policy is vague, defining certain crimes as more serious or less serious by example rather than rule, and the company does not say how its decisions are made or by whom (or what). Proprietary algorithms and algorithmic decision-making are invisible, human decision-making is opaque, actual decisions about the type and length of banishment at times do not match the company's published policy, and its decisions are not subject to appeal. This policy is paradigmatic of a shifting landscape in which private companies are tasked with designing and imposing collateral consequences fully at their own discretion and with little or no public oversight. As discussed in the previous chapter, the system of collateral consequences codified in law is deeply flawed. However, private collateral consequences are designed and imposed wholly outside of judicial or legislative processes. It is Airbnb as a corporate entity, rather than legislators, the public, or even its own members, that determine things like the seriousness or severity of crimes or types of crimes and the post-sentence sanctions that people with criminal convictions should face. Airbnb's criminal ban is an example of how the boardroom is increasingly fashioned as a quasi-judicial body whose purpose is to impose sanctions on those individuals it deems a risk, even when those individuals' crimes have already been adjudicated and punished by the courts.

Although Airbnb is not a courtroom, it is the arbiter of decisions about what consequences or penalties a convicted person will face. Like criminal defendants facing new charges, people with criminal records who are subject to banishment from Airbnb were convicted in a criminal justice system plagued by racial prejudice, coercive police tactics designed to impel confessions, and the inequity of the plea bargain.[2] Convictions won under such circumstances are used in the private sector almost universally and by default to impose new consequences in excess of both judicial sentences and collateral consequences codified in state and federal law. Whereas the Federal Rules of Evidence disallow the use of previous convictions to prove a defendant's character, Airbnb's 2018 criminal ban relies on the reasoning that criminal procedure is designed to mitigate—that a conviction is evidence of future offending. While there are numerous exceptions to these rules, the law contends, at least in principle, that previous criminal activity does not guarantee future criminal activity, and that only evidence related to the case at hand should be used to determine guilt.[3] Moreover, criminal procedure is relatively transparent, open to public debate, and subject to change based on shifting public sentiment, judicial opinion, legislation, and precedent. Unlike in the criminal justice system, however, there are no rules or systematized practices that employers, landlords, or other private interests must adhere to or apply when determining the probative or prejudicial value of previous convictions. Employers, landlords, and private companies have complete discretion to determine, using any methods they wish, or no methods at all, whether they believe that someone convicted of a crime poses a future risk. They may impose blanket bans on people convicted of any crimes or certain types of crimes, or they may categorize crimes according to severity, based on whatever criteria they wish. In opposition to the spirit, if not the outcome, of criminal procedure, these processes implicitly and often explicitly aver that a previous conviction guarantees future criminality.

Legal scholar Wayne Logan calls consequences of conviction not codified in state and federal law "informal collateral consequences." These include discrimination in housing and employment, general social stigma, and other forms of exclusion from and marginalization within any number of social and institutional contexts.[4] This chapter argues in contrast that Airbnb's 2018 criminal ban is paradigmatic of the policy-and-order society, of the way that many forms of extra-legal exclusion and marginalization are not at all informal but are rather codified in corporate policy and carried out with professional, managerial, and quasi-judicial expertise. While these policies and exclusions help to ensure that ex-offenders remain within the confines of the service ghetto, they also shape public perception of crime, risk, and justice. When the imposition of collateral consequences is outsourced to companies like Airbnb, punishment becomes an apolitical best practice that replaces the public negotiation of social norms with terms of service.

CORPORATE COMMUNITIES AND COMMUNAL EXCLUSIONS

Corporate policies that ban people convicted of crimes from accessing technology platforms are an example of how the boardroom is increasingly fashioned as a quasi-judicial body whose purpose is to assess the severity of crimes and to determine and impose the appropriate sanctions for those crimes, even though these crimes have already been adjudicated in a court of law, their perpetrators punished with court imposed sentences such as fines, terms of probation, and prison sentences, and further subjected to collateral consequences codified in state and federal law. While discrimination in excess of these sanctions against people with criminal records in housing and employment is longstanding, Airbnb's 2018 ban on people with criminal records as both hosts and guests is an index of the shifting landscape of exclusions and penalties in an increasingly technology-driven economy and society.

Airbnb has created an enormous professional market for short-term housing. In many cities, rental prices have increased exponentially as real estate is bought up en masse by corporate interests, realtors, and limited liability companies and transformed into short-term rental space under the guise of the sharing economy. As many discussion forum complaints among Airbnb hosts show, the platform is increasingly used as the short-term rental option of choice for people who are experiencing housing insecurity—and not just for vacation or travel lodging. Despite this, Airbnb's status as a platform—essentially as a middleman that connects private individuals who want to "share" their home with potential guests who want to stay in those homes—protects it from many of the legal obligations of realtors and property agents. For the same reason, the company relinquishes responsibility for screening guests. It encourages hosts to take responsibility for screening their own guests, suggesting that members "consider doing a web search and checking public government databases such as the U.S. federal or state sex offender registries for the name(s) of anyone with whom you interact offline."[5] Here, guidance that would bring landlords and leasing agents out of compliance with the Fair Credit Reporting Act (FCRA) is considered a best practice for guest screening—even though such information may be incorrect or outdated. A whole range of online services has emerged to help hosts conduct this screening process. On the home page of its website, the technology company Autohost claims to use a proprietary algorithm to "evaluate the risk level of guest reservations and, if necessary, [run] a complete background check on the guest." This background check "leverages the power of machine learning to comb through 300k databases in a split second to find a match for an individual."

Despite its position that members should engage in lateral surveillance by conducting their own background checks on potential guests, in 2018, Airbnb began banning people with criminal records from its site, as both hosts and guests. Under point 2.1.5 of its Updated Terms of Service, "Information We Collect from Third Parties," Airbnb acknowledges that it will now collect "background information" about members:

> For Members in the United States, to the extent permitted by applicable laws, Airbnb and Airbnb Payments may obtain reports from public records of criminal convictions or sex offender registrations. For Members outside of the United States, to the extent permitted by applicable laws and with your consent where required, Airbnb and Airbnb Payments may obtain the local version of police, background or registered sex offender checks. We may use your information, including your full name and date of birth, to obtain such reports.[6]

On one of its help pages, the company attempts to explain its policy on the use of criminal background checks.[7] This explanation is grounded in fears that guests with a criminal conviction pose a threat to hosts and is careful to explain that background checks, while necessary, are insufficient for determining such a threat. It warns that hosts should be skeptical of criminal background checks, noting that even a clean record is "never a guarantee that a person won't break the law in the future." It says nothing of the possibility that someone who has committed a crime in the past may not commit one in the future—implicitly framing the conviction as a mark of future criminality.

Airbnb outlines the kinds of criminal activity it finds unacceptable and the consequences for having committed them:

- Users with serious criminal histories may be removed or referred for further review if our checks show convictions within a certain time period.
- Less serious convictions will never result in removal (such as disorderly conduct or marijuana possession).
- Some other crimes may result in removal for a period of 14 years (such as felony burglary or felony larceny) or seven years (such as fraud or property damage) from the date of conviction.

- Severe crimes may result in removal for a longer period of time or even permanently (such as murder, terrorism, rape or child molestation).

It is impossible to tell from Airbnb's public documentation how determinations are made, for example by individuals or by algorithms, or what criteria the company uses to make such determinations. It is entirely possible that there are no systematized or formalized criteria and that cases are simply resolved according to individual employees' moral judgments. The opacity of the decision-making process means that Airbnb can determine on a case-by-case, ad hoc basis which offenses it considers serious and how perpetrators of these offenses should be further punished, as evidenced by the fact that at least some individual banishments, including my own, exceed the company's already vague set of guidelines.[8]

Both the types of crimes and the measures the company purports to take are ill-defined. In point one, Airbnb does not define what it means by "serious criminal histories," how long "a certain time period" is, what "referral" means, to whom such a referral might be made, or whether removal is temporary or permanent. While it uses examples in point two to illustrate what it means by "less serious convictions"—disorderly conduct or marijuana possession—it is impossible to know how the company determines what serious and non-serious offenses are, or what other crimes might constitute them. Moreover, many states' criminal codes do not have a statute specifically for marijuana possession, making it impossible for Airbnb to determine which kind of drug was the object of a drug possession conviction without inspecting the arrest reports of every potential member convicted of such a crime.

After permanent banishment for serious crimes, the next level of criminal severity comes with a fourteen-year period of removal, followed by a seven-year period of removal for "some other crimes." Like the company's quasi-definitions of crime types, whether these numbers are arbitrary or evidence-based, and the extent to which it actually follows its own guidelines, is impossible to know—since the company has every right to keep its records private. While most states do not place limits on the criminal history information that can be obtained by landlords, some management companies do follow guidance issued by HUD that suggests limiting background checks to a "reasonable period of time," which is often interpreted to mean ten years. In employment contexts, most states do not place a time limit on reporting criminal convictions, although about a dozen states follow a seven-year rule, meaning that consumer background reports cannot report information to potential employers about convictions that are more than seven years old. In many cases, Airbnb may plan to ban members well into a future in which their crimes would not be identifiable via these same background checks if used by employers or landlords. In this way, Airbnb's criminal ban is even more excessive and punitive than those found in many employment contexts and in the traditional housing market. Whether or not employers or landlords follow their policies is also difficult to assess, but the policies themselves at least symbolize compliance with progressive interpretations of antidiscrimination law. In contrast, an intentionally ill-defined policy such as Airbnb's is an ideal way to ensure that the company can exercise broad discretion in making case-by-case decisions grounded in personal, moralistic judgments while avoiding the appearance of racial, ethnic, or class bias.

Corporate policies that address factors beyond the criminal conviction are not without their problems, not least of which are that the conviction continues to be seen as proof of criminality rather than a result of structural inequalities, and that rehabilitation is usually defined as normative performance in the capitalist marketplace. Moreover, what these policies actually mean and whether or not employers follow them are difficult to determine. In its 2012 survey of employers, the Society for Human Resources Management asked employers how and why they used criminal background screenings in the hiring process. Survey respondents cited any number of factors they might consider when encountering an applicant with a criminal record. Eighty-four percent of respondents said that the severity of criminal activity—apparently as defined by the respondent—would be very influential in their decision-making process, while 76 percent said the number of convictions would be. Sixty-nine percent cited the relevance of the criminal activity to the position as being very influential, while 51 percent said the length of time since the criminal activity occurred would influence their decision, and 37 percent would be influenced by the age of the candidate when the criminal activity occurred (i.e., in adulthood versus in youth).[9] Regardless of company policies, hiring managers have the discretion to make subjective interpretations about the severity of crimes and crime types, and to decide what rehabilitation means and how it is demonstrated. While overtly acknowledging that criminal convictions may be inadequate to determine the qualifications of a job candidate, renter, or community member, policies that promote ad hoc decision-making often provide hiring managers, landlords, and other administrators with the means to exclude individuals and groups in ways that appear race- and class neutral. These companies can facilitate the increased social exclusion of former offenders—a group that is disproportionately Black and socioeconomically disadvantaged—by leveraging ostensibly neutral, technical, and colorblind expertise.

Because technology companies are so reliant on algorithms to make decisions, they may appear less prone to interpersonal bias than landlords and employers, who expressly make moral decisions about the qualifications of job candidates and the suitability of potential renters. However, as *New York Times* journalists Sheera Frenkel and Cecilia Kang explain in their recent book documenting Facebook's failure to protect users' privacy, technology companies are not at all immune from personal, ad hoc decision-making. In one particularly salient vignette, the authors describe how the company handled the massive influx of dis- and misinformation on the network during the Trump era. While Facebook historically had maintained a policy banning hate speech, its "definition of what constituted it was ever evolving," and it had no real methodology for determining what counted as hate speech. Facebook content moderators were simply expected to "know it when [they] see it," much like judges who know collateral consequences (not to mention "obscenity") when they see them and, more recently, lawmakers who know lynching when they see it.[10] Like Airbnb's criminal ban that relies on definitions-by-example, Facebook's early speech policies, Frenkel and Kang explain, "boiled down to 'If something makes you feel bad in your gut, take it down.' These guidelines were passed along in emails or in shared bits of advice in the office cafeteria. There were lists of previous examples of items Facebook had removed, but without explanation or context behind those decisions. It was, at best, ad hoc."[11] The company's "evolving" speech policy, often constituted by ad hoc decision-making by content moderators, had not changed much in the decade leading up to the 2016 election cycle when "Facebook executives were creating the basis for a new speech policy as a knee-jerk reaction to Donald Trump."[12]

Like Facebook's knee-jerk reaction to Donald Trump, Airbnb's criminal ban seems to have been precipitated by criminal or criminal-like behavior among guests—such as theft and vandalism. But there does not seem to be much evidence that these behaviors were disproportionately committed by people who had criminal records. Indeed, by any measure, the predictive logic of the criminal record is inexact, with some recent evidence suggesting that most people have engaged in some form of law-breaking, and that many habitually violate the law.[13] Not only do half of all crimes in the United States go unreported, half of those crimes that are reported remain unsolved.[14] In 2019, according to the FBI, only 45.5 percent of reported violent crimes and 17.2 percent of reported property crimes were solved—where being solved may only mean that an arrest has been made.[15] There is no way to know how many of these crimes may have been committed by people who already had a criminal record, but it is likely that a significant number of people have broken the law, or have habitually broken the law, but do not have a criminal record. This is part of the reason that Airbnb warns users not to rely solely on the information contained in commercial background reports when making decisions about renters: it is not only those people with criminal records who present a probable risk to the safety and security of the community, and hosts should conduct their own research to learn just what *type* of person they might be renting to.

Although Airbnb has spent years developing policies to stem racial discrimination on the platform, the company provides a number of guidelines to help hosts determine what constitutes the right type of guest, beyond their criminal history, and many of these are raced, classed, and gendered. The Airbnb magazine is one of the ways the company shapes an image of itself and its members and assists hosts in identifying other normative members of the community. While it purports to "[celebrate] humanity wherever it exists: across borders, time zones, languages, and skin tones," the magazine's target audience, according to its media kit, is college-educated millennials with a median annual household income of $95,000. In attempting to reach two audiences at once—hosts and guests—the magazine presents an ideal form of neoliberalism in which there is no distinction between buyer, seller, or product, and in which all parties to a transaction are perfectly branded units of individual enterprise. It is part travel magazine, part advertising vehicle, part strategy and branding column. For guests, Airbnb promises belonging in once-foreign places, namely by providing access to homes, families, and communities that wish to facilitate that belonging: "Airbnb Magazine amplifies the local perspective and positions travel as transformative. It's accessible, immersive, and champions connection and connectivity by focusing on people, especially in the local 'host' community." For hosts, Airbnb ostensibly provides relief from "a world that is increasingly digital and transactional," even as members transact business on its digital platform, and the belonging offered is a commodity that can be perfected and sold by following the magazine's advice.[16]

It is not only hosts who must brand themselves as "authentic" members of a local community. Guests, too, are not only encouraged through sleek advertising and editorials to conform to a certain ideal, but through the use of publicly accessible reviews from their hosts, are hounded into this ideal and punished when they fail to adopt it. These reviews serve as evidence for future hosts to gauge the subjective qualities of their guests to determine the extent to which they conform to these ideals. Some of my own reviews as a guest in Airbnb properties noted that I was a "fantastic [guest] in every respect: friendly, tidy, responsive and interesting," "fun to talk to and . . . easy to get along with," and "clean, friendly and respectful." Such quality-of-life metrics are not only entirely subjective but are often a coded way of identifying members of in- and out-groups that are inherently raced and classed. For both hosts and guests, who are, of course, the same people, being successful means being a normative member of society—a society whose norms are shaped by Airbnb—and branding oneself as a tidy, interesting, friendly, respectful, college-educated member of the aspirational class.

Not that branding oneself is protection from banishment for people convicted of crimes. This is because the criminal record is a heuristic for determining out-group members—those who are not tidy, interesting, friendly, and respectful college-educated members of the aspirational class. As such, it supersedes any evidence to the contrary. The criminal record is evidence that a person has been convicted of a crime, but it also constructs a much more specific raced, classed, and gendered subject—what Katherine Russell-Brown calls the *criminalblackman*.[17] For Airbnb and its members, the criminal ban is a race- and class-neutral way to mitigate risk that nevertheless crafts a raced and classed community, albeit in opposition to the *criminalblackman*. The tidy, interesting, friendly, respectful (and white) college-educated member of the aspirational class is Airbnb's target demographic because it is the demographic from which Airbnb can extract the most wealth and political capital. It is the demographic more likely to own desirable property, respect private property in ways that privilege the transfer of wealth from the poor to the rich, and to assume the right of Airbnb as a corporate entity to conduct its business, manage and exploit its users, and generate revenue in the marketplace however it wishes.

LEGAL AMBIGUITIES AND THE PRESUMPTION OF RISK

There has been some broad public sentiment in recent years that the discrimination facing people convicted of crimes, especially in employment and housing, is too harsh. Many local and state jurisdictions have responded to these concerns. Pennsylvania's Clean Slate Act, signed into law in 2018, for example, automatically limits public access to as many as thirty million records, although most of these are related to summary and low-level misdemeanor convictions.[18] "Ban the box" laws remove the question of criminal history from job applications in order to limit discrimination during the early stages of hiring, although they do little to mitigate discrimination later in the hiring process: by 2020, 94 percent of employers conducted background checks on some or all employees.[19] The European Court of Justice proposed a somewhat more radical solution in 2014 when it ruled that search engines would, upon request, be required to remove irrelevant or out-of-date information, including information about some criminal convictions. The ruling was codified in Article 17 of the European Union's General Data Protection Regulation (GDPR) as the "right to erasure" and is better known in the United States as the "right to be forgotten." Despite providing some significant privacy protections for individuals convicted of crimes in Europe, it remains the purview of the private corporations who own these search engines to determine, with broad discretion, whether the requests they receive are legitimate, and whether the information contained in the requests is a matter of public interest. As the *New York Times* reports, "Google has become a quasi-judicial authority on the right to be forgotten, determining what constitutes private information or not."[20]

While the GDPR does not apply within the United States, American media companies have begun grappling with the so-called right to be forgotten. A 2019 episode of *Radiolab* listens in on a series of deliberations at the offices of Cleveland.com, the major online news outlet serving the Cleveland, Ohio, news market.[21] The journalists and other staff members at Cleveland.com were interested in taking up the challenge posed by European regulators to balance individuals' rights to privacy and the public's right to access information, and the *Radiolab* episode follows the debate that unfolds. This conversation is instructive not because it necessarily mirrors the conversations happening in boardrooms but rather because it represents a popular way of thinking about justice and is illustrative of public discourse about the treatment of criminals by private companies in American society. These journalists, who care about the fair treatment of people with criminal records, therefore act as a sort of bellwether, encapsulating how it has become a matter of course to negotiate policy-and-order not in terms of *whether* companies should have the right to impose collateral consequences but only in terms of *how* they should.

As their debate unfolds, it soon becomes apparent that this will not be an analysis of legal principles or rights but a discussion about whether various requests for removal should be granted. The journalists then make these determinations in an ad hoc way, fashioning rules and normative claims as they go along: One person was young when he committed a crime. One crime is too serious to warrant forgetting, while a very similar crime is not too serious because it was committed by someone in college. The next crime should be forgotten because some arbitrary period of time has elapsed since its commission. The episode pays scant attention to the structuring inequities of the criminal justice system, such as selective policing and prosecution, coerced confessions, and plea bargains. Aside from an introduction to the basic principles behind the EU's right to be forgotten, specific laws and legal principles—such as sentencing guidelines, collateral consequences, and due process—were almost entirely absent from the discussion. In their place were a set of questions that called on these particular individuals, much like hiring managers and landlords, to rely on their common sense and whatever incomplete information could be found online about their subjects, to craft a set of judgments about the extent to which particular individuals had paid their debt to society and deserved to be forgotten.

In addition to a lack of attention to the legal processes that determine guilt and sanctions, several other important questions never emerge for the reporters making decisions about convicted people's right to be forgotten or for the producers of the *Radiolab* episode. First, the Cleveland.com staff never wonder why the completion of a court-imposed sentence is an insufficient criterion for forgetting. Each of the cases addressed by the Cleveland.com staff had already been adjudicated in a court of law, the individuals involved had already served sentences, and they were already subject to the collateral consequences applicable to their jurisdictions. These factors—the price already paid—were ignored in favor of deliberating in an ad hoc way about the risk individuals pose after these penalties have been applied, potentially in perpetuity. For the Cleveland.com staff, the imposition of additional penalties in the form of employment and housing discrimination corresponds roughly to the logic of collateral consequences in the courts insofar as they are framed as serving a preventive or public safety function rather than a punitive one.

Second, their deliberations did not address the appropriateness of five (or one or ten or one hundred) people in a boardroom readjudicating crimes or imposing additional penalties for crimes already adjudicated and punished. While the Cleveland.com staff did not see themselves as arbiters of guilt, they were, and their decisions hinged radically on whether each of them, according to their own common sense and moral judgments, believed particular individuals who had committed crimes presented a risk to society, and whether they deserved some measure of forgiveness or forgetting. This same responsibility was then transferred onto the human resources administrator, who, as the journalists seemed to understand it, is tasked with the difficult job indeed of sifting through the detritus of the internet to determine whether any potential employee poses a risk to the safety and security of the company as community. The staffers and the show's producers seemed to take for granted that the human resources administrator is the primary stakeholder in debates about individuals' rights. The concern that dominated reporters' discourse was whether employers would have access to job candidates' criminal histories should this information be scrubbed from the internet. In each instance, the journalists weigh an individual's right to be forgotten not with the public's right to know about a crime but with their future employer's. This propensity to conflate corporate and public interest is part of a larger trend in which private corporations are not only increasingly responsible for determining what is *in* the public interest but are actually fashioned *as* the public.

Finally, the conversation in the Cleveland.com boardroom assumes that the media is the only resource for the corporation-as-public to obtain information about potential employees' criminal histories. This conversation never manages to acknowledge that such information is a matter of public record, easily accessible through states' now largely unified justice systems and through consumer background reports. Indeed, making hiring decisions based on incorrect or outdated information—which is what internet searches often yield—is illegal and the major reason that employers use consumer background report agencies in the first place, since consumer background report agencies must comply with the FCRA. Employers take a significant risk relying even on information obtained in public records, such as court filings, since, in so doing, they take on the burden of FCRA compliance rather than transferring that risk to for-profit consumer background report agencies.

Taken together, these elisions represent a series of assumptions and misunderstandings about the laws and legal processes that govern the treatment of criminal defendants in the courts, and the state-based and other institutional exclusions to which people convicted of crimes are subject. They also represent a series of assumptions and misunderstandings about the laws that govern the employment relation and that protect potential employees. The dominant way of thinking about privacy and risk in the Cleveland.com boardroom mirrors the logic of private employers and the consumer background report industry insofar as it privileges the employment relation above all others and frames the employee as a persistent risk to the employer's bottom line. It also promotes the view that adjudicating and imposing sanctions for current and potential behavior is best handled not in the courtroom but in the boardroom.

Part of the reason for the dominance of these assumptions is a lack of enforcement of the laws protecting employees and job candidates. In the case of using outdated or incorrect information in hiring decisions in violation of the FCRA, for example, there is little government oversight of hiring practices within private companies. Such illegality is likely only to be uncovered through civil litigation, in the already unlikely event that a job candidate learns which criteria were used in a hiring decision. Such litigation is extremely unlikely not only because most people (rightly) believe that their chances of winning a lawsuit are slim but also because employment issues are increasingly seen as belonging outside the realm of law and rights. This belief—that employment issues are outside the realm of law and rights—is an aspect of what Lauren Edelman calls the managerialization of law.

In *Working Law*, Edelman describes how ambiguities in the law— and especially in civil rights and antidiscrimination law—provide organizations, both public and private, with the opportunity to interpret laws in ways that favor existing organizational goals and policies. Her theory of symbolic civil rights suggests that "organizational policies that symbolize diversity have become widely accepted indicia of compliance with civil rights laws, irrespective of their effectiveness." Organizational policies are seen as a form of compliance with civil rights laws, even though they may "represent little more than cosmetic compliance." When courts accept these symbols as compliance with the law, they begin to defer to corporations' own standards of civil rights compliance, which Edelman calls legal endogeneity—the process by which the law is "influenced by the social fields that it seeks to regulate."[22]

> Judges defer to symbolic structures because the widespread acceptance of the idea that organizations' antidiscrimination policies and procedures constitute nondiscrimination makes it difficult for them to discern workplace practices that deviate from or undermine those formal policies. If the presence of these policies always meant that organizations were following the law, then judicial reliance on organizations' symbolic structures would not be a problem. But when judges infer nondiscrimination from the presence of policies that managers ignore, when they look at the presence of diversity training programs rather than whether organizations are in fact diverse, and when they infer fair and rational governance from personnel manuals that do not govern the daily lives of organizations, then law tends to condone practices that deviate from legal ideals.[23]

Prison disciplinary and grievance procedures were an aspect of mid-century civil rights transformations and were developed in response to public and judicial activism that sought to amend the arbitrary systems of governance and discipline that dominated the prison at that time. Edelman argues that, like prison grievance procedures, corporate grievance procedures "signified attention to due process, a principle that has always been central to the public legal order but was antithetical to the arbitrary governance systems that had prevailed in the early industrial organizations." Nonetheless, grievance procedures—whether in the prison or in the human resources office—are not due process, which can only be realized within the public legal order and not within other organizations. However, "by adopting antidiscrimination policies that *resembled* statutes, EEO offices that *resembled* administrative agencies, and grievance procedures that *resembled* courts, organizational governance took the form of (and thus could benefit from the ready legitimacy of) the public legal order."[24] The existence of grievance procedures and their broad acceptance as mechanisms of due process transforms organizations into quasi-judicial bodies—bodies that are taken to be judicial and sometimes perform the roles of the judiciary even though they are not and do not.

Edelman notes that prison administration is paradigmatic of how internal policies are not only accepted as compliance with the law but are actually adopted by the courts as models of compliance. Courts deferred to internal grievance procedures to the extent that a series of laws, beginning with the Civil Rights of Institutionalized Persons Act (CRIPA) of 1980 and culminating with the Prison Litigation Reform Act (PLRA) in 1996, actually codified that deference: "Under PLRA, federal judges are all but mandated to defer to prison grievance procedures." Like the prison grievance procedure and the requirement codified in the PLRA to exhaust all internal dispute mechanisms before pursuing legal action, "the internal grievance procedure [within other institutions, such as workplaces] has been one of the most effective tools in the management arsenal for combating the threat of litigation."[25]

Pursuing civil rights claims in court is one of the primary ways in which individuals insist on their rights and make claims on the state. "EEO law," Edelman maintains, "depends on ordinary citizens who experience discrimination to mobilize the law by taking action to invoke their legal rights."[26] When public law is supplanted by organizational processes—such as diversity policies and grievance and disciplinary procedures—these policies come to be seen as, and eventually become, the (only) path to remedying discrimination. This process results in a managerialization of legal consciousness, which Edelman defines as "the process through which people increasingly understand EEO law in managerialized terms and understand the presence of organizations' symbolic structures as constituting compliance with EEO law." It is not just judges, employees of individual companies, or individual renters but the broader public that, "as legal consciousness becomes managerialized," come to "understand the presence of symbolic structures not simply as tools designed to achieve legal compliance but rather as the achievement of legal ideals."[27] Legal endogeneity and managerialized legal consciousness affect "whether and how aggrieved employees pursue legal redress, how plaintiffs' lawyers frame legal complaints, and how management lawyers frame their defenses." One of the most significant problems with a managerialized legal consciousness is that it "depresses rights mobilization," since "employees accept the rhetorical framing of legal constructs and, therefore, see their complaints as beyond the bounds of law." At least in part as a result of judicial deference to organizational policies and the concomitant managerialization of legal consciousness, "most employees who believe that their rights have been violated do nothing."[28]

There are corollary ambiguities in criminal law and procedure that result in another form of managerialized legal consciousness, in which private companies are vested with the quasi-judicial authority to adjudicate and impose penalties for crimes. The Bureau of Justice Statistics (BJS) found that between 2006 and 2010, more than 50 percent of violent crimes—rape, sexual assault, robbery, and aggravated assault— went unreported to law enforcement. Victims of violent crime who responded to the BJS survey cited fear of retaliation, lack of confidence in the police's ability to help, and a belief that their victimization was not important enough as reasons for not reporting their victimization. But the most common reason of all, cited by 34 percent of respondents, was that they dealt with their victimization in another way, for example by reporting it to an employer. While on average, just over half of violent crimes go unreported to police, 76 percent of violent crime victimizations that took place at schools went unreported, where fully half of victims dealt with their victimization in another way, such as by reporting it to school officials.[29] In such cases, human resources officers and school administrators, rather than judges or juries, are tasked with adjudicating violent crimes and imposing penalties for them.

When human resources officers and school administrators, among others, are vested with the quasi-judicial authority to adjudicate crimes and impose penalties for them, legal consciousness in the realm of criminal law and procedure is depressed and deformed. The discourse of the Cleveland.com journalists about the right to be forgotten is one example of how, in the cultural imaginary, legal expertise regarding crime and criminal justice is reduced to managerial expertise. The journalists' understanding of a specific law and its potential application within the United States relied not on legal principles, criminal codes, or case law but on managerialized common sense to make moralistic judgments about the seriousness or severity of crimes. They did not develop a process or procedure to make these judgments but instead formulated rules as they went along, modifying criteria for each case based on what they perceived to be important features of each individual's character or personality. Especially because these journalists were sympathetic to the barriers to reentering society that people convicted of crimes face, and because they agreed with the principles undergirding the right to be forgotten, their process reflects the ambiguities present in criminal law and procedure that allow judges and juries to use previous convictions as evidence of character, despite the intention of criminal procedure rules to protect defendants. On the other hand, they acknowledged neither these ambiguities in the law nor their manifestation in the boardroom.

These journalists' understanding about how people convicted of crimes should be treated in society was based not on legal principles but on a popular understanding of the criminal conviction as evidence of future risk—an understanding that has been shaped significantly by the consumer background report industry, whose continued growth necessitates undermining the principle of presumptive innocence that is foundational to criminal procedure. In considering the consequences of a permanent criminal record, they did not consider academic research about the detrimental effects of collateral consequences or the vast, albeit divided, body of literature on the causes and consequences of recidivism.[30] Nor did they reference the body of case law governing the state-based imposition of collateral consequences, even though they frequently deployed the "formalistic fiction," as Joshua Kaiser describes it, that separates collateral consequences from punishments.[31] Perhaps most importantly, they never suggested that they—or employees of Google or other search engines—might not be the most appropriate parties to make decisions about the severity of crimes and the types of sanctions that people with criminal convictions should face, or that these decisions had already been made by judges and juries.

GHETTOS, GIG WORK, AND TERMS OF SERVICE

Many people who leave prison will be relegated to what Alessandro De Giorgi calls the "service ghetto": "a self-contained space, bordered on all sides by gentrifying uptown neighborhoods, which local authorities have designated as the ideal location for homeless shelters, transitional houses, community clinics, women's shelters, halfway houses, SRO hotels, and rehabilitation programs."[32] Excluded from normative models of work and housing, ex-offenders become the products to be circulated within the prisoner reentry industry.[33] This funneling of ex-offenders into knowledge-economy service ghettos is made possible in part because of the legal discrimination they face in housing and employment—which is in turn made possible through the use of consumer background reports as a best practice. Airbnb's criminal ban extends these exclusions, making it difficult or impossible for people with criminal convictions not only to rent in the new short-term housing market but to find work in the gig economy, a critical alternative to the traditional economy whose barriers to entry are increasingly high. Banishment from Airbnb means banishment from a potential source of income, since the banished are also prohibited from becoming hosts.

It is not only ex-offenders, however, who must endure the consequences of the company's decisions and decision-making processes. Outsourcing the imposition of collateral consequences to entities such as Airbnb transforms this method of punishment into an apolitical best practice that substitutes the public deliberation of social norms with terms of service, ultimately transforming the sharing economy into its own kind of service ghetto and its users into potential hustlers and quasi-citizens.

By 2021, approximately 36 percent of Americans were earning at least some of their income in the gig economy.[34] While ex-offenders are mostly barred from using platforms like Airbnb, Uber, and TaskRabbit, these companies, as Alexandrea Ravenelle's ethnographic research suggests, also promote the kinds of activities and lifestyles historically associated with criminality. One of Ravenelle's informants calls working in this economy a form of hustling. Although gigs in the sharing economy are (often) legal hustles, they share features with illegal hustling, such as a decreased ability to earn a living wage, the need to work long hours or be always on-call, impoverishment of rights and access to the state, and loss of symbolic capital within the hegemonic, white, middle-class social milieu that values saving, investment, status, and accumulation of wealth.[35] As the field of economic activities that produce a reasonable standard of living shrinks, more and more people find themselves hustling to make ends meet, and some would rather "lie to their family and friends . . . than admit they drive for Uber or clean homes via TaskRabbit."[36] Under neoliberal political and economic conditions, the stigma of criminality attaches itself even to those who may not have been convicted of crimes—even as companies like Airbnb insist on the potential of the gig economy to transform people into members of the aspirational class. Moreover, apps like TaskRabbit may actually promote criminal activity, since users can easily hire a Tasker to pick up and deliver packages whose contents are unknown.[37] Because many gig workers struggle to make ends meet, they may not have the luxury of passing up work, even if they think it might be illegal. And whereas platforms like Airbnb provide hosts with flexibility in terms of when they want to work and which guests they want to host, other apps—like Uber and Lyft, TaskRabbit and Instacart—may penalize gig workers for not accepting jobs, legal and illegal alike, or accepting them too slowly.

Airbnb makes and enforces normative claims about the nature of community and work, including how access to community must be policed and how it is constituted by individual units of enterprise making financial transactions in the free market, all while paying platforms a 14–16 percent fee to do so. Although companies like Autohost, Quickstay, "a growing Airbnb property management company," and Guesty, "an end-to-end solution for professional short-term property managers" operating on Airbnb, belie the company's stated business model of helping individuals supplement their income by "sharing" extra space in their homes, non-professionals continue to use the platform, and they must do so in ways that conform to the policies and "community standards" devised by the company.[38] However, as Ravenelle documents, non-professionals who work in the gig economy increasingly do so on a full-time or 24/7 on-call basis, as a first source of income rather than as a supplementary one. While the sharing economy "[promises] to transcend capitalism in favor of community," she observes, for non-professional gig workers, it actually "resembles the early industrial age, where workers worked long hours in a piecemeal system, workplace safety was nonexistent, and there were few options for redress."[39]

Airbnb also resembles early industrial-age employers in its enforcement of morality. These employers, such as the Ford Motor Company, likewise defined and policed normative behavior: "Workers were eligible for Ford's famous $5 wage only if they kept their homes clean, ate diets deemed healthy, abstained from drinking, used the bathtub appropriately, did not take in boarders, avoided spending too much on foreign relatives, and were assimilated to American cultural norms."[40] These were also the types of normative behaviors and values that the modernist penitentiary was designed to inculcate in its prisoners—and the reason Foucault describes the penitentiary as an institution "situated on the borders of morality and penality."[41] The penitentiary's emergence as a key site in the negotiation of the capitalist social contract coincided with other midcentury institution building, including the enactment of federal laws codifying rights for workers and setting some limits on employers' authority over their employees, making practices like Ford's all but obsolete. But since the criminal justice and penal systems have abandoned the project of inculcating normative behavior in favor of pursuing an actuarial vision of justice, the private company once again serves as a default institution for monitoring, policing, and punishing the behavior it defines as immoral, undesirable, or nonnormative. Those midcentury worker protections have been replaced by private contracts and at-will employment, the latter of which, Elizabeth Anderson explains, "entitles employers to fire workers for any or no reason, [and] grants the employer sweeping legal authority not only over workers' lives at work but also over their off-duty conduct." Diminishing workers' legal rights endows the employer—or, perhaps better, the private firm—with powers traditionally reserved for the state. In contrast to the early twentieth century, however, the neoliberal state, in its managerial function, now mandates companies exercise such authority over their workers and contractors. As a result, "employers' authority over workers, outside of collective bargaining and a few other contexts, . . . is sweeping, arbitrary, and unaccountable—not subject to notice, process, or appeal. The state has established the constitution of the government of the workplace."[42]

Even more so than in the traditional employment context, gig workers find themselves in a legalistic gray zone where they are considered independent contractors rather than employees. Gig economy "workers find themselves outside even the most basic workplace protections regarding discrimination and sexual harassment, the right to unionize, and even the right to redress for workplace injuries. The sharing economy is upending generations of workplace protections in the name of disruption and returning to a time when worker exploitation was the norm."[43] In this relationship, the independent contractor is totally dependent on the platform for their ability to work at the same time they can make no claims on the platform—either in terms of wages and benefits or in terms of legal rights. The platform model gives Uber, TaskRabbit, and Airbnb absolute control over the terms of the employment relation, which has actually transformed the employment relation into a terms-of-service relationship. In stripping workers of their legal rights and dictating the terms of the employment relation, platforms also become the default institutions where labor rights are negotiated—and where they can only be negotiated in favor of the platforms, since they are the only parties to the transaction with financial capital, political power, or legal standing.

Like the traditional employment relation, the contractual relationship between platforms and users is seen as one in which both parties freely and willingly consent to conducting business with each other. If users do not like Airbnb's terms of service, they can simply opt not to use the service. The problem with this rationale is similar to the problematic rationale that governs the traditional employment relation. Legally, employees are seen as free and willing participants in the employment contract, able to opt in or out at will. This is a constituent ingredient of economic-political freedom in neoliberal theory. As Milton Friedman explains, businesses must be private, such that individuals are the parties to any legal contracts. Thus, "individuals are effectively free to enter or not enter into any particular exchange, so that every transaction is strictly voluntary." However, as Friedman goes on to clarify, an absence of "physical coercion" is what constitutes the "strictly voluntary" nature of entering into an exchange. He does admit that monopoly can limit freedom by reducing the range of choices that consumers and employees have.[44] Ultimately, however, "the employee is protected from coercion by the employer because of other employers for whom he can work."[45] So long, in other words, as a range of employers exists, employees should be considered voluntary parties to the employment relation and therefore free.

Airbnb is similarly framed as a service that individuals can opt into or out of at will. The company does not physically coerce people to list their homes on the platform, and in the eyes of the law, hosts could just as easily rent out a room or apartment using some other listing or advertising method, and guests could just easily find and rent those rooms or apartments elsewhere. But when one company dominates a sector to the exclusion of all others—as Airbnb has done in the home-sharing economy—or when all companies within a sector practice the same kinds of exclusionary and (non-physically) coercive techniques, the "freedom" to opt in or opt out is more like the freedom to withdraw from the market altogether. Likewise, it is meaningless to take issue with Airbnb's criminal ban, or its antidiscrimination policy, its fee structure, or its terms of service. Users have no right to contest these policies or terms, and the only alternative to consenting to them is being banished from the community oneself.

Airbnb is more than a company or platform. Nofar Sheffi describes it as "a domain, a complex political association" that produces and standardizes "forms, actions, terms of engagement, and subjectivities." The company's principles "impose limits on the exercise of power by public institutions, but also define modes of participation and courses of action, constituting political subjectivities." Writing about the steps Airbnb has taken to stem discrimination on the site and its adjudicative processes when discrimination is brought to its attention by users, Sheffi articulates how the company produces and reproduces itself as a political platform through policy that functions as law. Although framed as a set of rights and responsibilities, the legal and political arrangement between Airbnb and its users is a two-party contract. Thus, while framing nondiscrimination as a "right," the company can only adjudicate "claims" of discrimination by excluding the claimant from adjudicative processes. "Beyond establishing a series of bilateral contractual relations between a service provider and each of its users and regulating the use of the platform, the Airbnb Terms of Service agreement is the epitome of [a] new social contract" that is constituted by consumer–service provider relationship. In agreeing to terms of service, what members actually agree to is "to mind their own business and to stay out of the relations between the corporate entity and other members."[46]

The "terms of service" that define the contractual relationship between users and technology companies—from Airbnb to Facebook to Uber to Amazon to Acorns to Expedia to Grubhub to eBay to Etsy to retail chains, banks, and restaurants—insist that users relinquish any number of their legal rights, not least of which is the right to pursue litigation for negligence or wrongdoing, all in the name of the contract being voluntary. But agreeing to technology companies' terms of service is only voluntary in the narrowest sense of the word. It is extremely difficult to live in the world without access to the goods and services that exist only or mostly online. In other words, it is extremely difficult to live in the world today without relinquishing a wealth of legal rights, and without giving consent to technology firms to dictate which legal rights individuals can enjoy. Consenting to their authority to adjudicate behavior, impose post-sentence sanctions, and dictate the terms of the social contract may in some ways be an extension of the nullification of legal personhood effected through clicking "I agree."

In the next chapter, these explicit and implicit authorizations will be shown to contribute to broader cultural transformations in how things like criminality, legal rights, and due process are imagined. More specifically, it analyzes how the ideas that circulate around "cancel culture" proceed from the view that the boardroom is better equipped than the courtroom to define and delimit legal rights, adjudicate civil rights claims and criminal behavior, and impose penalties, sanctions, and collateral consequences.

5. Neoliberal Vigilantism, Cancel Culture, and the Post-Juridical Turn

Crime is increasingly figured as a debt that can never be repaid. The law manufactures this debt through an ever-expanding catalogue of sometimes permanent sanctions for ex-offenders. The consumer background report industry manufactures this debt by trafficking in the ideology of perpetual risk in order to sell the criminal record as a product on the open market. Employers, landlords, and tech firms manufacture this debt by crafting policies that ensure people with criminal records are permanently banned from decent housing and desirable workplaces, as well as, increasingly, gigs in the sharing economy and access to leisure. Blanket bans on people with criminal records in employment contexts, the private housing market, and platforms like Airbnb fashion "the convict" as a perpetual risk to institutional safety, and to society more broadly. The easy banishment of other, noncriminal, users from social media platforms also suggests that private companies are increasingly vested with the authority to define acceptable speech and behavior far in excess of criminality and to punish those behaviors they find unacceptable. The combination of at-will employment, degradations in legal and political personhood, and the managerialization of legal consciousness means that employers are also increasingly able to exercise draconian control over their employees' behavior—their use of drugs, alcohol, and cigarettes, their exercise, and their speech—and to punish those behaviors they find undesirable.

In this way, people living in the United States today are not only required to abide by the laws of the state but also by the terms of their employers' demands and by the terms of service of the corporations where their speech and behavior take place. For a great number of people, the law is replaced by a limit defined by private employers and companies like Airbnb and Facebook. This limit may, and often does, include particular laws. But it may also include a range of other behaviors, such as hate speech and bullying but also political organizing, drug and alcohol use, cigarette smoking, poor financial decision-making, obesity, untidiness, and noisiness. The punishment for unacceptable behavior as defined by employers and other private corporations can be, like that facing people with criminal records, loss of employment or housing and banishment from other private spaces. Private governments conflate criminality with other forms of misconduct or undesirable behavior, and they impose sanctions on a great deal more people than even the criminal justice system has access to. These institutions subvert and deform the law, transforming their ideas about acceptable or normative behavior into a new kind of legal regime—which is in fact a policy regime—and their disciplinary techniques or tactics into a dominant mode of punishment.

The transfer of quasi-judicial authority from the courtroom to the boardroom transforms how the law, judicial processes, and rights are understood and mobilized. At the same time, neoliberalism, in degrading public institutions and the very notion of the public, exploits (real) popular fears and anxieties—those borne of the failure of the state to guarantee safety and justice—to secure the political power of these private governments. In the wake of these transformations, renewed forms of vigilantism have emerged to contend with these failures. One feature of neoliberalism has been the transfer of responsibility for policing and surveillance from the state to individuals. During the 1980s, television shows like *America's Most Wanted* encouraged viewers to collaborate with law enforcement to solve crimes.[1] Implicitly, this show and others like it suggested that police were insufficiently prepared to apprehend some of the country's most violent predators. Other shows, like *Cops*, which has been on air since 1989, bring viewers into patrol cars and onto the streets where they can vicariously apprehend, and enact violence on, some of those same (racialized) "predators." But the consumer background report industry ushered in a new era of lateral surveillance. As Nora Draper argues, the industry "capitalizes on contemporary anxieties . . . to normalize lateral surveillance and self-monitoring as essential parts of everyday life, thereby pressing ordinary people into the role of digital detectives."[2] She contends that the management of risk by individuals is part of a broader trend in which "responsibilities for safety traditionally assigned to state actors have been pushed onto ordinary citizens."[3] The tech revolution has only accelerated this trend: Apps like Nextdoor and Neighborhood (by Ring, the home security equipment company owned by Amazon) provide crime alerts and allow individuals to report suspicious activity to produce a crowdsourced version of policing. The app Citizen offers similar services as well as "24/7 access to a trained Protect Agent who can discreetly help, silently monitor your live location and audio, alert other users, call 911, monitor heart rate through your Apple watch and more."[4]

This chapter traces the relationship between "cancel culture" and these other forms of lateral surveillance. While there is no easy or singular definition of cancel culture, one assumption this chapter makes is that cancellation is a form of sanction necessitated by the failures of the state and other institutions to secure safe and just conditions, especially for women and racial and sexual minorities. Emerging from racial and gender justice activism like the #MeToo and Black Lives Matter movements, cancellation was a radical alternative to the pervasive dismissal of the criminal victimization and civil rights violations of women, people of color, and LGBTQ people by and within powerful institutions. In some iterations, however, cancel culture has mirrored the ideological positions and rhetorical strategies of the corporate boardroom and the consumer background report industry even as it promotes progressive social justice causes. Moreover, the practices and punishments that constitute cancel culture do not begin or end with activism against racism, misogyny, transphobia, and other forms of bigotry. Rather, when viewed as a technique of punishment rather than a form of protest, resistance, or identity politics, a range of other behaviors might be seen to fall under its purview. The online investigations, adjudications, and punishments levied against alleged criminals, for example, are rarely taken to be an aspect of cancel culture, even though the methods, discourses, and techniques of punishment applied in these cases are strikingly analogous. To take an example from the introduction of this book, the calls for an American Airlines passenger to be permanently banned from public transportation after allegedly assaulting a flight attendant seems to have had nothing to do with anything remotely resembling identity politics. Yet, the desired outcome among those calling for his banishment was quite similar to the desired outcome of those who sought the cancellation of Louis C. K., Dave Chapelle, J. K. Rowling, or Ellen DeGeneres: private companies were called on to cancel the alleged assaulter's access to "public" transportation—a call that American Airlines, in this case, complied with—just as they were called on to cancel the book contracts, comedy specials, and television shows of other perceived bad actors. By untethering, at least partially, this technique of punishment from its widely perceived status as an aspect of America's culture wars, this chapter aims to address how cancel culture functions as a mode of justice that responds to the failures of the state and other public institutions under neoliberalism to secure the conditions for a functioning and just society even as it rearticulates the terms of the neoliberal social contract.

A NEW MODEL OF INFAMY

Cancel culture is a contested term. While the conservative right rallies against cancel culture as a punitive movement that chills political speech, many liberal and progressive media commentators and public intellectuals suggest that cancel culture is little more than a disorganized, ineffectual, and largely inconsequential group of individuals whose voices are being elevated by the right. Others go so far as to call it a myth—a way that those on the conservative right of the American political spectrum vilify those who promote social justice causes.[5] In this view, cancel culture is mostly a fiction made up by conservative pundits to malign movements like #MeToo and Black Lives Matter. By casting these movements as unreasonable and punitive, and unreasonably punitive, right-wing ideologues seek to undermine the causes such movements promote, such as gender and racial justice.

While cancel culture resists easy definitions and may even be difficult to identify in practice, there is a segment of the population that believes that individuals who engage in certain behaviors—be they criminal, racist, sexist, homophobic, or transphobic—should be permanently shunned, banned, boycotted, or deplatformed. For its proponents, cancellation is seen as a valid path to sanctioning bad actors. At the outset of the #MeToo movement, entertainment industry figures like Harvey Weinstein faced public scrutiny as women in the industry came forward with stories of longstanding sexual harassment, abuse, and assault. While #MeToo activists called for traditional justice—arrest, conviction, and prison sentences—they also underscored the historical failure of the criminal justice system to hold individuals like Weinstein accountable for their alleged criminal behavior. As such, some of these activists believed that alternative sanctions were a necessary path to justice and called on private companies and the public to cancel figures like Weinstein. For many of its proponents, cancellation is viewed as a way to hold public figures accountable for their harms when the bodies traditionally assigned that role fail to do so.

Before people could be canceled, cancellation mostly referred only to television shows that failed to get picked up for another season: a show was canceled when its ratings weren't high enough.[6] When people are canceled, it means that their personal ratings, or the ratings of their personal brands, drop—and that, as a result, studios or employers will elect not to pick them up for another season. Because cancel culture emerged as a response to the abuses of the rich and the powerful, and often the famous, especially in the entertainment industry, the metaphor of cancellation evokes a certain kind of poetic justice. If neither the criminal justice system nor the entertainment industry would impose justice, then some other collective would have to. In the context of the rich, the powerful, and the famous, the cancellation of contracts, the removal of films and television shows from streaming sites, their removal from films or television shows they had acted in—these were acts of punishment that fit the criminal, as it were, if not the crime.

Popular media sources continue to frame cancellation as a fate affecting culture industry moguls. A BuzzFeed list of "celebs" canceled in 2020 featured Ellen DeGeneres (for creating a toxic work environment), J. K. Rowling (for espousing anti-trans views), and Anna Wintour (for not supporting Black employees). But its list of celebrities also included much more minor pop culture figures, such as reality television personalities and YouTubers.[7] The collapsing of YouTubers with Ellen DeGeneres, who headed a media empire for two decades and whose net worth is estimated to be in the range of $370 million, and Anna Wintour, the editor-in-chief of *Vogue* and current artistic director of that magazine's parent company, Condé Nast, who sat at #48 on Forbes' list of most powerful women in 2018, is indicative of how cancel culture ultimately cannot account for differences in scale. If rich and powerful culture industry figures were the initial targets of cancellation, the standards applied to them soon came to be applied to others. It was not just Harvey Weinstein but social media influencers, and eventually people who were not public figures at all, who faced the same consequences for their alleged bad behavior. Because they do not hold the same kind of material or symbolic power as Ellen DeGeneres or Anna Wintour, YouTubers and social media influencers are not in a position to meaningfully impact the structural causes and consequences of racism, ethnocentrism, sexism, homophobia, and transphobia. Their biases are personal and their influence largely interpersonal. The public need not accept speech or behavior that is racist, sexist, homophobic, or culturally insensitive. However, cancellation—in what might be thought of as its ideal form—should punish individuals and effect systemic change by reducing the symbolic and material power of those who abuse that power. YouTubers and social media influencers, let alone private individuals, simply do not have the kind of symbolic or material power that cancellation putatively seeks to reduce.

Collapsing these two different types of individual subjects—one with institutional power to abuse and one without—and applying the same penalties to their respective crimes or misconduct is an aspect of contemporary justice that both resembles and transforms what Foucault describes in his lectures on the punitive society as the model of infamy. As discussed in chapter 3, Foucault identifies in those lectures a transformation during the eighteenth century in the way the criminal is figured first as someone who transgresses against or harms another person and later as someone who harms all of society.[8] Foucault identifies within this new paradigm four principles and three models of "actual punishment" that should be able to exist within a society where the criminal is figured as a social enemy.

The first principle is a relativity of penalties. Since strong societies are more capable of withstanding crime than weak societies, the punishments for crime within a stronger society will be more lenient than those within a weaker society. The result of the first principle is "that there cannot be any universal model of penalties." Since penalties exist along a spectrum, the need for a second principle arises, which is that penalties should be "commensurate with the attacks on society," or commensurate with the crime. Because punishment in the social enemy paradigm is geared towards disarmament—or ensuring that the criminal does not continue committing crimes—the principle of supervision is introduced. Whether disarmament takes the form of re-habilitation or disablement, the convicted criminal must be supervised across the term of his sentence. Finally, in addition to disarmament, a goal of punishment is to dissuade others from attacking society in the same way. As a fourth principle, then, punishment must be "public and infallible."[9]

Foucault goes on to describe three models of actual punishment that can accommodate these principles: the model of infamy, the model of talion, and the model of slavery. The model of infamy is based on "shame that marks the guilty person" and which "is first of all a reaction of the whole society."[10] In the model of infamy, there is no need for a juridical structure at all, since the person who transgresses against society is judged by each individual he encounters at every moment. The model of talion, on the other hand, promotes an equivalence between offense and punishment: talion "in effect . . . is a penalty that, in its nature and strength, is exactly correlative with the offense itself; through it, society succeeds in turning the attack made on it back against the criminal." This model reflects the Old Testament logic of an eye for an eye: the criminal's punishment exactly replicates the crime committed. Finally, the model of slavery is one of "hard and public labor" that offers society a form of reparation: a term of slavery represents "the pact of the individual's reformation as a member of society; it is the forced re-edition of the social contract between the criminal and society."[11]

Foucault's purpose in these lectures is to explain the birth and consolidation of the prison as a model of punishment. He contrasts the prison to each of these three models—which have a natural basis, as it were, in the existing social order—to the penitentiary, which does not. In other words, the model of punishment that became dominant during the nineteenth century—the prison—does not actually correspond to any existing (or possible) models of punishment. Rather, the prison was imposed on the system of justice, and on society, from the outside—imposed by itself. The prison, a technique of punishment "situated on the borders of morality and penality," emerged spontaneously from the interests of the petite bourgeoisie.[12] The practices and institutions that developed around this technique of punishment became the basis for new forms of knowledge about crime and criminals. The study of how to punish and the effects of punishment were the basis for a new discipline of penology. The study of criminals as the objects of this punishment became the basis for the new discipline of criminology, whose "discourse . . . makes it [scientifically] possible to define the offender as aggressive and describe punishment as a process of rehabilitation, of social reintegration."[13] This aggressive and dangerous—and ultimately pathological—subject of nineteenth-century penal and criminological discourse forms the basis for a medical, and finally juridical, knowledge about crime and the criminal. For Foucault, the medical, scientific, and juridical knowledges that emerge in response to this technique of punishment eventually supplant and foreclose other possible epistemes.

If the prison supplanted and foreclosed other possible epistemes for much of the nineteenth and twentieth centuries, the social and political transformations constitutive of neoliberalism—and the technologies that have emerged alongside them—have given birth to new ones, or at least transformed and precipitated the reemergence of older ones. While neoliberalism was made possible in part by the reductions of legal and political personhood effected by the prison—and especially by mass incarceration—it has also produced new knowledge about criminals and other bad actors, and it has produced new or transformed techniques of punishment. Moreover, the prison is increasingly viewed as an institution that does not work. This is true of both progressives, who tend to the prison as a tool of racial subordination, and of conservatives, who tend to highlight its failure to mitigate crime. From this perspective, cancel culture may represent an alternative to the prison, which is, after all, an imposed and "unnatural" technique of punishment that never truly responded to the social, political, and economic conditions on which it was imposed.

Cancel culture represents a transformation of social relations such that justice in the neoliberal digital age more closely resembles the justice constitutive of the model of infamy than it does that of the penitentiary. Even though we are living in the era of mass criminalization and incarceration such that fully one-third of Americans have some sort of criminal record, cancel culture represents an emerging—or re-emerging—form of popular justice divorced altogether from the law and other juridical structures.[14] Cancel culture is by no means a dominant mode of justice in the United States, but it does more closely resemble forms of popular or vigilante justice that are more traditional or endemic to the culture. This mode of justice has long been revered in pop culture icons like the superhero. Batman, as a paradigmatic example, not only takes justice into his own hands but reveals actual law enforcement to be bungling and incompetent: In the original television series, Commissioner Gordon was helpless to solve any case other than the most mundane street crimes, rushing to his iconic red phone at the first sign of any real danger. Batman is a reminder that the vigilante was a "natural" part of the originary American "Old West" system of justice when law enforcement was either nonexistent or in its infancy. John Walsh, the founder and host of *America's Most Wanted*, is considered by some to be a Batman figure—a real-life, righteous vigilante. The Crime Museum in Washington, DC, certainly does, noting that "more than 1,000 fugitives, including 15 criminals from the FBI's 10 Most Wanted List, have been captured due to the crime tips that have been reported to trained operators who work on-site."[15] At least since the 1980s, every individual has been encouraged to act as a vigilante— sometimes to enforce the law, but always to be a crime fighter qua police informant.[16]

A recent Netflix documentary series illustrates how this vigilantism has evolved and transformed in the digital age. The 2021 four-part series *Crime Scene: The Vanishing at the Cecil Hotel* follows the 2013 disappearance in Los Angeles of twenty-one-year-old Vancouver native Elisa Lam.[17] The first three episodes rely heavily on the testimony of so-called web sleuths, whose research into and theories about the case are presented alongside the testimony of police investigators and potential witnesses. With few leads in the early days of the investigation, the police released a four-minute video of Lam in an elevator on the day of her disappearance. Lam's behavior in the video is so beguiling that an online community formed to investigate and share their theories of the case.

The series indicts a culture of online rumor mongering in the figure of a Mexican death metal artist named Morbid (Pablo Vergara), whom the online community of web sleuths targeted as Lam's killer. The "evidence" they used to convict him included the content of his stage persona, for example performing in front of photos of a serial killer; a song that he had written about drowning; a music video in which an actress is running from danger; and a selfie the artist had taken with the caption "the killer is me."[18] While Morbid had indeed been a guest at the Cecil during the same *month* as Lam's stay, his stay had occurred a year prior to her disappearance. Once the online accusations took hold, however, Morbid faced significant harassment, including death threats, and his social media accounts were eventually shut down. The series ultimately presents the singer as a victim of online conspiracy theories who, because of the harassment he received, eventually tried to take his own life. The conspiracy theorists explain how such theories took hold—and none of them express regret over their harassment or Morbid's suicide attempt. The sleuths saw their "evidence" as valid and their online community as a valid response to the lack of information about and progress on the case. They believed not only that they were qualified to solve a crime—despite lacking any physical evidence themselves—but, implicitly, that the police were not. The sleuths, moreover, not only demonstrate a lack of faith in the ability of the police to solve the crime but promote a conspiracy about a police coverup. Law enforcement is not only incompetent, in other words, but also corrupt. As a consequence, internet chat rooms and message boards are a more appropriate forum to hold a public trial and sentencing—and this well before the pathology report had been completed. The police ultimately concluded that there had been no foul play in the death of Elisa Lam.

What happened to the death metal artist Morbid does not fit neatly into the right-wing vision of cancel culture as a movement designed to punish politically incorrect speech, and it is instructive for precisely this reason. If the so-called culture wars have framed cancellation as a phenomenon that pits ideologues against one another, what happened in the Lam investigation reveals a different and perhaps more structuring aspect of cancel culture. In this view, cancel culture is not fundamentally about the identity of victims or offenders, or even about types of transgressions, but is rather a form of punishment. The online investigation, adjudication, and sentencing in the Lam case is one of at least three modes of justice operating in the United States in the twenty-first century. The state's use of mass surveillance, arrest, detention, and supervision coexists alongside a system of policies and procedures primarily used by private interests to shape the neoliberal social contract. Blanket bans, employment contracts (or lack thereof), and terms of service dictate what normative behavior is and how non-normative behavior should be punished. Cancel culture represents a third type of justice, which more closely resembles Foucault's model of infamy.[19] In this model, "the shame that marks the guilty person is first of all a reaction of the whole of society; furthermore, society has no need here to delegate its right to judge to any authority; it judges immediately by its own reaction." Cancel culture resembles the model of infamy because those accused of bad or criminal behavior are not tried or punished by any legal authority but by, in effect, the internet, by web sleuths and all of the individuals who encounter the "criminal" online at any—and every—moment. The model of infamy represents a kind of "penal utopia," since "judgment in the juridical sense of the term would be entirely reduced to judgment in the psychological sense; the judgment will be nothing other than the totality of the individual judgments of the citizens." Foucault further describes infamy as "an ideal penalty inasmuch as it varies from society to society; each society establishes the intensity of infamy to be allocated to each crime. Thus, there is no need for court or code. One does not have to say in advance that this act will be allocated this penalty. Infamy corresponds at every moment point by point to each crime."[20]

Cancel culture reflects "the dissolution of judicial power into the collective judgment of individuals" insofar as it does not require a court or a legal code.[21] The infamous are judged by a collection of individuals on social media, or in the broader society, who also establish the intensity of infamy to be allocated to each crime—on an ad hoc basis and with no need to say in advance which acts will be considered transgressions. Any act might be condemned as a transgression against society, and the infamy of any alleged predator corresponds at every moment point by point to each transgression or crime. The collection of individuals on social media not only establishes the criteria by which any act might be considered a transgression, act by act, but also establishes the intensity of infamy to be allocated to each transgression. This combination of vigilante crime fighting and the imposition of penalties based on the psychological judgment of individuals is an extension of an originary American justice, but it is also "the only punishment in which the system of penalties accords exactly with the penal principle of the criminal-social enemy. It is a transparent punishment: only the gaze and murmur, the instantaneous and possibly constant judgment of each and all constitutes this kind of permanent court."[22]

The popular justice that exists today in the form of cancel culture, however, is also significantly different from the popular justice that Foucault describes. The major feature these two justices share is the dissolution of judicial power and the collective judgment of individuals. However, the model of infamy is opposed to stigmatization or branding. Whereas some models of punishment marked or branded the criminal for life, ensuring that he could not escape his punishment, the model of infamy "leaves only a memory and not traces," is revocable, and therefore allows for reconciliation.[23] While cancel culture avoids formal juridical power, one of its foundations is the permanence of information in the form of the internet as an archive. This makes identifying past transgressions possible and all but eliminates the possibility of their being forgotten. In this way, cancel culture is preceded by the cultural trend described in the previous two chapters: criminals —and other bad actors, such as people with bad credit scores or who have been evicted from their homes—are figured as permanently flawed and irredeemable. Indeed, cancellation is also often framed explicitly as a permanent condition: those who commit bad acts are irredeemable and should be permanently excluded from their social, economic, and professional networks.

For this reason, cancel culture disrupts another important feature of the model of infamy, as described by Foucault, which is the possibility of establishing varying degrees of the intensity of infamy. The infamy imposed by cancel culture is both permanent and static, at least in principle. The degree of infamy is not so much a reflection of acts themselves or even the judgment of individuals but is rather a reflection of the type or form of punishment that is available. There is only one punishment according to cancel culture, as evidenced by debates that emerge around potential targets of cancellation. These do not usually consider the degree to which or period of time during which a person should be canceled but rather only whether or not they should be canceled. There is no difference in punishment between sexual assault and a racial slur, between sexual harassment and dressing as a Native American for Halloween—and therefore there can be no difference in the degree of infamy allocated to any offender. All punishments are essentially the same, and for this reason, all crimes are essentially the same. When a single tactic is used to punish all transgressions, all transgressions, and all of the people who commit them, come to be treated as equivalents. Despite its extremely moralistic and sometimes dogmatic dimensions, cancel culture takes one aspect of the neoliberal actuarial justice model to its extreme logical conclusion. If, under this model, "there is no fundamental difference between the murderer and the traffic violator,"[24] cancel culture posits that there is no difference between the murderer, the traffic violator, the serial sexual abuser, the transphobic YouTuber, or the teenager who publishes a racist tweet. The law, strictly speaking, has no bearing on whether an individual should be brought to justice. In this model of ideal justice, where legal codes are unnecessary, any act might constitute a limit whose punishment is always the same, but it is always impossible to know in advance which acts will constitute such a limit. Moreover, in contrast to the protections from retroactive applicability of new laws offered by the Fifth Amendment, the new "laws" of cancel culture almost always apply retroactively—such that behaviors that were largely considered acceptable when they were performed, sometimes many decades in the past, are subject to the same judgment and the same penalties as those performed under the current set of norms.

The unknowability of both the limit and the prospect of punishment is reminiscent of the legal system of collateral consequences—in which penalties are codified but, for many of them, there is no guarantee either way whether any individual offender will face them. It is also predicated on this system, and on the ways in which the unknowability of penalties and the arbitrariness of their enforcement make the terms of the social contract opaque for both offenders and the general public. It is also predicated on the outsourcing of justice to quasi-judicial authorities such as prison administrators, compliance officers, and human resources managers. In both public and private settings, the grievance procedure and disciplinary hearing have replaced the courtroom adjudication of many civil and some criminal matters. This is especially true for matters related to civil rights, such as racial and gender discrimination, sexual harassment, and even sexual assault. Title VII and Title IX offices exist for good reason. Sexual harassment and gender-based discrimination are not criminal offenses; their adjudication by these offices replaced a system in which sexual harassment and gender-based discrimination were fully legal and were not adjudicated or punished at all. Moreover, the removal of this adjudication from the public was by design, so that victims of sexual harassment and discrimination could seek redress for their grievances without becoming victims of public shaming or workplace retaliation. The boardroom adjudication of criminal violations obviates guilt and innocence, but the boardroom adjudication of civil violations forecloses public knowledge and debate about these violations. It also makes termination of employment the default and sometimes only consequence for what might constitute serious crimes such as sexual assault and rape. One consequence of this system has been that workplaces and universities continue to shield themselves from accountability for reproducing the conditions in which civil and criminal violations take place. In her recent study of this phenomenon, Sarah Ahmed describes how so many of her interlocutors, university students and faculty members, all of whom had filed institutional complaints, were dragged through labyrinthine processes designed to ignore or silence those complaints or, if their complaints were eventually acknowledged, pressured into signing non-disclosure agreements that would protect their universities from public scrutiny.[25] While victims of harassment and other workplace violence should be protected, removing the adjudication of criminal behavior and behavior that violates civil rights from the public or even shared institutional settings can both harm victims of workplace violence and decrease our ability to define, negotiate, and respond to violence.

To take the #MeToo movement as a case in point, activists' allegations have been diverse, and some have been troubling for the way they frame certain behaviors as criminal. In attempting to craft a unified voice responding to the sexual violence that women face, some contributors to the discourse have conflated illegal behavior, such as harassment—and in some cases personally objectionable behavior, such as being asked out on a date or being asked for consent for sex—with criminality. A 2017 survey conducted by YouGov and *The Economist* found that 17 percent of people ages 18–24 considered a man asking a woman out for a drink to be sexual harassment.[26] In its reporting about the survey, *The Economist* noted that while some behaviors, such as unwanted touching, are widely accepted forms of harassment, "there is no clear consensus on exactly which behaviors cross the line."[27] Cultural norms shift—as they should—regarding what constitutes sexual harassment, sexual assault, and other forms of sexual violence, and the insidious violence of and harm caused by all forms of sexual harassment and violence should not be denied. However, removing the negotiation of these norms from public settings and reducing or eliminating adjudicative processes for resolving them can lead to confusion both about the relationship between laws and other norms, and about where and how these laws and norms can be negotiated. Not only do the terms of the social contract become more opaque as private institutions become responsible for resolving complaints of civil rights violations and criminality, but adjudicating and punishing them become matters of individual psychological judgment exercised by compliance officers, members of disciplinary boards, and human resources managers.[28]

Whereas Foucault's model of infamy is based on each individual's judgment at every encounter with the criminal, cancel culture blends individual judgment with a new form of sociality on the internet. In the largely two-sided world of online debate, where character limits and other formal constraints imposed by social media companies make longform argumentation and the nuance associated with it increasingly unpopular, it is very difficult to propose alternatives to a simplistic, binary model in which individuals are either good or bad, in which they either deserve punishment or do not (although most do). The algorithmic amplification by Twitter and Facebook of the most partisan and divisive voices makes it appear as though there is, and then ultimately creates, a reality in which there can only be two diametrically opposed "sides" to any argument. These constructed sides have been described by many scholars and media commentators as tribes, and the demand to unwaveringly agree with one's tribe as a new form of tribalism. In this model, even minor dissent from the dominant view may associate one with the opposing tribe, therefore singling out such dissenters for condescension, derision, harassment, or shunning. The rationality of cancellation thus imposes itself not just on individuals who commit certain offenses against others (or against society). Rather, anyone who disagrees with the dominant logic of their "side" and its judgment about infamy is subjected to the same degree of infamy as any other offender and to the same punishment—because there is neither any other degree of infamy nor any other punishment.

CANCEL CULTURE AND THE CULTURE WARS

In 2019, Harvard University rescinded its offer of admission to Kyle Kashuv, a survivor of the Marjory Stoneman Douglas High School shooting in Parkland, Florida. Kashuv was 16 at the time of the shooting and became in its aftermath an outspoken political conservative and gun rights activist. After Kashuv was admitted to Harvard, a series of social media posts surfaced in which he espoused explicitly racist views. The posts were published when Kashuv was 16 and featured his repeated use of racial slurs. Writing for *Forbes*, Michael T. Nietzel, president emeritus of Missouri State University, proposed that Harvard was right to rescind Kashuv's offer. Nietzel deploys the rhetoric of rights to assert that Harvard, as a private university, is legally entitled to admit or deny admission to whomever it wants, although the bulk of his argument consisted mostly of moral condemnation for Kashuv.[29] The collapsing of rights with moral imperative is a common strategy among liberal proponents of cancel culture that actually promotes the values of the conservative agenda.

Conservative complaints about cancel culture frequently center on the suppression of speech and the chilling effect of deplatforming or otherwise punishing individuals who espouse "unpopular" (i.e., racist, sexist, homophobic, or transphobic) views. One liberal response to these complaints is to assert the right of private organizations to impose their own rules—despite longstanding complaints that such organizations infringe on individuals' rights. In other words, private companies' restrictions on speech are seen as anathema to the so-called liberal agenda, except when such restrictions target those actors who are seen as enemies of that same agenda. Indeed, as Nietzel himself points out, Harvard's right to "decide which students will be admitted [is] a privilege of private institutions that conservatives usually defend."[30] Nietzel is not wrong in his estimation of conservatives' hypocrisy, although he fails to acknowledge the hypocrisy of a liberal discourse that engages in the same tactics. Both engage respectively in the discourse of rights or redemption, depending on which better defends or supports its current cause. Kashuv, for his part, and in keeping with such arguments of convenience, did not generally contest that Harvard was within its legal rights to deny him admission. While subscribing to a liberal identity politics that shuns racism, sexism, and homophobia, Nietzel drew on a much more conservative line of argumentation—one that asserted the legal rights of a private institution over the interests of individuals. On the other side, while subscribing to the opposite kind of (white) identity politics, Kashuv drew on the more progressive discourse of forgiveness and rehabilitation prevalent among proponents of criminal justice reform to implicitly contest the terms of a social contract that privileges the legal rights of private institutions over the rights of individuals.

Another Harvard admissions scandal further highlights the ways in which identity features in the deployment of these concepts. In 2017, Michelle Jones, who had served more than twenty years at Indiana Women's Prison for the murder of her four-year-old son, was accepted into Harvard's Department of History as a PhD student. Despite her imminent release and a significant record of public scholarship, the administration ultimately overrode the department's decision and denied her admission to the university. Jones eventually accepted an offer from NYU, but her Harvard admissions scandal generated significant backlash and public debate, especially among mainstream liberals and progressives, not about the rights of private institutions to admit whomever they want but about rehabilitation and forgiveness. Elizabeth Hinton, a faculty member in the Harvard department that had recruited Jones, was quoted in the *New York Times* about the case, noting that Jones's rejection called into question the extent to which society "really [believes] in the possibility of human redemption."[31]

The popular debates about Kashuv and Jones reflect the contemporary state of America's culture wars, itself an outcome of a neoliberal ethos that has transformed the basic tenets of democracy and governance and the meaning of rights. Both "sides" of the political spectrum —Democratic Party–style liberalism that foregrounds individual rights and civil liberties, and Republican Party–style neoconservatism that foregrounds individual obligations—"focus on free subjects as a basic rationale and target of government."[32] As a result, the only possible focus of popular debates about punishment and forgiveness is rights as they are inscribed in the liberal tradition, even as the "free subject" of liberalism has been transformed into an economic unit the basic rationale for which is institutional risk. The two "sides" of an argument about rights, when the rights of individuals and private institutions are at odds, as they always are, can only be resolved by shifting the debate away from the very rights that are at the center of that debate (by, for example, invoking redemption or rehabilitation).

British philosopher Piers Benn has recently described the contemporary online culture wars as a kind of popularity contest: "To their loyal followers, who grow in numbers with every retweet or share, the individuals who carry out [internet] shaming are brave and righteous. They expose others who err in thought, word, or deed."[33] Among Benn's criticisms of this culture is that the sword cuts both ways. For all the righteous defenders of progressive causes, there are just as many right-wing ideologues ready to shame their counterparts in the same way. The sheer volume of these kinds of communications on social media creates a "[spiral] of shaming and animosity" that forecloses the possibility of nuanced public discourse about complicated political issues.[34] A resulting tribalism reduces all individuals of the opposing political persuasion to static caricatures motivated by hate: "Opponents of certain opinions think those who hold those opinions are bad people—in extreme cases, not merely ordinarily flawed, but repellent, poisonous, and disgusting"[35]—criminal even. Political opinions, in other words, are conflated with moral character, such that those with whom we disagree politically become worthy of perpetual moral condemnation.

On the conservative right, cancel culture is often viewed as the inevitable outcome of years of political correctness, which it frames as a form of thought policing. However, while right-wing ideologues may be the most vocal about so-called PC culture, one 2018 study conducted by the nonprofit group More in Common found that as many as 80 percent of all Americans, across the political spectrum, "believe that political correctness had gone too far."[36] This more bipartisan view was on display when, in March of 2021, twenty-seven-year-old Alexi McCammond was canceled for racist and homophobic tweets she had published when she was seventeen. McCammond had apologized for the tweets in 2019, the same year she was named the emerging journalist of the year by the National Association of Black Journalists, but they reemerged in 2021 when she was hired as the editor-in-chief of *Teen Vogue.* According to reporting from the *New York Times,* the leadership at Condé Nast—the parent company of *Teen Vogue*—had discussed the tweets with staff as part of the vetting process. After her appointment, however, photos surfaced of the seventeen-year-old McCammond dressed as a Native American for Halloween. McCammond was condemned online, both for her tweets and her choice of costume, and she ultimately resigned her post.

McCammond's cancellation drew condemnation from liberal critics of cancel culture, who viewed her detractors as overzealous and the consequences of her behavior as overly harsh. Even among some proponents of cancellation, the cancellation of McCammond, a young woman of color who had disavowed and apologized for a series of ten-year-old behaviors performed as a teenager, was a bridge too far.[37] While few liberal commentators sought to defend Kyle Kashuv's blatant racism, many came to the defense of McCammond, using the same kinds of arguments that Kashuv used in his own defense—and they relied on the same kinds of reasoning that employers, landlords, and other private companies use to make determinations about whether or not certain criminals deserve to be given a "second chance." Those who disagreed with McCammond's fate questioned the justification for canceling someone based on actions that were a decade old, and especially actions that happened when she was a teenager. (Few of these same commentators came to the defense of Kashuv, despite his offenses also having occurred when he was a minor.)

While often framed as aspects of America's culture wars and the increasing racial and partisan polarization of American society, these debates about forgiveness, forgetting, rehabilitation, and redemption can also be understood as acts of adjudication. While undoubtedly speaking to the shifting ideological and political practices related to "woke" culture, identity politics, and partisan divides, these debates at the same time mirror those taking place in the corporate boardroom— for example in the development of Airbnb's vague banishment policy, the application of the European Union's right to be forgotten, or the decision-making processes of human resources managers who must decide whether an otherwise qualified applicant with a criminal record should be hired. The logic or rationality of the corporate boardroom has penetrated public discourse about who deserves punishment, as has the mode of identifying and adjudicating undesirable behavior. In much the same way that Facebook executives crafted policy as knee-jerk reactions to Donald Trump, and in much the same way its moderators simply had to recognize unacceptable speech when they saw it, cancel culture is a form of justice in which each person not only is responsible for "knowing it when they see it"—*it* being any behavior that transgresses a limit that is unknowable in advance—but also for doing the work of adjudicating and sentencing it. Moreover, the punishment itself—cancellation—and the fact that there is only one punishment, reflects the corporate model in which all criminals, regardless of crime and other contextual factors, are subject to the same punitive technique: banishment. In this way, the public negotiation of norms and values increasingly relies on unacknowledged, ill-defined

decision-making processes that are opposed to public debate and negotiation, and the basis for which is the commonsense psychological
judgment of individuals.

BANISHMENT, BEST PRACTICES, AND THE
PSYCHOLOGICAL JUDGMENT OF INDIVIDUALS

Foucault defines banishment, following Claude Lévi-Strauss, as a "punitive tactic [that] involves prohibiting an individual's presence in
communal or sacred places, removing or prohibiting all the laws of
hospitality concerning him."[38] For Lévi-Strauss, banishment results in
a type of social death where the banished individual is fully excom-
municated from society. Foucault argues, however, that the notion of
banishment is too broad and too vague to describe the historically and
culturally specific phenomena and practices that constitute punishment in modern society. Rather, banishment is but one of four major
tactics that Foucault suggests historically have constituted punishment.
More important than banishment in modern societies is the imposition of restitution or the organization of redemption. In contrast to
banishment, this tactic is characterized by bringing the offender back
into the web of symbolic relations by creating a debt or obligation. Banishment "involves breaking all ties with the individual, all the ties by
which he is held within power," whereas a system of restitution and
redemption "involves holding the offender to a network of obligations
that are multiplied and intensified in comparison with the traditional
network of obligations of his existence."[39]

Foucault writes of Lévi-Strauss's notion of banishment that "there
is no exile, no confinement that does not include, along with what is
generally described as expulsion, a transfer, a reactivation of the very
power that imposes, constrains, and expels." He uses the example of
the psychiatric institution to describe how the discursively constructed
mad subject is both removed from society and at the same time rein-
tegrated in a new way.

Through the very operation of ... expulsion, [the psychiatric hospital]
is a center of the constitution and reconstitution of a rationality that is

imposed in an authoritarian way in the framework of relations of power within the hospital, and that will be reabsorbed outside the hospital itself in the form of a scientific discourse that circulates outside as knowledge about madness, for which the condition of possibility of it being rational is, precisely, the hospital.[40]

In the hospital, the mad subject is acted upon by the rationality of the institution, power is exercised over him, and outside the hospital, knowledge about him is circulated in discourse. It is through this process that "a political relationship that structures the whole life of a psychiatric hospital is converted into a discourse of rationality, through which precisely the political authority—the basis on which the hospital is able to function—is strengthened."[41]

While the penitentiary has sometimes been characterized as a tactic of exclusion or banishment, for Foucault it functions much more like the psychiatric hospital: prisoners in one sense are removed from society, but in another sense, they are transformed into discursive objects and reincorporated into a system of knowledge, a discourse of rationality, about crime and criminality that strengthens the political authority of the state vis-à-vis its ability to contain and transform those same prisoners. The basis of the rationality for "scientific" knowledge about criminals circulated outside the prison—in the form of criminology, psychology, and psychiatry, for example—is the prison.

Transformations in the prison system since the 1970s, as well as broader economic and social conditions, mean that the kind of knowledge produced about crime and criminals is significantly different from the kind that was produced through much of the nineteenth and twentieth centuries. The prison has transformed since the 1970s according to the logics of neoliberalism into a model of actuarial justice constituted not by the transformation of prisoners into citizens or productive workers but by the mitigation of risk at the level of population. The prison and criminal justice system continue to produce knowledge about prisoners and crime, but the knowledge they produce is increasingly actuarial. The focus on crime rates rather than, for example, the psychological motivation of criminals, means that the knowledge produced is geared towards justifying the use of containment strategies to mitigate risk. This knowledge in turn is circulated not only as scientific discourse—among statisticians and economists, for example—but increasingly as best practices circulated within the private sector. As described in chapter 3, employers and landlords may rely on little more than their common sense or instincts to determine which job applicants they hire and tenants they accept. But these instincts are deeply influenced by the knowledge that circulates among professional organizations and trade groups, which are in turn informed by the knowledge produced about crime and criminals by statisticians, economists, and security experts. The prisoner reentry industry likewise relies on actuarial knowledge about rates of recidivism to promote and provide commonsense or best practice "solutions" for former prisoners, like life skills and parenting classes, "job training," and quasi-correctional services, like halfway houses. The prisoner reentry industry, along with landlords, employers, and other private companies such as Airbnb, relies on actuarial knowledge and subscribes to its rationality not as a political choice but as a best practice.

If the prisoner reentry industry deploys this knowledge and these best practices to transform the ex-offender into a commodity to be traded in the open market, the private sector—in the form of employers, landlords, and companies like Airbnb—exercises banishment in a way that is much more consistent with the kinds of banishment described by Lévi-Strauss. Banishment from Airbnb does not include any element of restitution, redemption, or bringing the offender into a network of obligations, but rather only "involves breaking all ties with the individual" and quite literally "prohibiting all the laws of hospitality concerning him."[42] While the state mobilizes actuarial knowledge in order to effect changes at the level of the population, private companies mobilize this knowledge to promote the kinds of banishments and exclusions that predominated in the Middle Ages. Far from being informed political or moral decisions, however, policies that banish people convicted of crimes rely on common sense gleaned from ostensibly neutral, technical expertise. This expertise is transformed into a rationality whose expression and output are institutional best practices. The effect, if not the intent, of corporate policies banishing people with criminal records is to craft "communities" constituted by members who subscribe to a neoliberal worldview that privileges the rights of corporations (and other private institutions) over individuals. For those who do not, there is no possibility of redemption or reincorporation into the community. They are simply banished from these particular societies and reincorporated elsewhere—within the criminal justice system and adjacent prisoner reentry industry.

Erik Nordenhaug and Jack Simmons have drawn attention to the ways in which best practices have replaced moral and political debate and led to impoverishments in institutions' ability to respond to challenges. They examine how, "in our methodically bound culture as a whole, the teaching of rules, codes, policies, professional procedures as well as the existence of ethics committees and legal advisors . . . [are] replacing the internal voice of moral reasoning in the individual."[43] They cite as one key example of this trend the inadequacy of medical institutions to respond to pressing situations that depart from those they experience on a day-to-day basis. Describing the events that happened at one hospital during Hurricane Katrina, including patients being given lethal doses of narcotics so that staff members and other patients could escape the disaster, Nordenhaug and Simmons agree that institutional mechanisms are inadequate to "addressing extraordinary professional and institutional challenges." They argue, however, that the inadequacy of medical institutions to respond to pressing ethical challenges is just one "symptom of a general trend in professional ethics."[44] They diagnose this general trend by suggesting that "the ideal of professionalism efficiently encourages students and clinicians in the health professions to avoid the difficult process of internalizing moral reasoning (while still achieving the desired effect of moral behavior) by following prescribed protocols and procedures that come from hired cricket voices of moral reasoning emanating from professional standards boards, ethics offices and committees, and legal departments." This version of ethical training not only in health care but across most industries, they continue, "reduces to the lesson that professional standards, codes, policies, rules, and the established procedures of institutions and professions must be followed while on the job." Practitioners, in other words, are trained not in how to conduct moral or ethical reasoning or exercise moral or ethical judgment but only to perform a certain version of ethical conduct. As a result, "the professionally trained clinician, performing her duties within the range of policies and codes that regulate professional conduct, is characterized as behaving ethically without having internalized a non-methodological rationality capable of producing or discovering moral standards or applying those standards to new situations."[45]

Ethics training has been reduced in many cases to compliance training, and compliance with ethical standards in many cases is little more than a mechanism for reducing institutional risk. The problem with this feature of professionalization is not only that compliance and ethics are not the same thing, but rather that institutionalizing compliance with what amounts to best practices in the name of ethics degrades and deforms the practice of ethics. "Over time," when compliance training replaces ethical training, this can "alter our motivations and thinking about ethics and redirect our activities."[46] This phenomenon has resonances with the managerialization of legal consciousness, as discussed in the previous chapter: the problem with private corporations being granted the authority to interpret and define civil rights law is not only that civil rights law can be perverted, circumvented, or obfuscated; rather, individuals begin to see private corporations as the final arbiter of civil rights claims, which depresses the actual mobilization of rights in the courts.[47] In the case of professional ethics, for Nordenhaug and Simmons, it is not only that institutional needs are privileged over the needs of patients (in medical settings) or clients (for example in legal settings), but that compliance-based systems actually depress the adoption and mobilization of moral or ethical judgment. Finally, also like the use of grievance and disciplinary procedures to adjudicate civil rights claims in the corporate boardroom, compliance with institutional rules and norms ultimately is not a choice but an obligation. Individuals must comply with the best practices of their institutions because they would otherwise be out of a job.

Individuals, then, are coerced into complying with institutional rules, codes, and norms—with best practices—under the guise of and as a substitute for ethics and ethical decision-making. The "outsourcing of ethical behavior" or moral reasoning is deeply embedded within all institutions, ranging from the medical profession to the university to the courtroom. Professionalization essentially entails the internalization of institutional rules, codes, and norms: the "professional," whether faculty member, judge, or medical doctor, "by definition . . . must represent the latest words, standards and methods of the profession."[48] This internalization of externally imposed rules, codes, and norms is tantamount to the adoption and internalization of best practices—or the replacement of ethical reasoning with ostensibly neutral and technical expertise. The (obligatory) acceptance of these rules, codes, and norms means that individual judgment is replaced by the rote application of organizational or institutional best practices. The opinions of individual human resources managers, for example, about how people with criminal convictions should be treated, the severity of crime types, or the role that length of time since conviction should play in hiring decisions is not, from this view, based on a thorough examination of the criminal justice system or on ethical reasoning that attends to questions about how human value, rehabilitation, or redemption might be evaluated. Rather, it comes from a set of rules, codes, and norms—best practices—that are crafted by professional organizations such as the Society for Human Resources Management. When the National Association for Independent Landlords describes why landlords should use criminal background screenings, it is quite simply, and without any ethical or political reasoning, because "you don't want a criminal in your home"—no matter what the circumstances of her conviction were, the type of criminal justice system that convicted her, the length of time that has elapsed since that conviction, or her post-conviction history.[49]

Nordenhaug and Simmons describe institutional rules, codes, and norms and the compliance mechanisms used to enforce them as "ethical devices." These are ethical shortcuts, as it were, that act as a kind of short circuit such that individual moral judgments can (and must) be avoided in favor of rote acceptance of best practices. In this way, a best practice can be thought of as a heuristic. Heuristics are problem-solving shortcuts whose primary benefit is the reduction of cognitive load. Reliance on the criminal record, as described in the last two chapters, can be considered a kind of heuristic because it eliminates the need to ask whether an individual is good, worthy, or respectable, and does the work of answering these questions without independent analysis or judgment. In their classic analysis of cognitive heuristics, Amos Tversky and Daniel Kahneman proposed that "people rely on a limited number of heuristic principles which reduce the complex tasks of assessing probabilities and predicting values to simpler judgmental operations."[50] In descriptions of their various studies, in which research subjects are presented with judgment-based tasks, they find that participants overwhelmingly ignore meaningful variables and instead rely on intuitive judgments, or heuristics, many of which are based on biases and stereotypes, leading to incorrect assessments.

A common heuristic that Tversky and Kahneman identify is representativeness. In one study, participants were asked to assess the probability that a certain individual was engaged in a particular occupation, based on a description of that individual. The description contained only details about the individual's personality and had nothing to do with the performance of any particular occupation. Nonetheless, participants disproportionately relied on stereotypes to categorize individuals into professions. A shy, withdrawn, helpful, meek, and tidy individual was judged to be a librarian (versus, for example, a pilot, farmer, or physician), since the probability that he is a librarian "is assessed by the degree to which he is representative of, or similar to, the stereotype of a librarian."[51] Tversky and Kahneman note that "the confidence [judgers] have in their prediction depends primarily on the degree of representativeness (that is, on the quality of the match between the selected outcome and the input) with little or no regard for the factors that limit predictive accuracy." Thus, a related heuristic is the illusion of validity: when the input matches a stereotype (like the description of a shy, withdrawn, but helpful individual that matches the stereotype of a librarian), judgers will believe in the accuracy of their prediction "even if the description is scanty, unreliable, or outdated."[52] The availability, retrievability, and familiarity with information often influence individuals' probabilistic judgments to a much greater extent than facts, analysis, statistics, or statistical reasoning. The disproportionate news reporting of Black people arrested for violent crimes has been widely critiqued for the way it sways the viewing public into believing that Black people are more likely to commit violent crimes.[53] From the perspective of heuristics, individuals who are inundated with these media reports may believe that Black people are more likely than white people to commit crimes because of the availability, retrievability, and familiarity with that information over information that accurately conveys crime statistics or that underscores the racialized operations of the criminal justice system.

Nordenhaug and Simmons identify a similar heuristic that has significant consequences for the way we think about moral or ethical agents. In their fallacy of composition, institutions are taken to be moral agents because they are composed of individuals who are moral agents. Using this heuristic to imbue corporations with ethical, and ultimately legal, personhood results, like most heuristics, in both factual errors and errors of reasoning. But these errors have much broader implications. Corporations' legal personhood not only makes them much more powerful. Rather, "the widespread acknowledgment of 'corporate personhood' . . . involves a transformation of human moral agency itself, meaning regular persons are also transformed by the existence of 'corporate personhood.'"[54] Not only do corporations become legal persons, but the legal personhood of actual people is eroded. In the context of their argument about professional ethics, Nordenhaug and Simmons believe that corporate personhood is an analogy for the way institutions, rather than people, are assumed to be responsible and ethical actors. In this case, not only do corporations and institutions (seem to) become moral agents, but in so doing, the moral agency of individuals is eroded. "Ultimately, the humanizing of professionalism requires [the institution] to 'think morally' and develop 'an artificial moral conscience' that stands independently of our individual moral sensibilities," and in fact stands above our individual and moral sensibilities. Individuals' moral and ethical agency, along with their legal rights and personhood, eventually become subsidiary to corporate and institutional norms, codes, rules, and procedures.[55]

While these features of contemporary social life impact professionals whose very professionalization is predicated on such obligations, another implication is that, at a broader level, the "psychological judgment of individuals," as described by Foucault in relation to the model of infamy as a system of justice, is, in the contemporary moment, also predicated on what amounts to obligatory compliance with best practices that appear to be one's own moral or ethical framework. The adoption of best practices as a replacement for ethical reasoning and political decision-making results in a broader cultural acceptance of certain norms that come not from personal reasoning or moral judgment but from trade groups, professional organizations, and other institutions. The psychological judgment of individuals in the context of cancel culture is not only predicated on new forms of sociality brought on by the algorithmic amplification of divisive speech on social media, but on heuristics that are adopted on the basis of availability, retrievability, and familiarity with information—all of which are significantly determined by trade groups and professional organizations but also by social media companies themselves. The lack of any formal adjudicative process or mechanism in cancel culture—whether the subject of cancellation is an alleged murderer like Morbid or an alleged sexual harasser like Louis C. K.—reflects the use of heuristics to adjudge guilt, but it also suggests that these heuristics can and do replace legal, ethical, and political reasoning and debate. In much the same way that professionals are trained not in how to exercise ethical judgment but only in how to perform a certain version of ethical conduct, the public, too, can sometimes rely on heuristics to perform a certain version of ethical conduct that conforms to the best practices of contemporary social media discourse.

When progressive and mainstream discourse, for example in the #MeToo movement, insists on believing the victim of sexual violence, it does so in large part because of the historical tendency to disbelieve women victims of sexual violence. However well-intentioned, and however much these same proponents insist that believing the victim does not presume the guilt of the accused, it absolutely must, logically speaking, presume that guilt. This is not to say that the accused are or are not guilty, nor does it suggest that women lie about their own victimization. Rather, the point is to highlight a logical paradox in the discourse of some progressive movements that results from the use of heuristics and the adoption of best practices formulated in the corporate boardroom. The presumption of innocence is both a legal right and a political ideal in the criminal justice system, even if it has been practiced irregularly. But it is neither a legal right nor a political ideal in the disciplinary hearing (no matter whether that disciplinary hearing takes place within a public institution like a prison or university or a private one like a workplace). Rather, disciplinary and grievance procedures, as Lauren Edelman argues, can do little more than symbolize attention to due process, since due process is something that exists only within the courtroom. The managerialization of legal consciousness that Edelman describes, which results from the widespread use of these procedures to resolve civil rights claims, means that concepts and practices like due process are degraded and deformed. They are replaced by compliance mechanisms or, as Nordenhaug and Simmons describe them, "ethical devices," which individuals rely on as heuristics that substitute their own individual psychological judgment.

When social conservatives decry cancel culture because of its "chilling effect" on discourse, it is easy to dismiss these claims as bigotry. After all, they are often posed in hyperbolic language that suggests any mention of race, ethnicity, and gender will result in cancellation. However, there is a great deal of popular discourse that does demonstrate intolerance towards debate. One of these is the "fact" asserted by many advocates of gender justice that all men who are accused of sexual violence should be presumed guilty. It is worth putting the formulation in these terms, not because women who accuse men of sexual violence should be disbelieved, but precisely because the discourse relies on a best practice of popular justice that does not include any adjudicative process, let alone due process. People accused of sexual violence, no matter the type or context, are presumed to be guilty of transgressing a limit whose punishment, cancellation—because there can be no other punishment—has itself become a best practice.

THE POST-JURIDICAL TURN

Cancel culture is perhaps taken most seriously by conservative media pundits who wish to discredit social justice causes. Many progressives, especially in the media, suggest that it is not worth taking seriously, or have elected to change its name to something less distasteful (for example, "call-out culture"). Cancel culture "warriors," many believe, represent a small and largely impotent but vocal minority. However cancel culture is defined, whoever constitutes its members, and whatever its size, there is a movement that has shifted public discourse about acceptable norms regarding race, gender, and sexuality. This movement's activities have included agitating against bigotry and sexual violence, shaming or deplatforming individuals who demonstrate bigotry or have a history of proven or alleged sexual violence, and pressuring organizations and institutions to sever their relationships with those individuals. These are all actions that might be considered positive ones under the terms of traditional social justice activism. Indeed, they emerged from these forms of activism. The terminology of cancel culture, however, seems to place a pallor over them—so much so that many on the left of the mainstream political spectrum deny its very existence. Whatever it is called, *something* happened to Alexi McCammond, Kyle Kashuv, Ellen DeGeneres, Anna Wintour, and the death metal musician Morbid, among many others. Variously, their television shows or employment contracts were canceled, they resigned from their positions, their admissions to university were rescinded, they were victims of online harassment and doxing, and their social media accounts were suspended.

In comparison to the severity of the legal, political, economic, and social consequences of a criminal conviction, cancellation may appear inconsequential. And it is true that the effects of cancellation for many may be insignificant. But for others, especially those without wealth and institutional power, being canceled—being fired from a job or denied admission to university, being harassed online or getting doxed—can result in significant material and symbolic losses. Whether individual cancellations appear as a significant loss of social standing or as an insignificant slap on the wrist may depend not only on the political affiliation of the observer but on the prior social standing, wealth, or power of the canceled subject. For Ellen DeGeneres and Anna Wintour, the material and symbolic effects of cancellation may be less than they are for someone like Michelle Jones or Kyle Kashuv, whose future job prospects and social standing may be seriously diminished by their Harvard admissions decisions.

Whether or not this kind of punishment is righteous, legitimate, effective, or even real will likely continue to be a matter of debate for some time. These debates about cancel culture, however, reflect popular anxieties about and disaffections with the administration of justice in the United States. For both Democratic Party–style liberals and Republican Party–style conservatives, the criminal justice system has failed, albeit for different reasons. For proponents of cancel culture, popular justice responds to the state's failures to hold the wealthy and the powerful accountable for misconduct, illegal behavior, and crime. It also responds to the failure of corporations and other private governments and their grievance and disciplinary procedures not only to guarantee civil rights properly speaking but to create just environments free of racism, ethnocentrism, sexism, homophobia, and transphobia.

If cancel culture is a reasonable response to the failures of corporations and the state to secure justice, however, it is also an expression or rearticulation of those failures. Cancel culture is not a literal return to the model of infamy in the sense of eliminating or replacing other modes of justice that have been prevalent in American society since its inception. It may better be formulated as a post-juridical mode of justice—in the sense that "post" implies in critical theories such as postmodernism. Postmodernism does not simply assert an "after" of modernism, or even a radical break from it, both of which imply a kind of erasure. Rather, postmodernism is not only predicated on modernism, it actually reproduces it through rearticulation and repetition.[56] The post-juridical order of cancel culture contests the terms of a disciplinary regime that fails to produce justice, but it cannot fail to repeat and rearticulate the terms of that same regime. In the process of repetition and rearticulation, this post-juridical order produces an ideal form, as it were, of the juridical order it wishes to break from. Cancel culture is a mode of popular or vigilante justice that has no recourse to legal codes or procedural rules, but which secures a "permanent court" whose punitive tactic promotes (even as it cannot realize) a form of banishment or exclusion in which the social enemy is neither rehabilitated nor reformed but erased.[57]

One notable example of cancel culture's quite literal erasure of the transgressing subject was the removal of Kevin Spacey from the film *All the Money in the World*, which had already completed filming in

2017 when Spacey was accused of a variety of sexually-based offenses against minors, ranging from making inappropriate advances to sexual assault. Even though Spacey had played a major supporting role in the film, director Ridley Scott made the decision "almost [immediately]" after the allegations emerged to reshoot all of his scenes using a different actor.[58] The Netflix drama series *House of Cards* made a similar, and similarly swift, decision when it halted production on the sixth season of the show. When the first episode premiered, Spacey's character, President Frank Underwood, had been killed off, invoked most prominently by his tombstone in the trailer for the season.

While Spacey has largely remained *persona non grata* in the entertainment industry since 2017, none of the sexual assault cases against him have been successful in either civil or criminal courts—sometimes because the statute of limitations had elapsed and other times because victims or witnesses had died or chosen not to identify themselves publicly. And for his own part, Spacey defies his public shunning by insisting that Frank Underwood is still alive in his annual "Christmas address" released on his personal YouTube page in the persona of his *House of Cards* character. In his 2018 message, wearing an apron covered in Santa Clauses, Spacey/Underwood impugns the public for forgoing due process and laments his "impeachment without trial."[59] At the same time, he wishes for the public to thank him for showing them a harsh truth about the world that others are afraid to acknowledge—as Frank Underwood often did when he broke the fourth wall in the television series. This "truth" is ambiguous: it may be one about the cynicism Frank Underwood is so frank about, a cynicism that excuses murder for the sake of a "greater good," or it may be another hard truth about the existence of predators, or the failure of cancel culture to hold people like Spacey accountable. His 2019 message, delivered in front of a fireplace decorated with stockings, is less ambiguous: he admonishes those who would "go on the attack" when someone does something they "don't like," and encourages us instead to "kill them with kindness."[60]

In 2021, just a few years after the initial allegations against him, Spacey was hired to act in an Italian film about a man wrongfully accused of child abuse. Spacey may have suffered some material consequences as a result of being temporarily exiled from the entertainment industry, but his wealth is intact and he will likely continue to work, if in Europe rather than Hollywood, much like other alleged sexual abusers, such as Woody Allen and Roman Polanski. Moreover, Spacey shows us not only that he denies the allegations against him but that he is unaffected by his cancellation. Rather, we, his imagined audience, should thank him for revealing to us that the only way to get ahead in society is by disavowing it—by maintaining a cynical distance that allows one to step on or over anyone who gets in the way.

Like many white (collar) criminals who face, or might face, traditional justice in the courts, Spacey is largely shielded from the material and symbolic consequences of punishment. In this way, cancel culture repeats and rearticulates the terms of the disciplinary regime it wishes to transcend. The consequences of being canceled are, like the consequences of conviction, unevenly distributed among those who lack social, political, and economic power. For them, the "gaze and murmur" may someday subside, but the material damage will have been done. For someone like the heavy metal artist Morbid, a resolution in the case of Elisa Lam results in the "web sleuths," who acted as his judge and jury, becoming bored with him—without remorse or even interest in his suicide attempt or the other consequences of his having been very publicly accused of murder. In contrast, the "permanent court" of gaze and murmur relishes the spectacle of the unresolved, in the spectacle of Kevin Spacey, for whom there can be no resolution in the "case," no final word as it were, on his guilt or innocence. Spacey's every public appearance provokes the gaze and the murmur anew. TMZ publishes paparazzi photos of him on set as they repeat the allegations against him.[61] ABC News reports on the "beleaguered [actor's]" bizarre Christmas videos as they repeat the allegations against him.[62] Vox speculates about the veracity of the Christmas videos as it repeats the allegations against him.[63] It is not that the allegations against Spacey are not newsworthy. Rather, in erasing Spacey, or in attempting to erase him, the permanent court at every moment actually ensures that the individual who transgresses a limit remains bound to society, even as it insists that there can be no rehabilitation or redemption. Where cancel culture insists on an exile or erasure, it can effect only "gaze and murmur," a visual and discursive performance of exile that actually brings the offender constantly back into the social consciousness as a demand for justice. As such, the post-juridical turn of cancel culture is not only a demand for justice, but as demand, is a constant rearticulation of the failure of liberalism to produce justice.

Postscript

In May of 2021, Texas Governor Greg Abbot signed into law one of the most restrictive abortion bans in the country prior to the overturning of *Roe v. Wade* in 2022. Senate Bill 8 (SB8), also known as the "Heartbeat Act," makes abortion illegal after a fetal heartbeat can be detected, usually around six weeks—well before most people know they are pregnant. SB8 went into effect on September 1, 2021. While a number of states have moved to restrict abortions after the detection of a fetal heartbeat, the law is unique in that it prohibits the state from enforcing it. Instead, it can only be enforced by private individuals, who are authorized to bring civil litigation against physicians who perform abortions that are illegal under the new law, as well as against anyone who "knowingly engages in conduct that aids or abets the performance or inducement of an [illegal] abortion."[1] Aiding and abetting may include paying, in whole or in part, for an abortion, but the language is sufficiently broad that any act of assistance might be considered illegal, such as when a friend, family member, or taxi or ride-share driver takes someone to a medical appointment. In contrast to the typical operation of civil proceedings, in which a judge or jury determines the extent of damages against a plaintiff, this Act provides that "if a claimant prevails in an action brought under this section, the court shall award . . . statutory damages in an amount of not less than $10,000 for each abortion that the defendant performed or induced in violation of this chapter, and for each abortion performed or induced in violation of this chapter that the defendant aided or abetted." While individuals who seek or have an abortion cannot be sued under the Act, the law provides significant financial incentive for private individuals to monitor, surveil, and police the behaviors of women, their family and friends, abortion providers, and other individuals such as ride-share and taxi drivers.

A day after SB8 went into effect, injunctive relief was sought in the US Supreme Court. The majority denied that relief. In his dissent, Chief Justice John Roberts summarized the case in the following way: "The legislature has imposed a prohibition on abortions after roughly

six weeks, and then essentially delegated enforcement of that prohibition to the populace at large. The desired consequence appears to be
to insulate the State from responsibility for implementing and enforcing the regulatory regime." While Chief Justice Roberts's and Justice
Breyer's dissents highlighted the state's attempt to circumvent the law,
Justices Kagan and Sotomayor were more attentive to the possible effects of delegating enforcement of the law to private individuals. Sotomayor writes that, "in effect, the Texas Legislature has deputized the
State's citizens as bounty hunters, offering them cash prizes for civilly
prosecuting their neighbors' medical procedures." Whereas the constitutional right to obtain abortion services meant only that the state
could not interfere with an individual's ability to procure an abortion,
the Texas law, "by prohibiting state officers from enforcing the Act directly and relying instead on citizen bounty hunters," seeks "to make
it more complicated for federal courts to enjoin the Act on a statewide
basis." Justice Kagan concurs, noting that the Court, in failing to provide injunctive relief, "rewards Texas's scheme to insulate its law from
judicial review by deputizing private parties to carry out unconstitu-
tional restrictions on the State's behalf." Among the dissenting justices,
Kagan most forcefully highlights the "wholly unprecedented" nature of
the law's enforcement mechanism.[2]

In his September 3 remarks, President Biden denounced the law in
similar terms, calling it a "vigilante system" that is "almost un-Amer-
ican," and in media interviews, legal scholars explained how the law's
enforcement mechanism was tantamount to a bounty system.[3] Cornell
University law professor Michael Dorf argued that the law promotes
"the creation of a kind of Stasi," "an East German-type society in which
everybody is informing on everybody else."[4] But while there are aspects
of this law that are novel, neither bounty hunters nor informants nor
vigilantes are unprecedented in American history, either in the recent
or distant past. Indeed, the metaphors used to describe the law's enforcement mechanism—bounty hunters, deputizing private citizens,
vigilantism—are effective precisely because they are well-established
cultural and socio-legal phenomena.

Republican Texas legislators may understand the contemporary cultural moment more clearly than their Democratic counterparts. Asking
private individuals to monitor, surveil, and inform on one another is a

natural extension of the post-1980s regime of lateral surveillance and of the vigilante justice that characterizes cancel culture—both of which have roots in a much older tradition of private policing and prosecution. As discussed in chapter 3, the extraordinary power of the prosecutor's office was developed over a short period of time beginning in the mid-nineteenth century. But alongside new systems of public policing and prosecution, bounty hunters like those employed by the Pinkerton National Detective Agency were a primary means of bringing to justice outlaws such as Jesse James, Butch Cassidy and the Sundance Kid, and the Younger brothers—all figures of American Old West folklore who continue to occupy the cultural imaginary through their representation in popular film and television. While the Pinkertons and other private mercenaries often worked with nineteenth-century law enforcement, they also served as evidence that law enforcement was inadequate to securing public safety. On the other hand, what "public safety" often meant was the protection of private property. The Pinkerton Agency began in the early 1850s as a small security force hired to protect the property of railroad companies. Writing in 1974, Theodore Becker argues that the distinction between public and private policing has always been murky, and that the goal of protecting private property has been at the heart of both projects.

Soon after its inception, Becker writes, "the modern police organization soon was recognized as insufficient to render self-defense totally unnecessary."[5] It was precisely because of this inadequacy—in an era in which, because of the very existence of public police, self-help was newly frowned upon—that private policing emerged. Thus, "the advent of modern police did not mark the demise of citizen self-help." Instead, "citizen self-help simply took a different form *for those who could afford it*."[6] Private policing did not end but rather in some ways began with the institution of public policing. The Pinkerton Agency continues to operate as a private security firm alongside thousands of others whose primary mission is to protect private property. Private security firms and services—ranging from multibillion dollar companies that protect other multibillion dollar companies to multibillion dollar companies like ADT that protect the private property of individual homeowners—not only supplement but act in lieu of the police, which, as an institution, is inadequate to fully securing either private property or public safety. Becker calls the use of private security firms, or private policing, "self-help once removed." In other words, private individuals continue to be responsible for securing the safety of their own persons and property, but rather than policing their own homes and neighborhoods, they outsource this work to private firms.

The direct self-help model, however, has not been completely eliminated—not only in matters of protecting private property but also in matters of public safety and national security. In Texas, as well as other border states like Arizona, California, and New Mexico, vigilante groups like the United Constitutional Patriots, Citizen Defenders, and the Minutemen police the US-Mexico border with spotlights, body armor, ATVs, and assault rifles. Sometimes they act as a deterrent for people wishing to enter the United States, but they, like private security firms, also sometimes work closely with law enforcement—in this case by contacting US Border Patrol and detaining migrants until federal agents arrive. While some law enforcement authorities vigorously oppose the use of private citizens to police the border—favoring instead, perhaps, the use of private military contractors—vigilante groups continue to thrive, not because they are agents of the state but precisely because they serve their own ostensible interests. Members of vigilante groups like the Patriots and Citizen Defenders defend their activities by describing how the situation at the southern border threatens their own economic interests and the interests of their communities.

There are not only resonances with but a direct line connecting groups like the Minutemen and Citizen Defenders with the paradigmatic form of American extralegal justice—lynching. Historically, while the Ku Klux Klan enjoyed the implicit and often explicit consent of the state, its primary tactic of racial terror had been extralegal adjudication and punishment of Black "crime"—a limit whose contours were defined in some cases by the state and in some cases by the Klan itself. While the extralegal terror exercised by the KKK was expressly racial, it was also pegged to the economic interests of whites. The desire for racial purity historically has also been a desire for the social, cultural, and economic supremacy of whites. In the 1970s, this desire found another expression when David Duke, then national director of the KKK, announced that its members would begin patrolling the

US-Mexico border with "band radios and legally registered weapons."[7] This action occurred during an important turning point for both the KKK and the broader white nationalist movement. Historian Kathleen Belew argues that, "unlike previous iterations of the Ku Klux Klan and white supremacist vigilantism, the [post-Vietnam era] white power movement did not claim to serve the state."[8] Rather, white nationalists, disaffected by the state's failure in Vietnam, as well as the "dramatic hard-won gains of feminism, civil rights, secularism, and gay liberation," came to understand themselves as revolutionaries against a state whose interests were opposed to their version of the ethnically homogenous nation.[9] By the late 1970s, the white nationalist movement began to position itself and its members not only as a nation but as a state. According to Belew, it adopted a more expressly military posture, its "activists [using] terminology, such as 'gooks,' associated with US soldiers in Vietnam; camouflage fatigues; civilian versions of the era's military weapons, as well as the genuine articles, sometimes illegally obtained; and training and combat methods modeled on soldiers' experience and US Army manuals."[10] David Duke's pronouncement that the KKK would begin patrolling the southern border is in some ways an acknowledgment that the group planned to assume more formally the role of the state, especially in its military and law enforcement functions.

Private bounty hunters and vigilante militia groups enforcing the law, then, are not only not extraordinary but well-established and, in some places, an accepted norm. This aspect of American culture belies the law-and-order rhetoric of politicians and also provides fertile soil for the normalization of extrajudicial policing and adjudication of criminal and other behavior—in the boardroom, at the border, on social media, and, in the case of Texas's Heartbeat Act, in the civil courtroom. Nor is the new Texas law unprecedented in socio-legal terms. During the colonial period through the nineteenth century, slave patrols were one of the primary forms of policing in North America, and these consisted entirely of private citizen bounty hunters hired to capture and return enslaved people. These slave patrols then served as the foundation for early state-based law enforcement. The Fugitive Slave Act of 1850 not only authorized private citizens to act as bounty hunters but required them to do so. Like slave patrols, Pinkerton agents later in the nineteenth century often enjoyed the support of the state and "seemed to carry the weight of the law."[11] This is because, in many contexts, they did determine the scope of acceptable behavior—even if that scope was essentially a reflection of the interests of the companies that hired them. Moreover, as S. Paul O'Hara explains, "the power of the Pinkerton agent in the Gilded Age does not suggest a weak state but rather shows a powerful but pragmatic state that demanded order but delegated its authority."[12] SB8 certainly goes against recent legal precedent, but in waiving its authority to enforce the law, promoting vigilantism, and deputizing private individuals to enforce the law, it is, culturally speaking, rather conventional. It is, contra President Biden's assertion, precisely "American." More recently, stand-your-ground laws have authorized private individuals to use deadly force in public, even when they could safely retreat from danger. By 2020, thirty-four states had enacted stand-your-ground laws under the logic that individuals should be authorized to defend themselves against violence. Implicitly, however, these laws acknowledge the inability of law enforcement to protect individuals from violence and suggest that individuals must interpret and enforce the law on their own behalf.

If, as Foucault describes it, the foundational or founding role of liberalism in the United States paves the way for an endogenous neo-liberalism, then the foundational or founding role of vigilante justice in American society also paves the way for the post-juridical justice exercised not only by vigilante groups like the Minutemen and Citizen Defenders, but also by landlords, employers, tech companies, security firms, and individuals on social media in the form of cancel culture. Ultimately, these forms of justice, characterized by the private policing and surveillance of behavior and adjudication and punishment of criminal and noncriminal behavior, are not only endorsed but mandated by the state as it outsources its authority to enforce the laws that it creates, as well as to interpret law and to define the limits of acceptable behavior in excess of the law. Contemporary post-juridicalism may have its roots in an endogenous, foundational American vigilante justice, but it was activated by a crisis. Neoliberalism—constituted in part by the transfer of symbolic, economic, cultural, and legal capital from individuals to corporations—is that crisis.

In the early 1970s, Foucault described capitalism and the penitentiary as "twin forms." Capitalism, he argues, reorganizes social life by
introducing "time as measure, and not only as economic measure in
the capitalist system, but also as moral measure."[13] The prison's adoption of time as a calculable phenomenon that can be used to quantify
the harm caused by crime and measure the amount of punishment for
that crime is directly related to the capitalist form, and to the capitalist
wage form in particular. Because the wage pays for time worked, rather
than for goods or labor, time is transformed into something with an
ostensibly quantifiable value.[14] The emergence of the penitentiary as a
"twin form" of capitalism did not simply eliminate all older forms of
punishment. Those who failed to conform to the logic of the penitentiary continued to face the kinds of punishment that dominated during earlier periods, such as corporal punishment. This was why, by the
mid-twentieth century, standardized grievance and disciplinary procedures were seen as a necessary remedy for the continued use of arbitrary, ad hoc punishment exercised by prison authorities. In this way,
the penitentiary rearticulated the failures of previous systems of punishment, albeit under the rubric of a new social contract that viewed
corporal punishment as despotic and inconsistent with liberal humanism. Instead, rather than using corporal punishment universally, it was
reserved for those deemed altogether incapable of entering the social
contract. Neoliberalism and the kinds of post-juridicalism described
in this book can similarly be thought of as twin forms.

The transfer of capital, power, legal personhood, and quasi-judicial
authority to corporations degrades the legal personhood of individuals and causes a managerialization of legal consciousness such that the
boardroom becomes a default, commonsense site for negotiating the
neoliberal social contract. These transformations in the adjudication
of behavior, imposition of penalties, and negotiation of the social contract result in correlative techniques of punishment that rearticulate
the failures of the juridical regimes that preceded them. As discussed
in chapter 4, for example, corporations have a long history of controlling and regulating the speech and behavior of their employees. The
Ford Motor Company offered a wage incentive only to employees
who adopted the company's own social and cultural norms, such as
maintaining a clean home, healthy diet, and respectable hygiene.[15] The

midcentury adoption of federal worker protections set some limits on employers' control over workers, but the failures of this regulatory regime are rearticulated under neoliberalism not as social and cultural norms but as ostensibly neutral, technical, and medicalized best practices. Smokers (as well as people considered obese, people who do not exercise enough, and so on) are penalized not by employers but by private insurance companies whose putative interest is health even as they profit from the nonnormative behavior of smokers. As a form of neutral, technical, medical expertise, the injunction against smoking constitutes an antipolitics in which smoking (as well as most matters of medical expertise) must be divorced from all social, political, legal, and historical contexts.[16]

In the context of criminal justice, the courts and other state institutions continue to play a significant role in punishing crime through the use of arrest, detention, and the imposition of collateral consequences. However, employers, landlords, and service providers adjudicate and readjudicate crimes and impose sanctions such as banishment through ad hoc decision-making processes informed by best practices. These best practices are a result of a decades-long process aimed at transforming all social phenomena—including crime—into market phenomena. The market-based valuation of crime—the actuarial justice model—suggests that "as with other market phenomena (e.g., employment, inflation), there is some nonzero level of crime that can be called a 'natural' rate."[17] The state asserts responsibility for managing the crime rate and the level of the population, but it is left to individuals and private companies to mitigate the risk associated with individual offenses. It is not only because the state is focused on the management of the population that individuals and companies must mitigate their own risks. Rather, this aspect of contemporary justice rearticulates the failures of the nineteenth century, when the state outsourced its law enforcement functions to private interests, who, if they could afford it, hired private mercenaries to protect their property. As with the medicalization of social and cultural norms, this process does not imply a simple adoption of nineteenth-century law enforcement practices. Rather, the bureaucratization of the criminal justice system attempted to abolish and amend those practices that promoted the ad hoc law- and decision-making of private mercenaries. The subsequent failures of this aspect of statification—namely that the state favored a criminal justice system that would adjust the population rather than protect private property or ensure public safety—meant that the failures of a system of private law enforcement, like the ad hoc adjudication and punishment of crimes, were constantly being rearticulated, albeit under new rubrics of risk mitigation, corporate responsibility to the public, and even civil rights.

One response to these rearticulated failures has been the popular justice of cancel culture, which insists that both the state and corporations have failed to produce the conditions for a functioning, democratic society, instead allowing race- and gender-based violence to flourish. This form of justice, articulated through boycott, banishment, and "calling out" as a type of public shaming, foregoes courts and criminal codes and establishes its own limits and punishments for transgressing them. This "dissolution of judicial power into the collective judgment of individuals"[18] aims to amend the failures of a criminal justice system, one of whose primary motivations has been to regulate the population in a way that promotes the optimal functioning of the market (for the capitalist class) instead of securing individuals' rights, for example to workplaces free from sexual harassment and violence. However, by foreclosing the possibility of a future in which a state might secure these conditions—in favor of dissolving juridical power into the collective judgment of individuals—it must rearticulate in new ways the failures of an originary American vigilante justice. Operating under the rubric of diversity, equity, and inclusion, it promotes a view that the tolerance and acceptance of cultural difference are not only separate from but more important than exercising rights and making claims on the state. Like the corporate regulation of bodies and habits, and the boardroom adjudication of misconduct and criminal activity, cancel culture articulates the previous failures of American vigilante justice, but within the context of a neoliberal rationality in which the legal personhood and quasi-judicial authority of corporations trump the legal personhood of individuals—and therefore their ability to exercise rights and makes claims on the state. "Successful" cancellation is predicated not on a shared sense of justice articulated through publicly-negotiated, rules-based democratic processes but on the ad hoc assessment of public opinion as apparently manifested in popular culture. It also requires book publishers, media conglomerates, production companies, universities, and other businesses to implement the boycotts or banishments of the offending individuals. Without these bodies to impose material punishments, being canceled means nothing at all.

The corporate regulation of bodies and habits, the boardroom adjudication of misconduct alongside illegal and criminal activity, and cancel culture share a belief in the state's inability to secure justice. Even though cancellation has proven somewhat impotent as a technique of punishment that might actually modify or correct the behavior of the individual bad actor, let alone institutions, cancel culture shares a commitment with corporations to developing new forms of non-state governance. But the forms of non-state governance that have actually emerged to replace the state are not democratic or communitarian institutions in which individuals might participate in collective governance. Rather, they are organizations that might be considered a "twin form" of civil society under neoliberalism: the philanthropic organizations, public-private partnerships, and service providers of the knowledge economy. These organizations transform surplus populations, such as ex-offenders and people experiencing homelessness, into products to be bought and sold among halfway houses, drug treatment facilities, psychological service providers, and job training programs. The productification of internet users—their transformation into commodities that can be bought and sold on the market—substantially mirrors the productification of ex-offenders in the reentry industry. And it is through this productification that companies like Facebook can craft new forms of non-state governance: users represent not a bloc of potential political power but capital that can be manipulated, mobilized, and exploited to position the company as a new form of government, replete with its own currency, laws, and national interests, and without any input or oversight from the people-products it ostensibly governs.

Notes

INTRODUCTION

1. Pete Muntean, "Assault on Flight Attendant 'One of the Worst' in Airline's History, American Airlines CEO Says," CNN, October 28, 2021, https://www.cnn.com/travel/article/american-airlines-flight-diverted-denver/index.html. By framing the story in the same terms as the airline, CNN's reporting implicitly endorses the company's unilateral decision-making.

2. Mitchell Dean and Kaspar Villadsen, *State Phobia and Civil Society: The Political Legacy of Michel Foucault* (Stanford: Stanford University Press, 2016), 21. Dean and Villadsen are skeptical of the large body of scholarship that considers Foucault "state phobic" in his refusal to develop a sustained theory of the state in favor of analyzing government and governmentality. They argue in contrast that Foucault's analysis of governmentality is precisely an analysis of the state.

3. Wendy Brown, *Undoing the Demos: Neoliberalism's Stealth Revolution* (New York: Zone, 2015), 9.

4. Michel Foucault, *The Birth of Biopolitics: Lectures at the Collège de France, 1978–79*, trans. Graham Burchell (New York: Palgrave Macmillan, 2008), 91.

5. Foucault, *Birth of Biopolitics*, 77.

6. On the corporate interpretation and adjudication of civil rights law specifically, see Lauren B. Edelman, *Working Law: Courts, Corporations, and Symbolic Civil Rights* (Chicago: University of Chicago Press, 2016).

7. Cedric J. Robinson, *Black Marxism: The Making of the Black Radical Tradition*, 2nd ed. (Chapel Hill: University of North Carolina Press, 2000).

8. Jasmyn Wimbish and Colin Ward-Henninger, "NBA-China Issue: Latest News on Daryl Morey's Hong Kong Tweet, What It Means for the League," *CBS Sports*, October 10, 2019, https://www.cbssports.com/nba/news/nba-china-issue-latest-news-on-daryl-moreys-hong-kong-tweet-what-it-means-for-the-league/.

9. Shannon Bond, "Hong Kong Protests Put US Businesses in a Tough Spot with China," *Morning Edition*, October 11, 2019, https://www.npr.org/2019/10/11/769193163/hong-kong-protests-put-u-s-businesses-in-a-tough-spot-with-china.

10. Milton Friedman, *Capitalism and Freedom*, Fortieth Anniversary ed. (Chicago: University of Chicago Press, 2002), ix.

11. Freedom to purchase is also a central tenet of Friedman's logic of small government: traditionally public services like schools, physical infrastructure, and sanitation are improved through privatization and their transformation into commodities to be bought and sold on the open market. The government might improve the lot of many, he admits, by providing such services, but it is only through privatization that such services might be subject to the kind of "experimentation which can bring tomorrow's laggards above today's mean." The greater the amount of government centralization, the fewer choices consumers have with regards to basic services. In contrast, less and more decentralized government means that if we don't like the services provided by our county or state, we can simply move to another one. Supposedly, the mere possibility of its consumer base moving away will motivate local governments to provide better services. Here, the government is figured not as a provider of services to a constituency but as a company attempting to retain its customer base. *Capitalism and Freedom*, 2–4.

12. Friedman, *Capitalism and Freedom*, 1.

13. Friedman, *Capitalism and Freedom*, 1–2. In Kennedy's address, it is not at all certain that serving one's "country" means serving one's state, as opposed to serving one's fellow citizens, who are also, for him, bound to the terms of a specifically European political heritage—one from which people of color and colonial subjects historically have been excluded. In the same address, he highlights the "cultural and spiritual origins we share" with our European forefathers and the importance of pride in "our ancient heritage." Although Friedman himself does not explicitly refer to a European social contract, his entire body of work is situated within the tradition of European liberalism and can be seen to function, therefore, as what philosopher Charles W. Mills describes as the racial contract. *The Racial Contract* (Ithaca: Cornell University Press, 1999).

14. Friedman, *Capitalism and Freedom*, 2.

15. Friedman, *Capitalism and Freedom*, 18, italics added.

16. Friedman, *Capitalism and Freedom*, 33.

17. Dario Melossi and Massimo Pavarini, *The Prison and the Factory: Origins of the Penitentiary System* (London: Macmillan, 1981), 56–58, 72.

18. Michel Foucault, *The Punitive Society: Lectures at the Collège de France, 1972–73*, trans. Graham Burchell (New York: Palgrave Macmillan, 2015), 70. See Michel Foucault, *Discipline and Punish: The Birth of the Prison*, trans. Alan Sheridan (New York: Vintage, 1995), 232–233. In contrast, Melossi and Pavarini argue that the punishment of imprisonment, of "doing time," is a direct result of capitalism's imposition of financial or monetary value on time.

19. Foucault, *Punitive Society*, 83.

20. National Inventory of Collateral Consequences of Conviction, https://niccc.nationalreentryresourcecenter.org.

21. In political theory, see, for example, Andrew Dilts, *Punishment and Inclusion: Race, Membership, and the Limits of American Liberalism* (New York: Fordham University Press, 2014); Elizabeth A. Hull, *The Disenfranchisement of Ex-Felons* (Philadelphia: Temple University Press, 2009); Claudio López-Guerra, *Democracy and Disenfranchisement: The Morality of Electoral Exclusions* (Oxford: Oxford University Press, 2014); Jeff Manza and Christopher Uggen, *Locked Out: Felon Disenfranchisement and American Democracy* (Oxford: Oxford University Press, 2008); Kealey McBride, *Punishment and Political Order* (Ann Arbor: University of Michigan Press, 2007).

22. Colin (Joan) Dayan, "Legal Slaves and Civil Bodies," *Nepantla: Views from the South* 2, no. 1 (2001): 3–39; Alec C. Ewald, "'Civil Death': The Ideological Paradox of Criminal Disenfranchisement Law in the United States," *Wisconsin Law Review* 2002, no. 5 (2002): 1045–1137.

23. Gabriel Chin, "The New Civil Death: Rethinking Punishment in the Era of Mass Incarceration," *University of Pennsylvania Law Review* 160 (2012): 1791.

24. The 2021 Florida Statutes, Title XXVIII, Chapter 379.

25. The 2020 Florida Statutes, Title XLVII, Chapter 961.

26. Nils Melzer, *The Trial of Julian Assange: A Story of Persecution* (London: Verso, 2022), 20. Melzer continues: "The purpose [of plea bargains] is to intimidate defendants to such as extent that they no longer invoke the presumption of innocence but accept a plea bargain, even if requires a false confession or testimony. It is the exact same rationale that characterizes torture. . . . Obviously, the overriding purpose of such a coercive criminal justice system is not to ensure truth or justice, but to enforce a maximum number of confessions—rightly or wrongly. Equally obviously, it is not conducive to developing or maintaining professional investigative skills; to reducing or eradicating crime, judicial error and arbitrariness; or to alleviating overcrowded prisons." False confessions are a separate but related issue, and one that makes agreeing to a plea even more likely. According to the National Registry for Exonerations, 12 percent of exonerees confessed to crimes they didn't commit. Among exonerees with mental illnesses or intellectual disabilities, 69 percent gave false confessions, versus only 8 percent without known mental illnesses or intellectual disabilities. "Age and Mental Status of Exonerated Defendants Who Confessed," April 18, 2022, https://www.law.umich.edu/special/exoneration/Documents/Age%20and%20Mental%20Status%20FINAL%20CHART.pdf.

27. Dilts, *Punishment and Inclusion*, 14.

28. Gabriel Chin, "Collateral Consequences and Criminal Justice: Future Policy and Constitutional Directions," *Marquette Law Review* 102, no. 1 (2018): 233–260; Sandra G. Mayson, "Collateral Consequences and the Preventive State," *Notre Dame Law Review* 91, no. 1 (2015): 301–362; Michael O'Hear, "Third-Class Citizenship: The Escalating Legal Consequences of Committing a 'Violent' Crime," *The Journal of Criminal Law and Criminology* 109, no. 2 (2019): 165–235; Victor J. Pinedo, "Let's Keep It Civil: An Evaluation of Civil Disabilities, a Call for Reform, and Recommendations to Reduce Recidivism," *Cornell Law Review* 102, no. 2 (2017): 513–545.

29. For nineteenth-century views on criminality, citizenship, and the social contract, see the debates that unfolded in the publication of the Pennsylvania Prison Society (formerly the Philadelphia Society for Alleviating the Miseries of Public Prisons), *The Journal of Prison Discipline and Philanthropy*.

30. Wayne Logan, "Informal Collateral Consequences," *Washington Law Review* 88, no. 3 (2013): 1104.

31. On the industry's market size and growth potential, see IBISWorld, "Background Check Services in the US—Market Size, 2004–2029," https://www.ibisworld.com/industry-statistics/market-size/background-check-services-united-states/.

32. For more on carceral technoscientific techniques deployed across a number of industries and other domains, such as surveillance, predictive policing, and credit scoring, see Ruha Benjamin, ed., *Captivating Technology: Race, Carceral Technoscience, and Laboratory Imagination in Everyday Life* (Durham: Duke University Press, 2019).

33. Howard S. Becker, *Outsiders: Studies in the Sociology of Deviance*, repr. ed. (New York: Free Press, 1966), 33.

34. National Inventory of Collateral Consequences of Conviction.

35. Ruth Wilson Gilmore (with Craig Gilmore), "Restating the Obvious," in *Abolition Geography: Essays towards Liberation*, ed. Brenna Bhandar and Alberto Toscano (London: Verso, 2022), 271. As David Graeber has described it, it is not only that the state achieves legitimacy through the market. Rather, the state is the first mover: markets are created by the state and must be continually recreated and managed by that same state. Modern economics rhetorically reverses the relationship between the state and the market, posing the market as something that precedes the state, and it is in this reversal that the state comes to be legitimated by the market. *Debt: The First 5000 Years* (Brooklyn: Melville House, 2014).

36. Gilmore, "Restating the Obvious," 276.

37. Ruth Wilson Gilmore, *Golden Gulag: Prisons, Surplus, Crisis, and Opposition in Globalizing California* (Berkeley: University of California Press, 2007), 122.

38. Elizabeth Anderson, *Private Government: How Employers Rule Our Lives (and Why We Don't Talk about It)* (Princeton: Princeton University Press, 2017), xi, 39, xix.

39. Laura Kipnis, *Unwanted Advances: Sexual Paranoia Comes to Campus* (New York: HarperCollins, 2017), 27, 30, 35.

40. Kipnis, *Unwanted Advances*, 17.

41. See Jillian C. York, *Silicon Values: The Future of Free Speech under Surveillance Capitalism* (London: Verso, 2020).

42. Sheera Frenkel and Cecilia Kang, *An Ugly Truth: Inside Facebook's Battle for Domination* (New York: Harper Collins, 2021), 193, 209.

43. Frenkel and Kang, *An Ugly Truth*, 124.

44. Libra Association, *Libra White Paper*, introduction. This version of the White Paper appears to have been mostly scrubbed from the internet, and the Libra website is no longer online. Libra was renamed Diem in 2020, and its new documentation focuses less than the previous one on the social, cultural, and political issues related to cryptocurrency. The original is archived at George Mason's Antonin Scalia Law School, https://sls.gmu.edu/pfrt/wp-content/uploads/sites/54/2020/02/LibraWhitePaper_en_US-Rev0723.pdf.

45. Libra Association, *Libra White Paper*, part 2.

46. Gary Gerstle, *The Rise and Fall of the Neoliberal Order: America and the World in the Free Market Era* (Oxford: Oxford University Press, 2022), 251. Trump's supporters, of course, were not exclusively, or even primarily, members of the working class; contrary to his populist messaging, middle-class, upper-middle-class, and wealthy white voters played a much more central role in his 2016 political success than working-class voters.

47. Wendy Brown, *In the Ruins of Neoliberalism: The Rise of Antidemocratic Politics in the West* (New York: Zone, 2015), 13, 11–14. See Citizens United v. Federal Election Commission, 558 U.S. 310 (2010); Masterpiece Cakeshop, Ltd. v. Colorado Civil Rights Commission, 584 U.S. ___ (2018); Burwell v. Hobby Lobby Stores 572 U.S. 682 (2014).

48. Although Anna Eskamani is staunchly in favor of reining in corporate power, her comments have the effect of promoting the conservative ideologies she otherwise condemns, such as those inscribed in *Citizens United*. "Two Florida State Representatives Debate Move against Disney's Self-Governing Status," CNBC Television, April 22, 2022, https://www.youtube.com/watch?v=oy5tBRri_SA.

49. Julilly Kohler-Hausmann, *Getting Tough: Welfare and Imprisonment in 1970s America* (Princeton: Princeton University Press, 2017), 15.

50. See Alessandro De Giorgi, "Back to Nothing: Prisoner Reentry and Neoliberal Neglect," *Social Justice* 44, no. 1 (2017): 83–120; Douglas E. Thompkins, "The Expanding Prisoner Reentry Industry," *Dialectal Anthropology* 34, no. 4 (2010): 589–604; Craig Willse, *The Value of Homelessness: Managing Surplus Life in the United States* (Minneapolis: University of Minnesota Press, 2015).

CHAPTER ONE. AN AMERICAN NEOLIBERAL REVOLUTION

1. Naomi Klein, *The Shock Doctrine: The Rise of Disaster Capitalism* (New York: Metropolitan Books, 2007), 7. For a similar, primarily economic, account of neoliberalism beginning with the Chicago School, see David Harvey, *A Brief History of Neoliberalism* (Oxford: Oxford University Press, 2005).

2. Wendy Brown, *Undoing the Demos: Neoliberalism's Stealth Revolution* (New York: Zone, 2015), 145.

3. Klein, *Shock Doctrine*, 285.

4. Chris Hedges, *Wages of Rebellion: The Moral Imperative of Revolt* (New York: Nation Books, 2015), 45–46.

5. Hedges, *Wages of Rebellion*, 48, 50.

6. Hedges, *Wages of Rebellion*, 50.

7. On how US intelligence agencies tap into the data mining operations of companies like Google and Facebook in order to surveil populations, see Bernard E. Harcourt, *Exposed: Desire and Disobedience in the Digital Age* (Cambridge, MA: Harvard University Press, 2015).

8. Ruth Wilson Gilmore (with Craig Gilmore), "Restating the Obvious," in *Abolition Geography: Essays towards Liberation*, ed. Brenna Bhandar and Alberto Toscano (London: Verso, 2022), 276.

9. Julilly Kohler-Hausmann, *Getting Tough: Welfare and Imprisonment in 1970s America* (Princeton: Princeton University Press, 2017), 3; Elizabeth Hinton, *From the War on Poverty to the War on Crime: The Making of Mass Incarceration in America* (Harvard University Press, 2016), 11.

10. Marie Gottschalk argues that an exclusive focus on the manufacturing crisis actually ignores broader trends in Black urban employment, especially since the 1940s, when the agricultural industry underwent significant restructuring. *Caught: The Prison State and the Lockdown of American Politics* (Princeton: Princeton University Press, 2016).

11. See Kimberlé Crenshaw, "Mapping the Margins: Intersectionality, Identity Politics, and Violence against Women of Color," *Stanford Law Review* 43, no. 6 (1991): 1241–1299.

12. Michel Foucault, *The Birth of Biopolitics: Lectures at the Collège de France, 1978–79*, trans. Graham Burchell (New York: Palgrave Macmillan, 2008), 178. See F. A. Hayek, *The Road to Serfdom*, repr. (1944; New York: Routledge, 2006), especially chapter 12, "The Socialist Roots of Nazism."

13. Foucault, *Birth of Biopolitics*, 193. For another account of the relationship between German ordoliberalism and American neoliberalism, see Pierre Dardot and Christian Laval, *The New Way of the World: On Neoliberal Society* (London: Verso, 2017).

14. Andrew J. Diamond and Thomas J. Sugrue, eds. *Neoliberal Cities: The Remaking of Postwar Urban America* (New York: New York University Press, 2020), 4.

15. Douglas Field, ed. *American Cold War Culture* (Edinburgh University Press, 2005), 4.

16. Paul Gootenberg, "Talking about the Flow: Drugs, Borders, and the Discourse of Drug Control," *Cultural Critique* 71, no. 1 (2009): 34.

17. Douglas Clark Kinder, "Bureaucratic Cold Warrior: Harry J. Anslinger and Illicit Narcotics Traffic," *The Pacific Historical Review* 50, no. 2 (1981): 171.

18. Kinder, "Bureaucratic Cold Warrior."

19. For a recent history of the use of the term "hyphenated Americans" in twentieth-century political rhetoric, see Sarah Churchwell, *Behold America: A History of America First and the American Dream* (New York: Bloomsbury, 2019).

20. Gootenberg, "Talking about the Flow," 25; Juan G. Tokatlian, "National Security and Drugs: Their Impact on Colombian-US Relations," *Journal of Interamerican Studies and World Affairs* 30, no. 1 (1988): 134, 136.

21. Kinder, "Bureaucratic Cold Warrior," 169.

22. Milton Friedman, *Capitalism and Freedom*, Fortieth Anniversary ed. (Chicago: University of Chicago Press, 2002), 21.

23. Jordan T. Camp, *Incarcerating the Crisis: Freedom Struggles and the Rise of the Neoliberal State* (Berkeley: University of California Press, 2016), 3.

24. Stuart Hall et al. examine the moral panic related to "muggings" in England during the 1970s. They argue that British media relied on many of the tropes central to US law-and-order discourses to explain the empirical phenomenon of muggings, including those about crime, criminality, and especially Black violence targeting whites. Because of the discursive creation of

a certain figure of racialized criminality, the criminal justice system both looks for and manufactures Black crime. *Policing the Crisis: Mugging, the State, and Law and Order*, 35th Anniversary ed. (London: Red Globe Press, 2013).

25. Angela Y. Davis, *Are Prisons Obsolete?* (New York: Seven Stories, 2003), 29. In some southern states, the plantation model of corrections dominated until the 1950s and 1960s, and it is still evident today in places like Louisiana's Angola Prison, the largest maximum-security prison in the United States which in 2021 housed some 6,300 prisoners, 76 percent of whom are Black.

26. Alex Lichtenstein, *Twice the Work of Free Labor: The Political Economy of Convict Labor in the New South* (London: Verso, 1996), 5.

27. Michelle Alexander, *The New Jim Crow: Mass Incarceration in the Age of Colorblindness* (New York: The New Press, 2012).

28. Camp, *Incarcerating the Crisis*, 15. For a history of moral panics and their relationship to law-and-order discourses, see Marie Gottschalk, *The Prison and the Gallows: The Politics of Mass Incarceration in America* (Cambridge: Cambridge University Press, 2006).

29. Bruce Western and Katherine Beckett, "How Unregulated is the US Labor Market? The Penal Institution as a Labor Market Institution," *American Journal of Sociology* 104, no. 4 (1999): 1032.

30. Ruth Wilson Gilmore, *Abolition Geography: Essays towards Liberation*, ed. Brenna Bhandar and Alberto Toscano (London: Verso, 2022); Jackie Wang, *Carceral Capitalism* (Cambridge, MA: Semiotext(e), 2018).

31. Ruth Wilson Gilmore, *Golden Gulag: Prisons, Surplus, Crisis, and Opposition in Globalizing California* (Berkeley: University of California Press, 2007).

32. Alessandro De Giorgi, *Re-Thinking the Political Economy of Punishment: Perspectives on Post-Fordism and Penal Politics* (New York: Routledge, 2006), 24; Western and Beckett, "How Unregulated Is the US Labor Market?," 1032.

33. Gilmore, *Golden Gulag*. While prison building did sometimes create economic growth, many new employees of small town and rural prisons, Gilmore notes, were not existing residents but transplants brought in to fill new jobs.

34. Judah Schept, *Progressive Punishment: Job Loss, Jail Growth, and the Neoliberal Logic of Carceral Expansion* (New York: New York University Press, 2015), 41.

35. Brett Story, *Prison Land: Mapping Carceral Power across Neoliberal America* (Minneapolis: University of Minnesota Press, 2019), 5.

36. E. Ann Carson, "Prisoners in 2013," Bureau of Justice Statistics, 2014, https://www.bjs.gov/content/pub/pdf/p13.pdf.

37. Sarah K. S. Shannon et al., "The Growth, Scope, and Spatial Distribution of People with Felony Records in the United States, 1948–2010," *Demography* 54, no. 5 (2017): 1795–1818.

38. Loïc Wacquant, *Punishing the Poor: The Neoliberal Government of Social Insecurity* (Durham: Duke University Press, 2009), 262.

39. Emma Bell, *Criminal Justice and Neoliberalism* (New York: Palgrave Macmillan, 2011), 4.

40. Hedges, *Wages of Rebellion*, 56.

41. Gilmore, *Golden Gulag*, 122, italics added.

42. Shannon et al., "Growth, Scope, and Spatial Distribution."

43. Owen Greenspan and Dennis DeBacco, "Survey of State Criminal History Information Systems, 2012," Bureau of Justice Statistics, 2014, https://www.ncjrs.gov/pdffiles1/bjs/grants/244563.pdf, 2.

44. Becki R. Goggins and Dennis A. DeBacco, "Survey of State Criminal History Information Systems, 2016: A Criminal Justice Information Policy Report," Bureau of Justice Statistics, 2018, https://www.ojp.gov/pdffiles1/bjs/grants/251516.pdf, 3.

45. Federal Bureau of Investigation, "Crime in the United States, 2016," https://ucr.fbi.gov/crime-in-the-u.s/2016/crime-in-the-u.s.-2016/topic-pages/persons-arrested"; Danielle Kaeble and Mary Cowhig, "Correctional Populations in the United States, 2016," Bureau of Justice Statistics, 2018, https://www.bjs.gov/content/pub/pdf/cpus16.pdf. The number of arrests dropped precipitously during the height of the COVID-19 pandemic, with the Office of Juvenile Justice and Delinquency Prevention estimating that there were approximately 7.6 million total arrests in 2020. Much of this drop was a result of decreases in federal arrests, many of which are related to immigration enforcement, which declined by 81 percent between March and April of 2020, and then another 25 percent between October 2020 and February 2021. Mark Motivans, "Federal Justice Statistics, 2021," Bureau of Justice Statistics, 2022, https://bjs.ojp.gov/sites/g/files/xyckuh236/files/media/document/fjs21.pdf.

46. Hedges, *Wages of Rebellion*, 55. See Hannah Arendt, *The Origins of Totalitarianism* (San Diego: Harcourt Brace, 1973), 245.

47. While addressing how domestic warfare and counterinsurgency tactics were used as early as the 1960s, especially against groups like the Black Panther Party, Harcourt argues that what makes these tactics "new and unique today is that the methods have been refined, systematized, applied across the

country, and, most importantly, have become dominant at a time when there is not even a semblance of domestic insurgency or revolution going on in this country." Bernard E. Harcourt, *The Counterrevolution: How Our Government Went to War against Its Own Citizens* (New York: Basic Books, 2018), 199–200, 203.

48. Dardot and Laval, *New Way of the World*, 7.

49. Kohler-Hausmann, *Getting Tough*, 1.

50. Gilmore, *Abolition Geography*, 203.

51. David Graeber, *Debt: The First 5000 Years* (Brooklyn: Melville House, 2014), 15.

52. Foucault, *Birth of Biopolitics*, 45, 116–121, 138–141. Foucault here is drawing on a specifically ordoliberal view of the state, which differs from the theories of neoliberalism prescribed by, for example, Friedrich Hayek and Milton Friedman. As Wendy Brown notes, however, "While ordoliberal prescriptions for a neoliberal state differ from those of Hayek and Friedman, the three schools of neoliberalism share a rejection of robust democracy and of the expansive notion of the political on which democracy rests." *In the Ruins of Neoliberalism: The Rise of Antidemocratic Politics in the West* (New York: Columbia University Press, 2019), 88.

53. Foucault, *Birth of Biopolitics*, 137.

54. Friedman, *Capitalism and Freedom*, 28.

55. Foucault, *Birth of Biopolitics*, 271.

56. Foucault, *Birth of Biopolitics*, 270. The idea of *homo oeconomicus*—economic man, or the rational man in pursuit of his own interest—is often attributed to John Stuart Mill, although many theories and critiques of the concept developed in the immediate aftermath of his "On the Definition of Political Economy; and on the Method of Investigation Proper to It." John Stuart Mill, *Essays on Economics and Society* (Toronto: University of Toronto Press, 1967), 309–339.

57. Foucault, *Birth of Biopolitics*, 275, italics added.

58. Foucault, *Birth of Biopolitics*, 276.

59. Patricia Ventura, *Neoliberal Culture: Living with American Neoliberalism* (New York: Routledge, 2012), 2.

60. Jason Read, for example, suggests that neoliberalism must be understood as a transformation "of human nature and social existence rather than a political program." "A Genealogy of Homo-Economicus: Neoliberalism and the Production of Subjectivity," *Foucault Studies*, no. 6 (2009): 26.

61. Dardot and Laval, *New Way of the World*, 3.

62. Byung-Chul Han, *Psychopolitics: Neoliberalism and New Technologies of Power* (London: Verso, 2017), 29.

63. Leela Fernandes, "Conceptualizing the Post-Liberalization State: Intervention, Restructuring, and the Nature of State Power," in *Feminists Rethink the Neoliberal State: Inequality, Exclusion, and Change*, ed. Leela Fernandes (New York: New York University Press, 2018), 4.

64. Klein, *Shock Doctrine*, 15.

65. Ventura, *Neoliberal Culture*, 4.

66. Gary S. Becker, *Human Capital: A Theoretical and Empirical Analysis with Special Reference to Education*, 3rd ed. (Chicago: University of Chicago Press, 1993), 16.

67. The private sector also plays an extremely important role in the investment in human capital. In Becker's theoretical treatment of education, on-the-job training is analyzed in much greater detail, and provides a more significant financial return on investment, especially in the context of marketable skills, than schooling. *Human Capital*, 29–51 (on-the-job training), 51–53 (schooling).

68. Friedman, *Capitalism and Freedom*, 2–4.

69. Gary S. Becker, "Crime and Punishment: An Economic Approach," *Journal of Political Economy* 76, no. 2 (1968): 169–217.

70. Gary S. Becker, François Ewald, and Bernard E. Harcourt, "Becker and Foucault on Crime and Punishment—A Conversation with Gary Becker, François Ewald, and Bernard Harcourt: The Second Session," University of Chicago Coase-Sandor Institute for Law and Economics Research Paper No. 654; University of Chicago Public Law and Legal Theory Working Paper No. 654; Columbia Law and Economics Working Paper No. 456, 2013, 14, italics in original.

71. Becker, Ewald, and Harcourt, "Becker and Foucault on Crime and Punishment," 16.

72. Friedman, *Capitalism and Freedom*, 24.

73. Foucault, *Birth of Biopolitics*, 271. François Ewald suggests that "Foucault saw in [Becker's] work the possibility of a critique of governmentality." In other words, in Ewald's estimation, among others, Foucault's analysis was not strictly a critique of neoliberalism but rather sought to grapple with the possibilities for how neoliberal theory and policy could challenge the persistent consolidation state power. The state, for Foucault, had become, from the eighteenth century, the dominant institution for producing knowledge of every kind, including, perhaps most urgently, about the criminal. *Homo*

oeconomicus, according to Ewald, represents for Foucault a very real alternative to *homo criminalis*. Becker, Ewald, and Harcourt, "Becker and Foucault on Crime and Punishment," 3–4.

74. Foucault, *Birth of Biopolitics*, 279.

75. For Becker, discrimination is seen through the lens of its economic costs and as a bug rather than a feature of American capitalism. Discrimination, for example, leads to lower wages for both whites and Blacks, which is economically suboptimal. What motivates discrimination, therefore, is a "taste for discrimination," which is non-pecuniary. This taste, like others, is "influenced by more fundamental variables" such as the intensity, duration, and level of contact between Blacks and whites, and it is on these variables that some intervention may lead to improved outcomes. Thus, it is again on the field of economic activity, but not on the market itself, which government should intervene. Gary S. Becker, *The Economics of Discrimination*, 2nd ed. (Chicago: University of Chicago Press, 1971), 154, 155–160.

76. Foucault, *Birth of Biopolitics*, 143.

77. Foucault, *Birth of Biopolitics*, 296.

78. Foucault, *Birth of Biopolitics*, 297. Here, Foucault uses Locke's definition of civil society as political society in his *Second Treatise of Government*.

79. Foucault, *Birth of Biopolitics*, 302.

80. Miguel Vatter, *The Republic of the Living: Biopolitics and the Critique of Civil Society* (New York: Fordham University Press, 2014), 1.

81. Foucault, *Birth of Biopolitics*, 297.

82. Foucault, *Birth of Biopolitics*, 296.

83. Michel Foucault, *The Punitive Society: Lectures at the Collège de France, 1972–73*, trans. Graham Burchell (New York: Palgrave Macmillan, 2015), 174.

84. Foucault, *Puntitive Society*, 173. In the American context, this purpose was a point of political contestation. Especially in the postbellum South, some white politicians charged that training Black "criminals" in capitalist production through prison discipline would serve to unfairly increase competition for jobs among more "deserving" whites. Lichtenstein, *Twice the Work of Free Labor*, 30.

85. This is one of the definitions of Foucauldian biopower, where the management of life becomes the express object of governmental power. The view in this book of these particular institutions as civil society probably reflects Michael Hardt's 1995 view of society slightly more than Foucault's, at least regarding the possibilities for civil society, if not the conditions underlying their (im)possibility. For Hardt, "the social," and one might add political, "conditions

necessary for civil society no longer exist." "The Withering of Civil Society," *Social Text*, no. 45 (Winter 1995): 40. As Mitchell Dean and Kaspar Villadsen suggest, any number of post-Foucauldian theories of civil society ignore "the fundamental question of what kind of active, sovereign state power needs to be exercised for the potentially lethal conflicts of civil society to be kept in check and for individuals to gain the capacities to participate and engage in social and political life." *State Phobia and Civil Society: The Political Legacy of Michel Foucault* (Stanford: Stanford University Press, 2016), 37.

86. Douglas E. Thompkins, "The Expanding Prisoner Reentry Industry," *Dialectal Anthropology* 34, no. 4 (2010): 589–604.

87. Craig Willse, *The Value of Homelessness: Managing Surplus Life in the United States* (Minneapolis: University of Minnesota Press, 2015), 9.

88. Alessandro De Giorgi, "Back to Nothing: Prisoner Reentry and Neoliberal Neglect," *Social Justice* 44, no. 1 (2017): 86.

89. Willse, *Value of Homelessness*, 13–14.

90. Brown, *Undoing the Demos*, 28.

91. Brown, *Undoing the Demos*, 42.

92. Brown, *Undoing the Demos*, 139.

93. Brown, *Undoing the Demos*, 141.

94. Wendy Brown, *Walled States, Waning Sovereignty* (New York: Zone, 2010), 22. As Harcourt maintains, the version of neoliberalism that predominates in the United States today is somewhat less radical than that proposed by Chicago School economists. This predominant neoliberalism is not so much a political philosophy as a more moderate ideology whose core tenets are the efficiency of the market and the inefficiencies of government. Bernard E. Harcourt, "Neoliberal Penality: A Brief Genealogy," *Theoretical Criminology* 14, no. 1 (2010): 80.

95. Shannon Bond, "Hong Kong Protests Put US Businesses in a Tough Spot with China," *Morning Edition*, October 11, 2019, https://www.npr.org/20 19/10/11/769193163/hong-kong-protests-put-u-s-businesses-in-a-tough-spot -with-china.

96. Patrick Radden Keefe reports that one of the FDA officials leading the approval and special status of OxyContin as "less addictive" later became an employee of Purdue with a salary of $400,000 per year. *Empire of Pain: The Secret History of the Sackler Family* (New York: Doubleday, 2021).

97. According to reporting, evidence in opioid legislation in West Virginia included an email chain with this language written by executives at AmerisourceBergen. Steve Inskeep, "West Virginia Trial May Establish Corporate

Liability for Opioid Crisis," *Morning Edition*, May 26, 2021, https://www.npr
.org/2021/05/26/1000400957/west-virginia-trial-may-establish-corporate-lia
bility-for-opioid-crisis.

98. John Irwin, *The Jail: Managing the Underclass in American Society*,
repr. (Berkeley: University of California Press, 2013), 25–41.

99. Joel A. Thompson and G. Larry Mays, eds., *American Jails: Public Policy Issues* (Chicago: Nelson-Hall, 1991), 1.

100. Micol Seigel, *Violence Work: State Power and the Limits of the Police*
(Durham: Duke University Press, 2018), 75. Harcourt similarly writes in the
context of the so-called surveillance state that the "amalgam of the intelligence
community, retailers, Silicon Valley, military interests, social media, the Inner
Beltway, multinational corporations, midtown Manhattan, and Wall Street
forms an oligarchic concentration that defies" simply defining the state against
private interests. *Exposed*, 65–66.

CHAPTER TWO. ADJUDICATING GUILT, INNOCENCE, AND
CITIZENSHIP IN THE NEOLIBERAL PRISON

1. Haines v. Kerner, 404 U.S. 519 (1972).

2. Wolff v. McDonnell, 418 U.S. 539 (1974).

3. Ruffin v. Commonwealth, 62 Va. 790, 21 Gratt. 790 (1871).

4. Katherine Q. Seelye, "A Nation Challenged: The Prisoners; First 'Unlawful Combatants' Seized in Afghanistan Arrive at US Base in Cuba," *New York
Times*, January 12, 2002, https://www.nytimes.com/2002/01/12/world/nation
-challenged-prisoners-first-unlawful-combatants-seized-afghanistan-arrive
.html.

5. Amy Kaplan, "Where is Guantánamo?," *American Quarterly* 57, no. 3
(2005): 834.

6. Kaplan, "Where is Guantánamo?," 834; Rasul v. Bush, 542 U.S. 466 (2004).

7. Kaplan, "Where is Guantánamo?," 836.

8. Kaplan, "Where is Guantánamo?," 836.

9. Kaplan, "Where is Guantánamo?," 837.

10. Kaplan, "Where is Guantánamo?," 838.

11. Kaplan, "Where is Guantánamo?," 841.

12. What counts as an *Insular Case* is a matter of some contention. Some
believe that either six, eight, or nine of the US Supreme Court cases decided
in 1901 should be considered a part of the *Insular Cases*, while others include
an additional series of cases decided between 1903 and 1914.

13. DeLima v. Bidwell, 182 U.S. 1 (1901); Downes v. Bidwell, 182 U.S. 244 (1901).

14. Juan R. Torruella, "Ruling America's Colonies: The *Insular Cases*," *Yale Law and Policy Review* 32, no. 1 (2013): 78.

15. Claribel Morales, "Constitutional Law—Puerto Rico and the Ambiguity within the Federal Courts," *Western New England Law Review* 42, no. 2 (2020): 248; see Neil Weare, "Why the *Insular Cases* Must Become the Next Plessy," *Harvard Law Review Blog*, March 28, 2018, https://blog.harvardlawreview.org/why-the-insular-cases-must-become-the-next-plessy/.

16. Torruella, "Ruling America's Colonies," 78.

17. Edgardo Meléndez, "Citizenship and the Alien Exclusion in the *Insular Cases*: Puerto Ricans in the Periphery of American Empire," *Centro Journal* 25, no. 1 (2013): 107.

18. Balzac v. Porto Rico, 258 U.S. 298 (1922), 318, cited in Torruella, "Ruling America's Colonies," 78.

19. Kaplan, "Where is Guantánamo?," 842.

20. Meléndez, "Citizenship and the Alien Exclusion," 107.

21. Downes v. Bidwell, 182 U.S. 244 (1901), 372, cited in Kaplan, "Where is Guantánamo?," 842.

22. Orlando Patterson, *Slavery and Social Death: A Comparative Study* (Cambridge, MA: Harvard University Press, 1982).

23. Alexa Koenig, "From Man to Beast: Social Death at Guantánamo," in *Extreme Punishment: Comparative Studies in Detention, Incarceration, and Solitary Confinement*, ed. Keramet Reiter and Alexa Koenig (New York: Palgrave Macmillan, 2015), 223, italics added.

24. Koenig, "From Man to Beast," 221.

25. People with mental illnesses are overrepresented in America's jails and prisons, although how mental illnesses are (over) diagnosed in prisons and the extent to which this is due to transinstitutionalization is contested. State hospitals faced many of the same criticisms that prisons today face: they were overcrowded, often provided inadequate care, were underfunded, and patients often suffered under horrendous conditions and extreme neglect. While conditions litigation sought to remedy these issues, funding adequate public mental health treatment was deemed too costly for states and the federal government, and by the 1980s, the state asylum had all but disappeared. While some blame declining numbers of state hospitals for the increasing incarceration of the mentally ill, others argue that increasing rates of incarceration were responsible for the rapid decline of the state hospital. See H. Richard Lamb

and Linda Weinberger, "The Shift of Psychiatric Inpatient Care from Hospitals to Jails and Prisons," *Journal of the American Academy of Psychiatry and the Law* 33, no. 4 (2005): 529–534; Seth J. Prins, "Does Transinstitutionalization Explain the Overrepresentation of People with Serious Mental Illnesses in the Criminal Justice System?," *Community Mental Health Journal* 47, no. 6 (2011): 716–722.

26. Malcolm Feeley and Van Swearingen, "The Prison Conditions Cases and the Bureaucratization of American Corrections: Influences, Impacts and Implications," *Pace Law Review* 24, no. 2 (2004): 434.

27. Feeley and Swearingen, "Prison Conditions Cases," 436.

28. Feeley and Swearingen, "Prison Conditions Cases," 438.

29. Raphael Ginsburg, "Mighty Crime Victims: Victims' Rights and Neoliberalism in the American Conjuncture," in *Cultural Studies and the "Juridical Turn,"* ed. Jaafar Aksikas and Sean Johnson Andrews (New York: Routledge, 2016), 194.

30. Ginsburg, "Mighty Crime Victims," 194–195. The family as the site of social and economic reproduction has been a central concern for socialist feminists, as well as for feminist political theorists. These concerns are redoubled, however, when accounting for race. Judith Butler writes that "African American kinship has been at once the site of intense state surveillance and pathologization, which leads to the double bind of being subject to normalizing pressures within the context of a continuing social and political delegitimation." In other words, the Black family cannot be the site of social and economic reproduction because it is surveilled, pathologized, and criminalized. In this way, it must be contained to protect the broader neoliberal social relation. "Is Kinship Always Heterosexual?" *differences: A Journal of Feminist Cultural Studies* 13, no. 1 (2002): 15.

31. John Irwin, *The Jail: Managing the Underclass in American Society*, repr. (Berkeley: University of California Press, 2013), 25–41.

32. Ginsburg, "Mighty Crime Victims," 171.

33. Milton Friedman, for example, writes that "we take freedom of the individual, or perhaps the family, as our ultimate goal in judging social arrangements." *Capitalism and Freedom*, Fortieth Anniversary ed. (Chicago: University of Chicago Press, 2002), 12. Wendy Brown has developed a sustained argument on the denial and dismantling of society in favor of the individual and the family, which she suggests undermines democracy. "If there is no such thing as society," she writes, "but only individuals and families oriented by markets and morals, then there is no such thing as social power generating hierarchies, exclusion, and violence, let alone subjectivity at the sites

of class, gender, or race." As a result, freedom is reduced to personal liberty and power to explicit coercion. "Reducing freedom to unregulated personal license in the context of disavowing the social and dismantling society," she continues, "anoints as free expression every historically and politically generated sentiment of (lost) entitlement based in whiteness, maleness, or nativism while denying these to be socially produced, releasing them from any connection to social conscience, compromise, or consequence." *In the Ruins of Neoliberalism: The Rise of Antidemocratic Politics in the West* (New York: Columbia University Press, 2019), 40, 45.

34. Ginsburg, "Mighty Crime Victims," 196.

35. Human Rights Watch, *No Escape: Male Rape in U.S. Prisons*, 2001, www .hrw.org/reports/2001/prison/.

36. Kimmett Edgar and Ian O'Donnell, "Assault in Prison: The Victim's Contribution," *British Journal of Criminology* 38, no. 4 (1998): 636.

37. *Haines v. Kerner.*

38. This form of discipline also has resonances with the military tribunal and the police internal investigation and disciplinary hearing, both of which feature processes for investigating, adjudicating, and punishing misconduct as well as crime, that are completely external to the criminal justice system. In these settings, as in the Title IX investigation and the prison disciplinary hearing, guilt and innocence are subsidiary to maintaining the institutional status quo.

39. 18 U.S.C. § 3771. Crime victims' rights.

40. Ginsburg, "Mighty Crime Victims," 181.

41. Ginsburg, "Mighty Crime Victims," 181–182.

42. See Meda Chesney-Lind and Lisa Pasko, *The Female Offender: Girls, Women, and Crime*, 2nd ed. (Thousand Oaks: Sage, 2003); Judith Ann Warner, *Women and Crime: A Reference Handbook* (Santa Barbara: ABC-CLIO, 2012).

43. Kathleen Ferraro, *Neither Angels nor Demons: Women, Crime, and Victimization* (Evanston: Northwestern University Press, 2006), 1.

44. Ginsburg, "Mighty Crime Victims," 183.

45. Stuart Hall, "The Neo-liberal Revolution," *Cultural Studies* 25, no. 6 (2011): 705–728.

46. Lauren Berlant, "Live Sex Acts (Parental Advisory: Explicit Material)," *Feminist Studies* 21, no. 2 (1995): 379–404.

47. Lauren Berlant, *The Queen of America Goes to Washington City: Essays on Sex and Citizenship* (Durham: Duke University Press, 1997), 5.

48. Berlant, *Queen of America*, 5.

49. Berlant, *Queen of America*, 4.

50. Berlant, *Queen of America*, 1.

51. See Andrew Dilts, *Punishment and Inclusion: Race, Membership, and the Limits of American Liberalism* (New York: Fordham University Press, 2014); Alison Young, *Imagining Crime* (Thousand Oaks: Sage, 1996).

52. Ben Harrison, *True Crime Narratives: An Annotated Bibliography* (Lanham: Scarecrow, 1997), xxxii.

53. Berlant, *Queen of America*, 1.

54. Pennsylvania Department of Corrections, *Pennsylvania DOC Inmate Handbook* (Harrisburg: Pennsylvania DOC, 2017), 24.

55. Amy D. Ronner, "The Cassandra Curse: The Stereotype of the Female Liar Resurfaces in *Jones v. Clinton*," *UC Davis Law Review* 31, no. 1 (1997): 123–129; Marilyn Yarborough and Crystal Bennet, "Cassandra and the 'Sistahs': The Peculiar Treatment of African American Women and the Myth of Women as Liars," *Journal of Gender, Race, and Justice* 3, no. 2 (2000): 625–657.

56. Jennifer L. Truman and Rachel E. Morgan, "Criminal Victimization, 2015," Bureau of Justice Statistics, 2016, https://www.bjs.gov/content/pub/pdf/cv15.pdf.

57. See Patricia A. Frazier and Beth Haney, "Sexual Assault Cases in the Legal System: Police, Prosecutor, and Victim Perspectives," *Law and Human Behavior* 20, no. 6 (1996): 607–628.

58. Patricia Williams writes that in contemporary America the "haves are entitled to privacy, in guarded, moated castles; have-nots must be out in the open-scrutinized, seen with their hands open and empty to make sure they're not pilfering." *The Alchemy of Race and Rights* (Cambridge, MA: Harvard University Press, 1991), 22.

59. Kimberlé Crenshaw's foundational legal analysis of intersectionality describes the ways in which the lives of people of color are subject to police scrutiny; considered to be always already criminals, communities of color have adopted a "generalized . . . ethic against public intervention, the product of a desire to create a private world free from the diverse assaults on the public lives of racially subordinated people." "Mapping the Margins: Intersectionality, Identity Politics, and Violence against Women of Color," *Stanford Law Review* 43, no. 6 (1991): 1257.

60. *Wolff v. McDonnell*, italics added.

61. While religious freedom is not absolute, for example as held in Turner v. Safley, 482 U.S. 78 (1987), the Religious Freedom Restoration Act of 1993 applies to federal prisoners, who are entitled to have access to religious literature per Sutton v. Rasheed, 323 F.3d (2003), and to participate in prayer and attend religious services per Mayweathers v. Newland, 258 F.3d (2001).

62. The Supreme Court has ruled that police do not have a constitutional obligation to enforce a restraining order. Jessica Gonzales called the police on her husband, against whom she had a restraining order. Police failed to respond, and he murdered their three children, Castle Rock v. Gonzales, 545 U.S. 748 (2005). Previously, in DeShaney v. Winnebago County, 489 U.S. 189 (1989), the Court had ruled that that county's social services agency's failure to protect a minor from abuse by his father did not constitute a violation of the Constitution.

63. Inmates have the right to access courts and that prisons must provide adequate resources for inmates to access them, namely, in the form of libraries. Prisons are not required to provide legal assistance. Bounds v. Smith, 430 U.S. 817 (1977).

64. Prison Litigation Reform Act (1996); Jacqueline Haley Summs, "Grappling with Inmates' Access to Justice: The Narrowing of the Exhaustion Requirement in *Ross v. Blake*," *Administrative Law Review* 69, no. 2 (2017): 469. PLRA was preceded by the Civil Rights of Institutionalized Persons Act (CRIPA) in 1980.

65. Van Swearingen, "Imprisoning Rights: The Failure of Negotiated Governance in the Prison Inmate Grievance Process," *California Law Review* 96, no. 5 (2008): 1354.

66. Swearingen, "Imprisoning Rights," 1354.

67. Swearingen, "Imprisoning Rights," 1354.

68. Summs, "Grappling with Inmates' Access to Justice," 468.

69. While some inmate handbooks outline the types of disciplinary measures that can be enforced—solitary confinement, loss of privileges—there is not usually an exact correspondence between infraction and discipline. In many cases, inmates must rely on precedent and word of mouth: certain infractions seem to result in cell restriction, while others result in thirty days of solitary; some infractions seem to result in the loss of visitation privileges, while others result in the loss of commissary privileges. More often than not, especially for minor institutional infractions—wearing improper attire on the floor, not locking in at count, nicking food from chow—disciplinary measures are determined by the attending officer on the spot. For more serious violations, a hearing may be scheduled, at which the inmate may or may not appear, and a disciplinary review board determines both culpability and disciplinary action.

70. Cook County Department of Corrections, *Inmate Information Handbook*, 2013. The internal statute of limitations for grievances at the Cook County Jail is fourteen days, excepting sexual discrimination or harassment, for which there is no time limitation.

71. Sentencing guidelines often give the appearance of neutrality while reinscribing racial disparities. Similarly, prosecutors have broad discretion to determine which charges are brought and against whom, and these decisions disproportionately work against people of color. See, for example, Paul J. Hofer, Kevin R. Blackwell, and R. Barry Ruback, "The Effect of Federal Sentencing Guidelines on Judge Sentencing Disparity," *Journal of Criminal Law and Criminology* 90, no. 1 (1999): 239–322. For more on prosecutorial discretion and judicial departures from sentencing guidelines, see Keith A. Wilmot and Cassia Spohn, "Prosecutorial Discretion and Real-Offense Sentencing: An Analysis of Relevant Conduct under the Federal Sentencing Guidelines," *Criminal Justice Policy Review* 15, no. 3 (2004): 324–343.

72. Julia Dressel and Hany Farid, "The Accuracy, Fairness, and Limits of Predicting Recidivism," *Science Advances* 4, no. 1 (2018), https://doi.org/10.11 26/sciadv.aao5580.

73. Robert Ferguson, *Inferno: An Anatomy of American Punishment* (Cambridge, MA: Harvard University Press, 2014), 23.

74. See Rainer Banse et al., "Pro-criminal Attitudes, Intervention, and Recidivism," *Aggression and Violent Behavior* 18, no. 6 (2013): 673–685.

CHAPTER THREE. CONSUMER BACKGROUND REPORTS AND THE MAKING OF NEOLIBERAL COPS AND ROBBERS

1. Alessandro De Giorgi, "Back to Nothing: Prisoner Reentry and Neoliberal Neglect," *Social Justice* 44, no. 1 (2017): 84.

2. De Giorgi, "Back to Nothing," 86; Douglas E. Thompkins, "The Expanding Prisoner Reentry Industry," *Dialectal Anthropology* 34, no. 4 (2010): 589–604.

3. Nora A. Draper, "Reputation Anxiety: Consumer Background Checks and the Cultivation of Risk," *Communication and Culture Critique* 12, no. 1 (2019): 36–52.

4. Joshua Reeves, "If You See Something Say Something: Lateral Surveillance and the Uses of Responsibility," *Surveillance and Society* 10, no. 3/4 (2012): 235–248; B. A. Glesner, "Landlords as Cops: Tort, Nuisance, and Forfeiture Standards Imposing Liability on Landlords for Crime on the Premises," *Case Western Reserve Law Review* 42, no. 3 (1992): 679–791.

5. Gabriel Chin, "The New Civil Death: Rethinking Punishment in the Era of Mass Incarceration," *University of Pennsylvania Law Review* 160 (2012): 1827.

6. Gabriel Chin, "Collateral Consequences and Criminal Justice: Future

Policy and Constitutional Directions," *Marquette Law Review* 102, no. 1 (2012): 247, 253.

7. Chin, "Collateral Consequences," 260.

8. Joshua Kaiser, "We Know It When We See It: The Tenuous Line between 'Direct Punishment' and 'Collateral Consequences,'" *Howard Law Journal* 59, no. 2 (2016): 343.

9. Kaiser, "We Know It When We See It," 343.

10. Kaiser, "We Know It When We See It," 360; United States v. Parrino, 212 F.2d 919 (2d Cir. 1954).

11. Kaiser, "We Know It When We See It," 351.

12. Kaiser, "We Know It When We See It," 363.

13. Chin, "New Civil Death," 1792, italics in original; Trop v. Dulles, 356 U.S. 86 (1958); Weems v. United States, 217 U.S. 349 (1910).

14. Chin, "New Civil Death," 1825.

15. Gilmore, *Golden Gulag: Prisons, Surplus, Crisis, and Opposition in Globalizing California* (Berkeley: University of California Press, 2007), 122.

16. Glesner, "Landlords as Cops," 681.

17. George J. Stigler, "The Optimum Enforcement of Laws," *Journal of Political Economy* 78, no. 3 (1970): 526.

18. Stigler, "The Optimum Enforcement of Laws," 528. Setha Low's ethnographic research has documented not only how the upper–middle class and wealthy elites use private security as a form of self-protection but also how these forms of securitization constitute a form of private government that is based on racial exclusions. *Behind the Gates: Life, Security, and the Pursuit of Happiness in Fortress America* (New York: Routledge, 2003); "Maintaining Whiteness: The Fear of Others and Niceness," *Transforming Anthropology* 17, no. 2 (2009): 79–92.

19. Clifford D. Shearing and Philip C. Stenning, "Modern Private Security: Its Growth and Operations," *Crime and Justice* 3 (1981): 204. As the authors note, however, the public/private distinction is not always clear cut. At universities and utility companies, the latter of which were mostly still public at the time of writing, policing may fall somewhere between public and private. Micol Seigel has more recently analyzed this fluid boundary between public and private policing, and public-private "hybrid" police forces. *Violence Work: State Power and the Limits of the Police* (Durham: Duke University Press, 2018), especially chapter 3.

20. Draper, "Reputation Anxiety," 37.

21. Draper, "Reputation Anxiety," 38.

22. Kline v. 1500 Massachusetts Avenue Apartment Complex, 439 F.2d 477 (D.C. Cir. 1970).

23. Glesner, "Landlords as Cops," 682.

24. Glesner, "Landlords as Cops," 692.

25. Texas House Bill 1188, Legislative Session 83(R), 2013.

26. Society for Human Resource Management, "Background Checking—The Use of Criminal Background Checks in Hiring Decisions," July 19, 2012, https://www.shrm.org/hr-today/trends-and-forecasting/research-and-surve ys/pages/criminalbackgroundcheck.aspx; HR Research Institute, Background Screening: Trends and Uses in Today's Global Economy, July 2020, https://pu bs.thepbsa.org/pub.cfm?id=459B8AB7-0CEA-625E-0911-A4A089DE5118#. Former Cook County Jail chaplain Jonathan Reuben Miller has documented through ethnographic research the toll that background checks take on former inmates in their search for housing, noting that many landlords may not even review applications submitted by people with criminal convictions. *Halfway Home: Race, Punishment, and the Afterlife of Mass Incarceration* (New York: Little, Brown & Company, 2021).

27. Michel Foucault, *The Punitive Society: Lectures at the Collège de France, 1972–73*, trans. Graham Burchell (New York: Palgrave Macmillan, 2015), 32–33. Foucault takes issue with the use of the language of transgression to describe crime. Chapter 5 of this volume addresses the relationship between transgression, the law, and the limit, and the different types of punishment operative in various social contexts in Foucault's discussion in *The Punitive Society*.

28. Andrew Dilts, *Punishment and Inclusion: Race, Membership, and the Limits of American Liberalism* (New York: Fordham University Press, 2014), 79.

29. Gary S. Becker, "Crime and Punishment: An Economic Approach," *Journal of Political Economy* 76, no. 2 (1968): 198–199.

30. Dilts, *Punishment and Inclusion*, 79.

31. Dilts, *Punishment and Inclusion*, 80, 82.

32. Michel Foucault, *The Birth of Biopolitics: Lectures at the Collège de France, 1978–79*, trans. Graham Burchell (New York: Palgrave Macmillan, 2008), 45, 116–121, 138–141.

33. As Gary Becker explains, it is not so much that individuals are rational actors, but rather that they must be subjected to economic analysis *as if* they are rational actors. Writing in the context of households, Becker notes that, of course, there is a "broad class of irrational behavior, including inert and impulsive behavior," but that these can "be encompassed by a model in which current choices were partly determined by past ones and partly by a

probability mechanism." Households must therefore be subjected to economic analysis as if they are rational *and* as if they are irrational. Thus, "negatively inclined demand curves result not so much from rational behavior per se as from a general principle which includes a wide class of irrational behavior as well." Essentially, "all behavior in this class [of irrational behavior] would reproduce the fundamental theorem of rational behavior." Becker argues that it is not households that are necessarily rational but the market itself. However, by subjecting households to the rationality of the market, the market can act on the field in which decisions are made by irrational or inert households, bringing them into the fold, as it were, of rational behavior: "Irrational units would often be 'forced' by a change in opportunities to respond rationally." "Irrational Behavior and Economic Theory," *Journal of Political Economy* 70, no. 1 (1962): 7, 4, 7, 12.

34. For more on neoliberal legality, especially insofar as the law is intended to make comprehensible the terms of the neoliberal social contract, and in particular the privileged place of the corporation under the law, see Honor Brabazon, ed. *Neoliberal Legality: Understanding the Role of the Law in the Neoliberal Project* (New York: Routledge, 2018).

35. Foucault, *Birth of Biopolitics*, 137.

36. Bernard E. Harcourt, "Neoliberal Penality: A Brief Genealogy," *Theoretical Criminology* 14, no. 1 (2010): 86.

37. Harcourt, "Neoliberal Penality," 85.

38. Dilts, *Punishment and Inclusion*, 80. As Richard Posner argues in 1985, "The pervasive emphasis placed in the criminal law on punishing harmless preparatory activity, on the mental state of the accused, and, related to both points, on the moral character rather than the consequences of behavior, suggests a decidedly noneconomic perspective." For Posner, all forbidden acts are actually economic inefficiencies, ones that do not increase the wealth of society. "An Economic Theory of the Criminal Law," *Columbia Law Review* 85, no. 6 (1985): 1194, 1195, 1197.

39. Malcolm Feeley and Jonathan Simon, "Actuarial Justice: The Emerging New Criminal Law," in *The Futures of Criminology*, ed. David Nelken (Thousand Oaks: Sage, 1994), 173–201.

40. Becker, "Crime and Punishment," 170, 173.

41. Becker, "Crime and Punishment," 174.

42. Becker, "Crime and Punishment," 183–185. Stigler concurs: "The professional criminal seeks income, and for him the usual rules of occupational choice will hold. He will reckon the present value of the expected returns and costs of the criminal activity and compare their difference with the net returns

from other criminal activities and from legitimate activities." "The Optimum Enforcement of Laws," 530.

43. Becker, "Crime and Punishment," 191–192. Becker provides a footnote referencing Jeremy Bentham as a source of inspiration: "The evil of the punishment must be made to exceed the advantage of the defense." Bentham, of course, was more concerned with moral than financial evils, and his moral economy was not market-based. In the same principle, he also discusses another necessity, which is the certainty of punishment. Here, "the more certain punishment is, the less severe it need be." *The Theory of Legislation*, 2nd ed. (London: Routledge & Kegan Paul Ltd., 1950), 325–326.

44. Dilts, *Punishment and Inclusion*, 73.

45. Feeley and Simon, "Actuarial Justice," 174.

46. Feeley and Simon, "Actuarial Justice," 175.

47. Bernard E. Harcourt, *Exposed: Desire and Disobedience in the Digital Age* (Cambridge, MA: Harvard University Press, 2015), 36.

48. Feeley and Simon, "Actuarial Justice," 178.

49. Kaiser, "We Know It When We See It," 243.

50. See Jenny Roberts, "Ignorance Is Effectively Bliss: Collateral Consequences, Silence, and Misinformation in the Guilty-Plea Process," *Iowa Law Review* 95, no. 1 (2009): 119–194.

51. Dilts, *Punishment and Inclusion*, 83.

52. Foucault, *Punitive Society*, 104.

53. Foucault, *Punitive Society*, 105. On governmentality as the conduct of conduct, see *Security, Territory, Population: Lectures at the Collège de France, 1977–1978*, trans. Graham Burchell (New York: Palgrave Macmillan, 2009), 389.

54. Foucault, *Punitive Society*, 105.

55. Foucault, *Birth of Biopolitics*, 77.

56. Alice Ristroph, "An Intellectual History of Mass Incarceration," *Boston College Law Review* 60, no. 7 (2019): 1966.

57. Ristroph, "Intellectual History," 1966–1967.

58. Robert H. Jackson, "The Federal Prosecutor," *American Institute of Criminal Law and Criminology* 3, no. 3 (1940): 3–6, quoted in Ristroph, "Intellectual History," 1967.

59. James B. Jacobs, *The Eternal Criminal Record* (Cambridge, MA: Harvard University Press, 2015), ix.

60. Jacobs, *Eternal Criminal Record*, x.

61. Fair Credit Reporting Act, 15 U.S.C § 1681, 1. The version of the Act cited here is the one compiled by the Federal Trade Commission for public distribution, revised September 2018.

62. FCRA, 1–2.

63. See, for example, Advance Market Analytics, *Background Investigation Comprehensive Study by Type (Cloud-based, Onpremise), Application (Commercial, Private), End-User Industry (Banking & Financial Sector, Government Agencies, Information Technology, Others), Service Type (Criminal Background Checks, Education & Employment Verification, Credit History Checks, Drug & Health Screening, Others) Players and Region—Global Market Outlook to 2024*, 2019. See Jacobs for a description of some of the major companies operating in the consumer background report space, some of the ways in which data is collected and distributed, as well as some of the more practical implications and challenges of relying on the consumer background report to assess risk. *Eternal Criminal Record*, 71–90.

64. Pre-Employ, "Child Welfare Services Hired a Convicted Murderer Revealing Gaps in Background Checks," https://www.pre-employ.com/news blog/child-welfare-services-hired-a-convicted-murderer-revealing-gaps -in-background-checks/.

65. Louis R. Mizell Jr. and Michael A. Gips, "Do Organizations Rely on Background Checks Too Much?," Society for Human Resources Management, December 10, 2020, https://www.shrm.org/resourcesandtools/hr-topics/tal ent-acquisition/pages/do-organizations-rely-on-background-checks-too-mu ch.aspx.

66. Matt Leingang, "Ohio State Shooter Had Complained that Bosses Weren't Fair," Cleveland.com, March 10, 2010, https://www.cleveland.com/me tro/2010/03/ohio_state_shooter_had_complai.html.

67. Mizell and Gips, "Do Organizations Rely on Background Checks Too Much?"

68. This individual was eventually indicted on drug trafficking and for obstruction of justice charges in relation to involvement with the cartel. The United States Attorney's Office, Southern District of Texas, "Press Release: USAO Employee Indicted for Conspiring to Obstruct Justice," July 22, 2020, https://www.justice.gov/usao-sdtx/pr/usao-employee-indicted-conspiring -obstruct-justice.

69. One may hear echoes of then-presidential candidate Donald Trump's promise not only to torture suspected terrorists but to murder their family members, for example during the March 3, 2016, Republic presidential debate. On "this zeal, this excess of terror" as a means of "winning over the masses," see Bernard E. Harcourt, *The Counterrevolution: How Our Government Went to War against its Own Citizens* (New York: Basic Books, 2018), 113.

70. The Americans with Disabilities Act may also provide a framework

for understanding how discriminating against people with criminal records is likely to have a disparate impact on people with disabilities, including, especially, people with substance use disorder. For a legal theory of the relationship between criminal records discrimination and disability-based discrimination, see Amanda Johnson, "Challenging Criminal Records in Hiring under the Americans with Disabilities Act," *Columbia Human Rights Law Review* 48, no. 3 (2017): 212–256.

71. Kate Linden Morris, "'Within Constitutional Limitations:' Challenging Criminal Background Checks by Public Housing Authorities under the Fair Housing Act," *Columbia Human Rights Law Review* 47, no. 2 (2016): 165. Quoted material from 42 U.S.C. § 13661(c)—Screening of applicants for federally assisted housing.

72. Valerie Schneider, "Racism Knocking at the Door: The Use of Criminal Background Checks in Rental Housing," *University of Richmond Law Review* 53, no. 3 (2019): 929.

73. Schneider, "Racism Knocking," 931.

74. Robin D. G. Kelley, *Yo' Mama's Dysfunctional! Fighting the Culture Wars in Urban America*, 10th Anniversary ed. (Boston: Beacon, 2008), 47.

75. Rebecca Oyama, "Do Not (Re)Enter: The Rise of Criminal Background Tenant Screenings as a Violation of the Fair Housing Act," *Michigan Journal of Race and Law* 15, no. 1 (2009): 192.

76. Oyama, "Do Not (Re)Enter," 186.

77. Chenoa A. Flippen, "Racial and Ethnic Inequality in Homeownership and Housing Equity," *The Sociological Quarterly*, 42, no. 2 (2001): 121–149; Lauren J. Krivo and Robert L. Kaufman, "Housing and Wealth Inequality: Racial-Ethnic Difference in Home Equity in the United States," *Demography* 41, no. 3 (2004): 585–605.

78. United States Department of Housing and Urban Development, *Housing Discrimination against Racial and Ethnic Minorities 2012* (Washington, DC: United States Department of Housing and Urban Development, 2013), xiv–xv.

79. Devah Pager, "The Mark of a Criminal Record," *American Journal of Sociology* 108, no. 5 (2003): 937–975; see Devah Pager, Bruce Western, and Naomi Sugie, "Sequencing Disadvantage: Barriers to Employment Facing Young Black and White Men with Criminal Records," *The Annals of the American Academy of Political and Social Science* 623, no. 1 (2009): 195–213.

80. US Department of Housing and Urban Development, *Office of General Counsel Guidance on Application of Fair Housing Act Standards to the Use of Criminal Records by Providers of Housing and Real Estate-Related Transactions*

(Washington, DC: United States Department of Housing and Urban Development, 2016), 2.

81. Griggs v. Duke Power Co., 401 U.S. 424 (1971).

82. Rigel C. Oliveri, "Beyond Disparate Impact: How the Fair Housing Movement Can Move On," *Washburn Law Journal* 54, no. 3 (2015), LexisNexis.

83. Peter E. Mahoney, "The End(s) of Disparate Impact: Doctrinal Reconstruction, Fair Housing and Lending Law, and the Antidiscrimination Principle," *Emory Law Journal* 47, no. 2 (1998): 411.

84. Michael Selmi, "Was the Disparate Impact Theory a Mistake?" *UCLA Law Review* 53 (2006): 705.

85. Robert Belton, "The Dismantling of the Griggs Disparate Impact Theory and the Future of Title VII: The Need for a Third Reconstruction," *Yale Law and Policy Review* 8, no. 2 (1990): 223–256; Wards Cove Packing Co. v. Antonio, 109 U.S. 2115 (1989).

86. Michael Selmi, "Proving Intentional Discrimination: The Reality of Supreme Court Rhetoric," *Georgetown Law Journal* 86, no. 2 (1997): 350.

87. American Apartment Owners Association, "Tenant Background Check," https://www.american-apartment-owners-association.org/tenant-screening-background-checks/.

88. National Association for Independent Landlords, "Criminal and Eviction Reports," https://landlordassociation.com/credit_reports.html#1.

89. Dilts, *Punishment and Inclusion*, 79.

90. For more on the concept of institutional exclusion, see David Thatcher, "The Rise of Criminal Background Screening in Rental Housing," *Law and Social Inquiry* 33, no. 1 (2008): 5–30.

CHAPTER FOUR. READJUDICATING CRIMES AND IMPOSING SANCTIONS IN AIRBNB'S NEOLIBERAL "COMMUNITY"

1. Airbnb Newsroom, "Fast Facts," https://press.airbnb.com/fast-facts/.

2. Anna Roberts, "Conviction by Prior Impeachment," *Boston University Law Review* 96, no. 6 (2016): 1979.

3. Rule 404(b) provides significant exceptions to the inadmissibility of prior convictions. Such "evidence may be admissible for another purpose, such as proving motive, opportunity, intent, preparation, plan, knowledge, identity, absence of mistake, or lack of accident." The robust exceptions to the inadmissibility of previous convictions outlined in Rule 404(b), as well as Rules 607, 608, and 609, act as backdoors that allow previous convictions into criminal proceedings. Legal scholars have written extensive criticism both about the

low bar for admitting past convictions into evidence, even when its probative value is questionable, and on the practice of impeaching criminal defendants based on prior convictions. See, for example, Anna Roberts, "Impeachment by Unreliable Conviction," *Boston College Law Review* 55, no. 2 (2014): 563–639; Anna Roberts, "Reclaiming the Importance of the Defendant's Testimony: Prior Conviction Impeachment and the Fight against Implicit Stereotyping," *University of Chicago Law Review* 83, no. 2 (2016): 835–891. Moreover, like many other legal principles, this one is obviated by the system in which the vast majority of criminal cases are now determined by plea arrangement.

4. Wayne Logan, "Informal Collateral Consequences," *Washington Law Review* 88, no. 3 (2013): 1103–1117.

5. Airbnb, "Does Airbnb Perform Background Checks on Members?" https://www.airbnb.com/help/article/1308/does-airbnb-perform-background-checks-on-members.

6. Airbnb, "Updated Terms of Service," January 21, 2019, https://www.airbnb.com/terms/privacy_policy.

7. Airbnb, "Does Airbnb Perform Background Checks on Members?"

8. It was my own banishment from Airbnb that prompted my inquiry into the company's policies. I was banished for life despite not being convicted of any crimes that resemble those described as warranting either permanent banishment or fourteen-year banishment. Because Airbnb's decisions are not a matter of public record, it is difficult to know how many people have been banished, for what time, and for what reasons.

9. Society for Human Resource Management, "SHRM Survey Findings: Background Checking—The Use of Criminal Background Checks in Hiring Decisions," https://www.shrm.org/hr-today/trends-and-forecasting/research-and-surveys/pages/criminalbackgroundcheck.aspx.

10. Sheera Frenkel and Cecilia Kang, *An Ugly Truth: Inside Facebook's Battle for Domination* (New York: Harper Collins, 2021), 13. Joshua Kaiser uses the (in)famous language of Supreme Court Justice Potter Stewart in describing how judges differentiate between punishment and collateral consequences. Justice Stewart declined to define "hard-core" pornography but claimed nonetheless that "I know it when I see it." "We Know It When We See It: The Tenuous Line between 'Direct Punishment' and 'Collateral Consequences,'" *Howard Law Journal* 59, no. 2 (2016): 341–372. See Jacobellis v. Ohio (Stewart, concurring), 378 U.S. 184 (1964), 197. Even more recently, this language has inflected debates about violence against Black people. In 2020, Senator Rand Paul objected to the Emmett Till Antilynching Act because, he claimed, it failed to adequately define lynching. He proposed that such a definition

include at least an attempt to do bodily harm. Then Senator Kamala Harris responded in a June 4 speech to Congress by saying that "it should not take a maiming or torture in order for us to recognize a lynching when we see it, and recognize it by federal law, and call it what it is, which is that it is a crime that should be punishable with accountability and consequence." The Act that was eventually introduced and then passed in the House of Representatives ultimately did include language that defined lynching as an act that resulted in serious bodily harm or death.

11. Frenkel and Kang, *An Ugly Truth*, 36.

12. Frenkel and Kang, *An Ugly Truth*, 14.

13. Michael J. Coyle, "Expanding Deviance toward Difference," in *The Death and Resurrection of Deviance*, ed. Michael Dellwing, Joe Kotarbe, and Nathan Pino (New York: Palgrave Macmillan, 2014), 68–84; Denise Woodall, "Interrupting Cultural Constructions of the Criminalized Other through a Revised Criminal Activities Checklist Classroom Exercise," *Teaching Sociology* 45, no. 2 (2016): 161–167.

14. John Gramlich, "Most Violent and Property Crimes in the US Go Unsolved," Pew Research Center, March 1, 2017, https://www.pewresearch.org /fact-tank/2017/03/01/most-violent-and-property-crimes-in-the-u-s-go-un solved/.

15. Federal Bureau of Investigation, "Crime in the United States, 2019," https://ucr.fbi.gov/crime-in-the-u.s/2019/crime-in-the.s.-2019/topic-pages /clearances. The FBI defines a case as being cleared—in other words, as being solved—when someone is either arrested, charged, or turned over to a court for prosecution, not when someone is convicted of a crime.

16. "2019 Media Kit," *Airbnb Magazine*, https://www.hearst.com/Documen ts/33329/97554/2019+Airbnb+Magazine+Media+Kit_2019+%281%29.pdf/f3a 0c436-f6ed-701a-11fc-2e8b6cd6c8c8.

17. Katherine Russell-Brown, *The Color of Crime: Racial Hoaxes, White Crime, Media Messages, Police Violence, and Other Race-Based Harms*, 3rd ed. (New York: New York University Press, 2021).

18. Act 56 of 2018 (Clean Slate Act). Pennsylvania General Assembly, Act of June 28, 2018, P.L. 402, No. 56. The records affected are still available to law enforcement.

19. HR Research Institute, Background Screening: Trends and Uses in Today's Global Economy, July 2020, https://pubs.thepbsa.org/pub.cfm?id=459B 8AB7-0CEA-625E-0911-A4A089DE5118#. See James B. Jacobs, *The Eternal Criminal Record* (Cambridge, MA: Harvard University Press, 2015), 6.

20. Adam Satariano, "'Right to Be Forgotten' Privacy Rule Is Limited by

Europe's Top Court," *New York Times*, September 24, 2019, https://www.nytimes
.com/2019/09/24/technology/europe-google-right-to-be-forgotten.html.

21. Molly Webster and Bethel Habte, prod., "Right to be Forgotten," *Radiolab*, August 23, 2019, https://www.wnycstudios.org/story/radiolab-right-be
-forgotten.

22. Lauren Edelman, *Working Law: Courts, Corporations, and Symbolic
Civil Rights* (Chicago: University of Chicago Press, 2016), 3, 11, 170.

23. Edelman, *Working Law*, 11.

24. Edelman, *Working Law*, 107, italics added.

25. Edelman, *Working Law*, 231, 234, 125.

26. Edelman, *Working Law*, 157

27. Edelman, *Working Law*, 155.

28. Edelman, *Working Law*, 153, 160, 159.

29. Lynn Langton, "Victimizations Not Reported to the Police, 2006–2010,"
Bureau of Justice Statistics, August 2012, https://bjs.ojp.gov/content/pub/pdf
/vnrp0610.pdf.

30. Recidivism is often defined as the commission of another crime, although is sometimes used to describe recommitment on technical violations
of probation or parole. Given the way in which convictions are used in policing to develop suspect lists and lineups, people with criminal convictions are
at risk of facing a higher incidence of arrest and conviction than people without criminal records, and their chances of being recommitted on technical
violations—for example for being out past curfew, for consuming alcohol, or
for being in the presence of other people with convictions—is extremely high.
One of the major problems with using recidivism as a metric of rehabilitation,
as Alessandro De Giorgi notes, is that "recidivism suppression prevails over
any meaningful institutional effort to improve former prisoners' economic
stability, well-being, physical and mental health, and civic integration." "Back
to Nothing: Prisoner Reentry and Neoliberal Neglect," *Social Justice* 44, no. 1
(2017): 93.

31. Kaiser, "We Know It When We See It," 243.

32. De Giorgi, "Back to Nothing," 86.

33. Douglas E. Thompkins, "The Expanding Prisoner Reentry Industry,"
Dialectal Anthropology 34, no. 4 (2010): 589–604.

34. *Gallup's Perspective on the Gig Economy and Alternative Work Arrangements*, Gallup, 2018, https://www.gallup.com/workplace/240878/gig-econo
my-paper-2018.aspx?thank-you-report-form=1.

35. Alexandrea J. Ravenelle, *Hustle and Gig: Struggling and Surviving in
the Sharing Economy* (Berkeley: University of California Press, 2019), 4. See

Bettylou Valentine, *Hustling and Other Hard Work: Lifestyles in the Ghetto* (New York: Free Press, 1978); Loïc Wacquant, "Inside the Zone: The Social Art of the Hustler in the Black American Ghetto," *Theory, Culture, and Society* 15, no. 2 (1998): 1–36.

36. Ravenelle, *Hustle and Gig*, 7–8.

37. Ravenelle, *Hustle and Gig*, 140–142.

38. Autohost, "Pricing," https://www.autohost.ai/pricing/; Guesty, "Features," https://www.guesty.com/features/.

39. Ravenelle, *Hustle and Gig*, 5–6.

40. Elizabeth Anderson, *Private Government: How Employers Rule Our Lives (and Why We Don't Talk about It)* (Princeton: Princeton University Press, 2017), 49.

41. Michel Foucault, *The Punitive Society: Lectures at the Collège de France, 1972–73*, trans. Graham Burchell (New York: Palgrave Macmillan, 2015), 105.

42. Anderson, *Private Government*, 53, 54.

43. Ravenelle, *Hustle and Gig*, 6.

44. Milton Friedman, *Capitalism and Freedom*, Fortieth Anniversary ed. (Chicago: University of Chicago Press, 2002), 14.

45. Friedman, *Capitalism and Freedom*, 14–15.

46. Nofar Sheffi, "We Accept: The Constitution of Airbnb," *Transnational Legal Theory* 11, no. 4 (2020): 502, 520.

CHAPTER FIVE. NEOLIBERAL VIGILANTISM, CANCEL CULTURE, AND THE POST-JURIDICAL TURN

1. B. A. Glesner, "Landlords as Cops: Tort, Nuisance, and Forfeiture Standards Imposing Liability on Landlords for Crime on the Premises," *Case Western Reserve Law Review* 42, no. 3 (1992): 679–791.

2. Nora A. Draper, "Reputation Anxiety: Consumer Background Checks and the Cultivation of Risk," *Communication and Culture Critique* 12, no. 1 (2019): 37.

3. Draper, "Reputation Anxiety," 38.

4. Citizen: Local Safety Alerts. Apple App Store, https://apps.apple.com/us/app/citizen-local-safety-alerts/id1039889567.

5. Nesrine Malik, *We Need New Stories: The Myths that Subvert Freedom* (New York: Norton, 2022).

6. The concept of cancelling a person may have its origins in Mario van Peebles' 1991 film *New Jack City* (Burbank, CA: Warner Bros. Pictures).

7. Ryan Schocket, "13 Celebs Who Were Actually Cancelled in 2020," *Buzzfeed*, January 3, 2021, https://www.buzzfeed.com/ryanschocket2/celebs-cancelled-in-2020.

8. Michel Foucault, *The Punitive Society: Lectures at the Collège de France, 1972–73*, trans. Graham Burchell (New York: Palgrave Macmillan, 2015), 68.

9. Foucault, *Punitive Society*, 67–68.

10. Foucault, *Punitive Society*, 68.

11. Foucault, *Punitive Society*, 69.

12. Foucault, *Punitive Society*, 105.

13. Foucault, *Punitive Society*, 178.

14. Philipp Wüschner has argued that Foucault's model of infamy is a useful analytic for understanding contemporary online behavior. In Foucault's reading, Wüschner explains, public, ritualistic shaming was replaced in the eighteenth century by the prison, which served to culturally reorient affect away from shame and towards guilt. Wüschner sees a return to shaming in online culture as a "somewhat problematic . . . form of resistance to the economy of guilt." "Shame, Guilt, and Punishment," *Foucault Studies*, no. 23 (2017): 86. A recent edited volume also examines how the economy of infamy, far from fully replacing the state apparatus of the prison, has continued to operate among individuals and families, informally as it were, in opposition to the economies of discipline that are paradigmatic of the nineteenth- and twentieth-century penal systems as described by Foucault. Nancy Luxon, ed., *Archives of Infamy: Foucault on State Power in the Lives of Ordinary Citizens* (Minneapolis: University of Minnesota Press, 2019).

15. Crime Museum, "Vigilantism," https://www.crimemuseum.org/crime-library/other-crime-topics/vigilante/.

16. One of the most striking features of the investigation into the January 6, 2021 Capitol riot investigation has been the widespread use of web sleuths by law enforcement agencies. Ryan J. Reilly has documented how the FBI has relied on these "sedition hunters," making the investigation, in essence, "crowdsourced." Reilly notes that the sleuths' "meticulously compiled dossiers are so in-depth that in some cases they effectively ghostwrote FBI affidavits." "The FBI's Secret Weapon in the Capitol Attack Manhunt," *HuffPost*, January 5, 2022, https://www.huffpost.com/entry/sedition-hunters-capitol-attack-online-sleuths-fbi-trump_n_6161da09e4b06a986bd00df1.

17. Joe Berlinger, dir., *Crime Scene: The Vanishing at the Cecil Hotel* (Netflix, 2021).

18. One review of the series describes the false accusations but is

sympathetic to the sleuths' interpretations of Morbid's behavior: "To be fair to the web sleuths, at first glance the videos Morbid posted do seem quite dark." "Morbid: Everything You Need to Know About the Man Falsely Accused of Killing Elisa Lam," February 18, 2021, Moviemaker.com, https://www.movie maker.com/morbid-pablo-vergara-death-metal-cecil-hotel-elisa-lam/.

19. A fourth may be what Bernard Harcourt calls the expository society— one in which we willingly expose the most intimate details of our lives to potentially thousands of companies through near-constant online interactions. He notes that "in these ways, ordinary life is uncannily converging with practices of punishment: The see-throughness of our digital lives mirrors the all-seeingness of the digital sphere." The pervasiveness of digital surveillance means, for Harcourt, that pleasure and punishment have become inseparable, and as our status as digital subjects concretizes, our status as legal and political subjects erodes. *Exposed: Desire and Disobedience in the Digital Age* (Cambridge, MA: Harvard University Press, 2015), 21–22.

20. Foucault, *Punitive Society*, 68.

21. Foucault, *Punitive Society*, 68.

22. Foucault, *Punitive Society*, 68.

23. Foucault, *Punitive Society*, 68. Foucault contrasts this model with the branding of slaves, who must always be brought back into the condition of their punishment.

24. Andrew Dilts, *Punishment and Inclusion: Race, Membership, and the Limits of American Liberalism* (New York: Fordham University Press, 2014), 80.

25. Sarah Ahmed, *Complaint!* (Durham: Duke University Press, 2021), 10–14, chapter 5.

26. The Economist/YouGov Poll, November 5–7, 2017–1500 US Adults, https://docs.cdn.yougov.com/ko2yooa1bx/econTabReport.pdf.

27. "Over-Friendly, or Sexual Harassment? It Depends Partly on Whom You Ask," *The Economist*, November 17, 2017, https://www.economist.com/gra phic-detail/2017/11/17/over-friendly-or-sexual-harassment-it-depends-partly -on-whom-you-ask.

28. See, for example, Laura Kipnis's description of several Title IX investigations carried out by individual investigators. She contends that some of these investigators ignore evidence, but more often, their decisions are based on biases and flawed assumptions about human relationships. *Unwanted Advances: Sexual Paranoia Comes to Campus* (New York: HarperCollins, 2017).

29. Michael T. Nietzel, "Harvard Was Right to Rescind Its Admission Offer

to Kyle Kashuv," *Forbes*, June 18, 2019, https://www.forbes.com/sites/michaelt
nietzel/2019/06/18/harvard-was-right-to-rescind-its-admission-offer-to-kyle
-kashuv/?sh=7ef9784768ab.

30. Nietzel, "Harvard Was Right."

31. Eli Hager, "From Prison to PhD: The Redemption and Rejection of Michelle Jones," *New York Times*, September 13, 2017, https://www.nytimes.com
/2017/09/13/us/harvard-nyu-prison-michelle-jones.html.

32. Aihwa Ong, *Neoliberalism as Exception: Mutations in Citizenship and
Sovereignty* (Durham: Duke University Press, 2006), 2.

33. Piers Benn, *Intellectual Freedom and the Culture Wars* (London: Palgrave Macmillan, 2021), 115.

34. Benn, *Intellectual Freedom*, 116.

35. Benn, *Intellectual Freedom*, 117.

36. Stephen Hawkins et al., *Hidden Tribes: A Study of America's Polarized
Landscape*, More in Common, 2018, https://hiddentribes.us, 98.

37. See, for example, Graeme Wood, "America Has Forgotten How to For-
give," *The Atlantic*, March 20, 2021, https://www.theatlantic.com/ideas/archive
/2021/03/america-has-lost-ability-forgive/618336/.

38. Foucault, *Punitive Society*, 6. See Claude Lévi-Strauss, *Tristes Tropiques*,
trans. John Russell (New York: Criterion, 1961). The Graham Burchell trans-
lation of Foucault's *The Punitive Society* translates Lévi-Strauss's concept as
exclusion.

39. Foucault, *Punitive Society*, 7.

40. Foucault, *Punitive Society*, 4.

41. Foucault, *Punitive Society*, 5.

42. Foucault, *Punitive Society*, 7, 6.

43. Erik Nordenhaug and Jack Simmons, "The Outsourcing of Ethical
Thinking," in *The Twenty-First Century and Its Discontents*, ed. Jack Simmons
(Lanham: Lexington Books, 2020), 15.

44. Nordenhaug and Simmons, "Outsourcing," 16. See Sheri Fink, *Five
Days at Memorial: Life and Death in a Storm-Ravaged Hospital* (New York:
Broadway Books, 2013).

45. Nordenhaug and Simmons, "Outsourcing," 16.

46. Nordenhaug and Simmons, "Outsourcing," 20.

47. Lauren B. Edelman, *Working Law: Courts, Corporations, and Symbolic
Civil Rights* (Chicago: University of Chicago Press, 2016).

48. Nordenhaug and Simmons, "Outsourcing," 26.

49. National Association for Independent Landlords, "Criminal and Eviction Reports," https://landlordassociation.com/credit_reports.html#1.

50. Amos Tversky and Daniel Kahneman, "Judgment under Uncertainty: Heuristics and Biases," in *Judgement under Uncertainty: Heuristics and Biases*, ed. Daniel Kahneman, Paul Slovic, and Amos Tversky, repr. (1982; Cambridge: Cambridge University Press, 2008), 3.

51. Tversky and Kahneman, "Judgment under Uncertainty," 4.

52. Tversky and Kahneman, "Judgment under Uncertainty," 9.

53. See, for example, Travis L. Dixon and Christina L. Azocar, "Priming Crime and Activating Blackness: Understanding the Psychological Impact of the Overrepresentation of Blacks as Lawbreakers on Television News," *Journal of Communication* 57, no. 2 (2007): 229–253; Travis L. Dixon and Keith B. Maddox, "Skin Tone, Crime News, and Social Reality Judgments: Priming the Stereotype of the Dark and Dangerous Black Criminal," *Journal of Applied Social Psychology* 35, no. 8 (2005): 1555–1570. More recently, Dixon found that news media in Los Angeles was more accurately representing the rate of Black offending but continued to underrepresent Black victimization. "Good Guys Are Still Always White? Positive Change and Continued Representation of Race and Crime on Local Television News," *Communication Research* 44, no. 6 (2017): 775–792. Other research illustrates how the media draws on cultural tropes to characterize prisoners, including disproportionately highlighting violent criminality among prisoners with the effect of downplaying the large portion of the prison population incarcerated for non-violent offenses. See, for example, Dawn K. Cecil and Jennifer L. Leitner, "Unlocking the Gates: An Examination of *MSNBC Investigates—Lockup*," *The Howard Journal* 48, no. 2 (2009): 184–199.

54. Nordenhaug and Simmons, "Outsourcing," 28.

55. Nordenhaug and Simmons, "Outsourcing," 30.

56. Jean-François Lyotard, *The Postmodern Condition: A Report on Knowledge*, trans. Geoff Bennington and Brian Massumi (Manchester: Manchester University Press, 1984).

57. Foucault, *Punitive Society*, 68.

58. Steve Rose, "Removing Kevin Spacey from Movie Was a 'Business Decision,' Says Ridley Scott," *The Guardian*, January 5, 2018, https://www.theguardian.com/film/2018/jan/05/removing-kevin-spacey-from-movie-was-a-business-decision-says-ridley-scott-all-the-money-in-the-world.

59. Kevin Spacey, "Let Me Be Frank," YouTube, December 24, 2018, https://www.youtube.com/watch?v=JZveA-NAIDI.

60. Kevin Spacey, "KTWK," YouTube, December 24, 2019, https://www.youtube.com/watch?v=WCuuKhjLBoQ.

61. "Kevin Spacey Filming New Movie, First Look on Set," *TMZ*, August

29, 2021, https://www.tmz.com/2021/08/29/kevin-spacey-filming-new-movie -first-look-on-set-sexual-assault-scandal/.

62. ABC News, "Kevin Spacey Releases Bizarre Christmas Video Message," YouTube, December 26, 2019, https://www.youtube.com/watch?v=FPBRloF GQ3M.

63. Aja Romano, "The Sexual Assault Allegations against Kevin Spacey Span Decades. Here's What We Know," *Vox*, December 24, 2018, https://www .vox.com/culture/2017/11/3/16602628/kevin-spacey-sexual-assault-allegations -house-of-cards.

POSTSCRIPT

1. Texas Senate Bill 8 (SB8), Sec. 171.208. Civil Liability for Violation or Aiding and Abetting Violation.

2. Whole Woman's Health et al. v. Austin Reeve Jackson, Judge, et al. on application for injunctive relief, 594 U.S. ___ (2021).

3. See law professor Elizabeth Sepper's interview, "University of Texas Law Professor Breaks Down the State's Unusual Abortion Ban," *Weekend Edition Sunday*, September 5, 2021, https://www.npr.org/2021/09/05/1034439272/uni versity-of-texas-law-professor-breaks-down-the-states-unusual-abortion-ban.

4. Nina Totenberg, "The Supreme Court Heads towards Reversing Abor- tion Rights," *NPR*, September 2, 2021, https://www.npr.org/2021/09/03/103373 3918/the-supreme-court-heads-toward-reversing-abortion-rights.

5. Theodore M. Becker, "The Place of Private Police in Society: An Area of Research for the Social Sciences," *Social Problems* 21, no. 3 (1974): 445.

6. Becker, "The Place of Private Police," 445, italics added. S. Paul O'Hara writes that in the nineteenth century, "because the aristocracy, the Crown, and the church were no longer able to provide order, and the state was not yet willing, private firms arose to deal with that need." *Inventing the Pinkertons or, Spies, Sleuths, Mercenaries, and Thugs* (Baltimore: Johns Hopkins University Press, 2016), 8.

7. "Ku Klux Klan Plans Border Patrol to Help Fight Illegal Alien Problem," *New York Times*, October 18, 1977, 80.

8. Kathleen Belew, *Bring the War Home: The White Power Movement and Paramilitary America* (Cambridge: Harvard University Press, 2018), 3.

9. Belew, *Bring the War Home*, 9.

10. Belew, *Bring the War Home*, 11.

11. O'Hara, *Inventing the Pinkertons*, 7.

12. O'Hara, *Inventing the Pinkertons*, 9.

13. Michel Foucault, *The Punitive Society: Lectures at the Collège de France, 1972–73*, trans. Graham Burchell (New York: Palgrave Macmillan, 2015), 83.

14. Dario Melossi and Massimo Pavarini, *The Prison and the Factory: Origins of the Penitentiary System* (London: Macmillan, 1981), 56–58, 72.

15. Elizabeth Anderson, *Private Government: How Employers Rule Our Lives (and Why We Don't Talk about It)* (Princeton: Princeton University Press, 2017), 49.

16. On best practices as an antipolitics, as discussed in chapter 1 of this volume, see Wendy Brown, *Undoing the Demos: Neoliberalism's Stealth Revolution* (New York: Zone, 2015), 139.

17. Andrew Dilts, *Punishment and Inclusion: Race, Membership, and the Limits of American Liberalism* (New York: Fordham University Press, 2014), 73.

18. Foucault, *Punitive Society*, 68.

Selected Bibliography

This bibliography includes cases and laws cited within this volume and references to the primary and secondary sources that informed the substance and range of the analysis. Popular source material such as podcasts, films, television shows, and newspaper and magazine articles have been cited in full within the notes.

CASES AND LAWS

18 U.S.C. § 3771. Crime victims' rights.
42 U.S.C. § 13661(c)—Screening of applicants for federally assisted housing.
The 2020 Florida Statutes, Title XLVII, Chapter 961.
The 2021 Florida Statutes, Title XXVIII, Chapter 379.
Act 56 of 2018 (Clean Slate Act). Pennsylvania General Assembly, Act of June 28, 2018, P.L. 402, No. 56.
Article 17 GDRP. Right to erasure ('right to be forgotten'), European Union General Data Protection Regulation, 2018.
Civil Rights of Institutionalized Persons Act (CRIPA) (1980).
Balzac v. Porto Rico, 258 U.S. 298 (1922).
Bounds v. Smith, 430 U.S. 817 (1977).
Brady Handgun Violence Prevention Act of 1993.
Burwell v. Hobby Lobby Stores, 572 U.S. 682 (2014).
Castle Rock v. Gonzales, 545 U.S. 748 (2005).
Citizens United v. Federal Election Commission, 558 U.S. 310 (2010).
DeLima v. Bidwell, 182 U.S. 1 (1901).
DeShaney v. Winnebago County, 489 U.S. 189 (1989).
Downes v. Bidwell, 182 U.S. 244 (1901).
Fair Credit Reporting Act, 15 U.S.C § 1681.
Fugitive Slave Act of 1850.
Griggs v. Duke Power Co., 401 U.S. 424 (1971).
Haines v. Kerner, 404 U.S. 519 (1972).
Jacobellis v. Ohio, 378 U.S. 184 (1964).
Jones-Shafroth Act of 1917.
Kline v. 1500 Massachusetts Avenue Apartment Complex, 439 F.2d 477 (D.C. Cir. 1970).

Masterpiece Cakeshop, Ltd. v. Colorado Civil Rights Commission, 584 U.S. ___ (2018).
Mayweathers v. Newland, 258 F.3d (2001).
Prison Litigation Reform Act of 1995.
Quality Housing and Work Responsibility Act of 1998.
Rasul v. Bush, 542 U.S. 466 (2004).
Religious Freedom Restoration Act of 1993.
Roe v. Wade, 410 U.S. 113 (1973).
Ruffin v. Commonwealth, 62 Va. 790, 21 Gratt. 790 (1871).
Sutton v. Rasheed, 323 F.3d (2003).
Texas House Bill 1188, Legislative Session 83(R) (2013).
Texas Senate Bill 8, Sec. 171.208 Civil Liability for Violation or Aiding and Abetting Violation.
Trop v. Dulles, 356 U.S. 86 (1958).
Turner v. Safley, 482 U.S. 78 (1987).
United States v. Parrino, 212 F.2d 919 (2d Cir. 1954).
USA PATRIOT Act, Public Law 107–56.
Wards Cove Packing Co. v. Antonio, 109 U.S. 2115 (1989).
Weems v. United States, 217 U.S. 349 (1910).
Whole Woman's Health et al. v. Austin Reeve Jackson, Judge, et al. on application for injunctive relief, 594 U.S. ___ (2021).
Wolff v. McDonnell, 418 U.S. 539 (1974).

REFERENCES

Ahmed, Sarah. *Complaint!* Durham: Duke University Press, 2021.
Alexander, Michelle. *The New Jim Crow: Mass Incarceration in the Age of Colorblindness.* New York: The New Press, 2012.
Anderson, Elizabeth. *Private Government: How Employers Rule Our Lives (and Why We Don't Talk about It).* Princeton: Princeton University Press, 2017.
Arendt, Hannah. *The Origins of Totalitarianism.* San Diego: Harcourt Brace, 1973.
Banse, Rainer, Judith Koppehele-Gossel, Lisa M. Kistemaker, Verena A. Werner, and Alexander F. Schmidt. "Pro-criminal Attitudes, Intervention, and Recidivism." *Aggression and Violent Behavior* 18, no. 6 (2013): 673–685.
Becker, Gary S. "Crime and Punishment: An Economic Approach." *Journal of Political Economy* 76, no. 2 (1968): 169–217.
———. *The Economics of Discrimination.* 2nd ed. Chicago: University of Chicago Press, 1971.

———. *Human Capital: A Theoretical and Empirical Analysis with Special Reference to Education.* 3rd ed. Chicago: University of Chicago Press, 1993.

———. "Irrational Behavior and Economic Theory." *Journal of Political Economy* 70, no. 1 (1962): 1–13.

Becker, Gary S., François Ewald, and Bernard E. Harcourt. "Becker and Foucault on Crime and Punishment—A Conversation with Gary Becker, François Ewald, and Bernard Harcourt: The Second Session." University of Chicago Coase-Sandor Institute for Law and Economics Research Paper No. 654; University of Chicago Public Law and Legal Theory Working Paper No. 654; Columbia Law and Economics Working Paper No. 456, 2013.

Becker, Howard S. *Outsiders: Studies in the Sociology of Deviance.* Reprint. New York: Free Press, 1966.

Becker, Theodore M. "The Place of Private Police in Society: An Area of Research for the Social Sciences." *Social Problems* 21, no. 3 (1974): 438–453.

Belew, Kathleen. *Bring the War Home: The White Power Movement and Paramilitary America.* Cambridge, MA: Harvard University Press, 2018.

Bell, Emma. *Criminal Justice and Neoliberalism.* New York: Palgrave Macmillan, 2011.

Belton, Robert. "The Dismantling of the Griggs Disparate Impact Theory and the Future of Title VII: The Need for a Third Reconstruction." *Yale Law and Policy Review* 8, no. 2 (1990): 223–256.

Benjamin, Ruha, ed. *Captivating Technology: Race, Carceral Technoscience, and Laboratory Imagination in Everyday Life.* Durham: Duke University Press, 2019.

Benn, Piers. *Intellectual Freedom and the Culture Wars.* London: Palgrave Macmillan, 2021.

Bentham, Jeremy. *The Theory of Legislation.* 2nd ed. London: Routledge & Kegan Paul Ltd., 1950.

Berlant, Lauren. "Live Sex Acts (Parental Advisory: Explicit Material)." *Feminist Studies* 21, no. 2 (1995): 379–404.

———. *The Queen of America Goes to Washington City: Essays on Sex and Citizenship.* Durham: Duke University Press, 1997.

Brabazon, Honor, ed. *Neoliberal Legality: Understanding the Role of the Law in the Neoliberal Project.* New York: Routledge, 2018.

Brown, Wendy. *In the Ruins of Neoliberalism: The Rise of Antidemocratic Politics in the West.* New York: Columbia University Press, 2019.

———. *Undoing the Demos: Neoliberalism's Stealth Revolution.* New York: Zone, 2015.

———. *Walled States, Waning Sovereignty.* New York: Zone, 2010.

Butler, Judith. "Is Kinship Always Heterosexual?" *differences: A Journal of Feminist Cultural Studies* 13, no. 1 (2002): 14–44.

Camp, Jordan T. *Incarcerating the Crisis: Freedom Struggles and the Rise of the Neoliberal State.* Berkeley: University of California Press, 2016.

Cecil, Dawn K., and Jennifer L. Leitner. "Unlocking the Gates: An Examination of MSNBC Investigates—Lockup." *The Howard Journal* 48, no. 2 (2009): 184–199.

Chesney-Lind, Meda, and Lisa Pasko. *The Female Offender: Girls, Women, and Crime.* 2nd ed. Thousand Oaks: Sage, 2003.

Chin, Gabriel. "Collateral Consequences and Criminal Justice: Future Policy and Constitutional Directions." *Marquette Law Review* 102, no. 1 (2012): 233–260.

———. "The New Civil Death: Rethinking Punishment in the Era of Mass Incarceration." *University of Pennsylvania Law Review* 160 (2012): 1789–1833.

Churchwell, Sarah. *Behold America: A History of America First and the American Dream.* New York: Bloomsbury, 2019.

Coyle, Michael J. "Expanding Deviance toward Difference." In *The Death and Resurrection of Deviance*, edited by Michael Dellwing, Joe Kotarbe, and Nathan Pino, 68–84. New York: Palgrave Macmillan, 2014.

Crenshaw, Kimberlé. "Mapping the Margins: Intersectionality, Identity Politics, and Violence against Women of Color." *Stanford Law Review* 43, no. 6 (1991): 1241–1299.

Dardot, Pierre, and Christian Laval. *The New Way of the World: On Neoliberal Society.* London: Verso, 2017.

Davis, Angela Y. *Are Prisons Obsolete?* New York: Seven Stories, 2003.

Dayan, Colin (Joan). "Legal Slaves and Civil Bodies." *Nepantla: Views from the South* 2, no. 1 (2001): 3–39.

Dean, Mitchell, and Kaspar Villadsen. *State Phobia and Civil Society: The Political Legacy of Michel Foucault.* Stanford: Stanford University Press, 2016.

De Giorgi, Alessandro. "Back to Nothing: Prisoner Reentry and Neoliberal Neglect." *Social Justice* 44, no. 1 (2017): 83–120.

———. *Re-Thinking the Political Economy of Punishment: Perspectives on Post-Fordism and Penal Politics.* New York: Routledge, 2006.

Diamond, Andrew J., and Thomas J. Sugrue, eds. *Neoliberal Cities: The Remaking of Postwar Urban America.* New York: New York University Press, 2020.

Dilts, Andrew. *Punishment and Inclusion: Race, Membership, and the Limits of American Liberalism.* New York: Fordham University Press, 2014.

Dixon, Travis L. "Good Guys Are Still Always in White? Positive Change and Continued Misrepresentation of Race and Crime on Local Television News." *Communication Research* 44, no. 6 (2017): 775–792.

Dixon, Travis L., and Christina L. Azocar. "Priming Crime and Activating Blackness: Understanding the Psychological Impact of the Overrepresentation of Blacks as Lawbreakers on Television News." *Journal of Communication* 57, no. 2 (2007): 229–253.

Dixon, Travis L., and Keith B. Maddox. "Skin Tone, Crime News, and Social Reality Judgments: Priming the Stereotype of the Dark and Dangerous Black Criminal." *Journal of Applied Social Psychology* 35, no. 8 (2005): 1555–1570.

Draper, Nora A. "Reputation Anxiety: Consumer Background Checks and the Cultivation of Risk." *Communication and Culture Critique* 12, no. 1 (2019): 36–52.

Dressel, Julia, and Hany Farid. "The Accuracy, Fairness, and Limits of Predicting Recidivism." *Science Advances* 4, no. 1 (2018). https://doi.org/10.1126/sciadv.aao5580.

Edelman, Lauren B. *Working Law: Courts, Corporations, and Symbolic Civil Rights*. Chicago: University of Chicago Press, 2016.

Edgar, Kimmett, and Ian O'Donnell. "Assault in Prison: The Victim's Contribution." *British Journal of Criminology* 38, no. 4 (1998): 635–650.

Ewald, Alec C. "'Civil Death': The Ideological Paradox of Criminal Disenfranchisement Law in the United States." *Wisconsin Law Review* 2002, no. 5 (2002): 1045–1137.

Feeley, Malcolm, and Jonathan Simon. "Actuarial Justice: The Emerging New Criminal Law." In *The Futures of Criminology*, edited by David Nelken, 173–201. Thousand Oaks: Sage, 1994.

Feeley, Malcom, and Van Swearingen. "The Prison Conditions Cases and the Bureaucratization of American Corrections: Influences, Impacts and Implications." *Pace Law Review* 24, no. 2 (2004): 433–475.

Ferguson, Robert. *Inferno: An Anatomy of American Punishment*. Cambridge, MA: Harvard University Press, 2014.

Fernandes, Leela. "Conceptualizing the Post-Liberalization State: Intervention, Restructuring, and the Nature of State Power." In *Feminists Rethink the Neoliberal State: Inequality, Exclusion, and Change*, edited by Leela Fernandes, 1–31. New York: New York University Press, 2018.

Ferraro, Kathleen. *Neither Angels nor Demons: Women, Crime, and Victimization*. Evanston: Northwestern University Press, 2006.

Field, Douglas, ed. *American Cold War Culture*. Edinburgh University Press, 2005.

Fink, Sheri. *Five Days at Memorial: Life and Death in a Storm-Ravaged Hospital.* New York: Broadway Books, 2013.

Flippen, Chenoa A. "Racial and Ethnic Inequality in Homeownership and Housing Equity." *The Sociological Quarterly* 42, no. 2 (2001): 121–149.

Foucault, Michel. *The Birth of Biopolitics: Lectures at the Collège de France, 1978-79.* Translated by Graham Burchell. New York: Palgrave Macmillan, 2008.

———. *Discipline and Punish: The Birth of The Prison.* Translated by Alan Sheridan. New York: Vintage, 1995.

———. *The Punitive Society: Lectures at the Collège de France, 1972-73.* Translated by Graham Burchell. New York: Palgrave Macmillan, 2015.

———. *Security, Territory, Population: Lectures at the Collège de France, 1977-1978.* Translated by Graham Burchell. New York: Palgrave Macmillan, 2009.

Frazier, Patricia A., and Beth Haney. "Sexual Assault Cases in the Legal System: Police, Prosecutor, and Victim Perspectives." *Law and Human Behavior* 20, no. 6 (1996): 607–628.

Frenkel, Sheera, and Cecilia Kang. *An Ugly Truth: Inside Facebook's Battle for Domination.* New York: Harper Collins, 2021.

Friedman, Milton. *Capitalism and Freedom.* Fortieth Anniversary ed. Chicago: University of Chicago Press, 2002.

Gerstle, Gary. *The Rise and Fall of the Neoliberal Order: America and the World in the Free Market Era.* Oxford: Oxford University Press, 2022.

Gilmore, Ruth Wilson. *Abolition Geography: Essays towards Liberation.* Edited by Brenna Bhandar and Alberto Toscano. London: Verso, 2022.

———. *Golden Gulag: Prisons, Surplus, Crisis, and Opposition in Globalizing California.* Berkeley: University of California Press, 2007.

Gilmore, Ruth Wilson (with Craig Gilmore). "Restating the Obvious." In *Abolition Geography: Essays towards Liberation,* edited by Brenna Bhandar and Alberto Toscano, 259–287. London: Verso, 2022.

Ginsburg, Raphael. "Mighty Crime Victims: Victims' Rights and Neoliberalism in the American Conjuncture." In *Cultural Studies and the "Juridical Turn,"* edited by Jaafar Aksikas and Sean Johnson Andrews, 170–205. New York: Routledge, 2016.

Glesner, B. A. "Landlords as Cops: Tort, Nuisance, and Forfeiture Standards Imposing Liability on Landlords for Crime on the Premises." *Case Western Reserve Law Review* 42, no. 3 (1992): 679–791.

Gootenberg, Paul. "Talking about the Flow: Drugs, Borders, and the Discourse of Drug Control." *Cultural Critique* 71, no. 1 (2009): 13–46.

Gottschalk, Marie. *Caught: The Prison State and the Lockdown of American Politics*. Princeton: Princeton University Press, 2016.

———. *The Prison and the Gallows: The Politics of Mass Incarceration in America*. Cambridge, MA: Cambridge University Press, 2006.

Graeber, David. *Debt: The First 5000 Years*. Brooklyn: Melville House, 2014.

Gramlich, John. "Most Violent and Property Crimes in the US Go Unsolved." Pew Research Center. March 1, 2017. https://www.pewresearch.org/fact-tank/2017/03/01/most-violent-and-property-crimes-in-the-u-s-go-unsolved/.

Hall, Stuart. "The Neo-liberal Revolution." *Cultural Studies* 25, no. 6 (2011): 705–728.

Hall, Stuart, Chas Critcher, Tony Jefferson, John Clarke, and Brian Roberts. *Policing the Crisis: Mugging, The State, and Law and Order*. 35th Anniversary ed. London: Red Globe Press, 2013.

Han, Byung-Chul. *Psychopolitics: Neoliberalism and New Technologies of Power*. London: Verso, 2017.

Harcourt, Bernard E. *The Counterrevolution: How Our Government Went to War against its Own Citizens*. New York: Basic Books, 2018.

———. *Exposed: Desire and Disobedience in the Digital Age*. Cambridge, MA: Harvard University Press, 2015.

———. "Neoliberal Penality: A Brief Genealogy." *Theoretical Criminology* 14, no. 1 (2010): 74–92.

Hardt, Michael. "The Withering of Civil Society." *Social Text* 45 (Winter 1995): 27–44.

Harrison, Ben. *True Crime Narratives: An Annotated Bibliography*. Lanham: Scarecrow, 1997.

Harvey, David. *A Brief History of Neoliberalism*. Oxford: Oxford University Press, 2005.

Hawkins, Stephen, Daniel Yudkin, Míriam Juan-Torres, and Tim Dixon. *Hidden Tribes: A Study of America's Polarized Landscape*. New York: More in Common. 2018. https://hiddentribes.us.

Hayek, F. A. *The Road to Serfdom*. 1944. 2nd edition, New York: Routledge, 2006.

Hedges, Chris. *Wages of Rebellion: The Moral Imperative of Revolt*. New York: Nation Books, 2015.

Hinton, Elizabeth. *From the War on Poverty to the War on Crime: The Making of Mass Incarceration in America*. Cambridge, MA: Harvard University Press, 2016.

Hofer, Paul J., Kevin R. Blackwell, and R. Barry Ruback. "The Effect of Federal

Sentencing Guidelines on Judge Sentencing Disparity." *Journal of Criminal Law and Criminology* 90, no. 1 (1999): 239–322.

Hull, Elizabeth A. *The Disenfranchisement of Ex-Felons.* Philadelphia: Temple University Press, 2009.

Human Rights Watch. *No Escape: Male Rape in U.S. Prisons.* 2001. www.hrw.org/reports/2001/prison/.

Irwin, John. *The Jail: Managing the Underclass in American Society.* Reprint. Berkeley: University of California Press, 2013.

Jackson, Robert H. "The Federal Prosecutor." *American Institute of Criminal Law and Criminology* 3, no. 3 (1940): 3–6.

Jacobs, James B. *The Eternal Criminal Record.* Cambridge, MA: Harvard University Press, 2015.

Johnson, Amanda. "Challenging Criminal Records in Hiring under the Americans with Disabilities Act." *Columbia Human Rights Law Review* 48, no. 3 (2017): 212–256.

Kaiser, Joshua. "We Know It When We See It: The Tenuous Line between 'Direct Punishment' and 'Collateral Consequences.'" *Howard Law Journal* 59, no. 2 (2016): 341–372.

Kaplan, Amy. "Where is Guantánamo?" *American Quarterly* 57, no. 3 (2005): 831–858.

Keefe, Patrick Radden. *Empire of Pain: The Secret History of the Sackler Family.* New York: Doubleday, 2021.

Kelley, Robin D. G. *Yo' Mama's Dysfunctional! Fighting the Culture Wars in Urban America.* 10th Anniversary ed. Boston: Beacon, 2008.

Kinder, Douglas Clark. "Bureaucratic Cold Warrior: Harry J. Anslinger and Illicit Narcotics Traffic." *The Pacific Historical Review* 50, no. 2 (1981): 169–191.

Kipnis, Laura. *Unwanted Advances: Sexual Paranoia Comes to Campus.* New York: HarperCollins, 2017.

Klein, Naomi. *The Shock Doctrine: The Rise of Disaster Capitalism.* New York: Metropolitan Books, 2007.

Koenig, Alexa. "From Man to Beast: Social Death at Guantánamo." In *Extreme Punishment: Comparative Studies in Detention, Incarceration, and Solitary Confinement,* edited by Keramet Reiter and Alexa Koenig, 220–241. New York: Palgrave Macmillan, 2015.

Kohler-Hausmann, Julilly. *Getting Tough: Welfare and Imprisonment in 1970s America.* Princeton: Princeton University Press, 2017.

Krivo, Lauren J., and Robert L. Kaufman. "Housing and Wealth Inequality:

Racial-Ethnic Difference in Home Equity in the United States." *Demography* 41, no. 3 (2004): 585–605.

Lamb, H. Richard, and Linda Weinberger. "The Shift of Psychiatric Inpatient Care from Hospitals to Jails and Prisons." *Journal of the American Academy of Psychiatry and the Law* 33, no. 4 (2005): 529–534.

Lévi-Strauss, Claude. *Tristes Tropiques*. Translated by John Russell. New York: Criterion, 1961.

Lichtenstein, Alex. *Twice the Work of Free Labor: The Political Economy of Convict Labor in the New South*. London: Verso, 1996.

Logan, Wayne. "Informal Collateral Consequences." *Washington Law Review* 88, no. 3 (2013): 1103–1117.

López-Guerra, Claudio. *Democracy and Disenfranchisement: The Morality of Electoral Exclusions*. Oxford: Oxford University Press, 2014.

Low, Setha. *Behind the Gates: Life, Security, and the Pursuit of Happiness in Fortress America*. New York: Routledge, 2003.

———. "Maintaining Whiteness: The Fear of Others and Niceness." *Transforming Anthropology* 17, no. 2 (2009): 79–92.

Luxon, Nancy, ed. *Archives of Infamy: Foucault on State Power in the Lives of Ordinary Citizens*. Minneapolis: University of Minnesota Press, 2019.

Lyotard, Jean-François. *The Postmodern Condition: A Report on Knowledge*. Translated by Geoff Bennington and Brian Massumi. Manchester: Manchester University Press, 1984.

Mahoney, Peter E. "The End(s) of Disparate Impact: Doctrinal Reconstruction, Fair Housing and Lending Law, and the Antidiscrimination Principle." *Emory Law Journal* 47, no. 2 (1998): 409–425.

Malik, Nesrine. *We Need New Stories: The Myths that Subvert Freedom*. New York: W. W. Norton, 2022.

Manza, Jeff, and Christopher Uggen. *Locked Out: Felon Disenfranchisement and American Democracy*. Oxford: Oxford University Press, 2008.

Mayson, Sandra G. "Collateral Consequences and the Preventive State." *Notre Dame Law Review* 91, no. 1 (2015): 301–362.

McBride, Kealey. *Punishment and Political Order*. Ann Arbor: University of Michigan Press, 2007.

Meléndez, Edgardo. "Citizenship and the Alien Exclusion in the *Insular Cases*: Puerto Ricans in the Periphery of American Empire." *Centro Journal* 25, no. 1 (2013): 106–145.

Melossi, Dario, and Massimo Pavarini. *The Prison and the Factory: Origins of the Penitentiary System*. London: Macmillan, 1981.

Melzer, Nils. *The Trial of Julian Assange: A Story of Persecution.* London: Verso, 2022.

Mill, John Stuart. *Essays on Economics and Society.* Toronto: University of Toronto Press, 1967.

Miller, Reuben Jonathan. *Halfway Home: Race, Punishment, and the Afterlife of Mass Incarceration.* New York: Little, Brown and Company, 2021.

Mills, Charles W. *The Racial Contract.* Ithaca: Cornell University Press, 1999.

Morales, Claribel. "Constitutional Law—Puerto Rico and the Ambiguity within the Federal Courts." *Western New England Law Review* 42, no. 2 (2020): 245–258.

Morris, Kate Linen. "'Within Constitutional Limitations': Challenging Criminal Background Checks by Public Housing Authorities under the Fair Housing Act." *Columbia Human Rights Law Review* 47, no. 2 (2016): 158–199.

National Inventory of Collateral Consequences of Conviction. https://niccc .nationalreentryresourcecenter.org.

National Registry for Exonerations. "Age and Mental Status of Exonerated Defendants Who Confessed." April 18, 2022. https://www.law.umich.edu /special/exoneration/Documents/Age%20and%20Mental%20Status%20F INAL%20CHART.pdf.

Nordenhaug, Erik, and Jack Simmons. "The Outsourcing of Ethical Thinking." In *The Twenty-First Century and Its Discontents*, edited by Jack Simmons, 15–37. Lanham: Lexington Books, 2020.

O'Hara, S. Paul. *Inventing the Pinkertons or, Spies, Sleuths, Mercenaries and Thugs.* Baltimore: Johns Hopkins University Press, 2016.

O'Hear, Michael. "Third-Class Citizenship: The Escalating Legal Consequences of Committing a 'Violent' Crime." *The Journal of Criminal Law and Criminology* 109, no. 2 (2019): 165–235.

Oliveri, Rigel C. "Beyond Disparate Impact: How the Fair Housing Movement Can Move On." *Washburn Law Journal* 54, no. 3 (2015). LexisNexis.

Ong, Aihwa. *Neoliberalism as Exception: Mutations in Citizenship and Sovereignty.* Durham: Duke University Press, 2006.

Oyama, Rebecca. "Do Not (Re)Enter: The Rise of Criminal Background Tenant Screenings as a Violation of the Fair Housing Act." *Michigan Journal of Race and Law* 15, no. 1 (2009): 181–222.

Pager, Devah. "The Mark of a Criminal Record." *American Journal of Sociology* 108, no. 5 (2003): 937–975.

Pager, Devah, Bruce Western, and Naomi Sugie. "Sequencing Disadvantage: Barriers to Employment Facing Young Black and White Men with

Criminal Records." *The Annals of the American Academy of Political and Social Science* 623, no. 1 (2009): 195–213.

Patterson, Orlando. *Slavery and Social Death: A Comparative Study.* Cambridge, MA: Harvard University Press, 1982.

Pinedo, Victor J. "Let's Keep It Civil: An Evaluation of Civil Disabilities, a Call for Reform, and Recommendations to Reduce Recidivism." *Cornell Law Review* 102 , no. 2 (2017): 513–545.

Posner, Richard A. "An Economic Theory of the Criminal Law." *Columbia Law Review* 85, no. 6 (1985): 1193–1231.

Prins, Seth J. "Does Transinstitutionalization Explain the Overrepresentation of People with Serious Mental Illnesses in the Criminal Justice System?" *Community Mental Health Journal* 47, no. 6 (2011): 716–722.

Ravenelle, Alexandrea J. *Hustle and Gig: Struggling and Surviving in the Sharing Economy.* Berkeley: University of California Press, 2019.

Read, Jason. "A Genealogy of Homo-Economicus: Neoliberalism and the Production of Subjectivity." *Foucault Studies*, no. 6 (2009): 25–36.

Reeves, Joshua. "If You See Something Say Something: Lateral Surveillance and the Uses of Responsibility." *Surveillance and Society* 10, no. 3/4 (2012): 235–248.

Ristroph, Alice. "An Intellectual History of Mass Incarceration." *Boston College Law Review* 60, no. 7 (2019): 1949–2010.

Roberts, Anna. "Conviction by Prior Impeachment." *Boston University Law Review* 96, no. 6 (2016): 1977–2036.

———. "Impeachment by Unreliable Conviction." *Boston College Law Review* 55, no. 2 (2014): 563–639.

———. "Reclaiming the Importance of the Defendant's Testimony: Prior Conviction Impeachment and the Fight against Implicit Stereotyping." *University of Chicago Law Review* 83, no. 2 (2016): 835–891.

Roberts, Jenny. "Ignorance Is Effectively Bliss: Collateral Consequences, Silence, and Misinformation in the Guilty-Plea Process." *Iowa Law Review* 95, no. 1 (2009): 119–194.

Robinson, Cedric J. *Black Marxism: The Making of the Black Radical Tradition.* 2nd ed. Chapel Hill: University of North Carolina Press, 2000.

Ronner, Amy D. "The Cassandra Curse: The Stereotype of the Female Liar Resurfaces in *Jones v. Clinton.*" *UC Davis Law Review* 31, no. 1 (1997): 123–129.

Russell-Brown, Katherine. *The Color of Crime: Racial Hoaxes, White Crime, Media Messages, Police Violence, and Other Race-Based Harms.* 3rd ed. New York: New York University Press, 2021.

Schept, Judah. *Progressive Punishment: Job Loss, Jail Growth, and the Neoliberal Logic of Carceral Expansion.* New York: New York University Press, 2015.

Schneider, Valerie. "Racism Knocking at the Door: The Use of Criminal Background Checks in Rental Housing." *University of Richmond Law Review* 53, no. 3 (2019): 923–947.

Seigel, Micol. *Violence Work: State Power and the Limits of the Police.* Durham: Duke University Press, 2018.

Selmi, Michael. "Proving Intentional Discrimination: The Reality of Supreme Court Rhetoric." *Georgetown Law Journal* 86, no. 2 (1997): 279–350.

———. "Was the Disparate Impact Theory a Mistake?" *UCLA Law Review* 53 (2006): 701–782.

Shannon, Sarah K. S., Christopher Uggen, Jason Schnittker, Melissa Thompson, Sara Wakefield, and Michael Massoglia. "The Growth, Scope, and Spatial Distribution of People with Felony Records in the United States, 1948–2010." *Demography* 54, no. 5 (2017): 1795–1818.

Shearing, Clifford D., and Philip C. Stenning. "Modern Private Security: Its Growth and Operations." *Crime and Justice* 3 (1981): 193–245.

Sheffi, Nofar. "We Accept: The Constitution of Airbnb." *Transnational Legal Theory* 11, no. 4 (2020): 484–520.

Smith, Adam. *An Inquiry into the Nature and Causes of the Wealth of Nations.* London: W. Strahan & T. Caddell, 1776. Reprinted and edited by Edwin Cannan. Chicago: University of Chicago Press, 1977.

Stigler, George J. "The Optimum Enforcement of Laws." *Journal of Political Economy* 78, no. 3 (1970): 526–536.

Story, Brett. *Prison Land: Mapping Carceral Power across Neoliberal America.* Minneapolis: University of Minnesota Press, 2019.

Summs, Jacqueline Haley. "Grappling with Inmates' Access to Justice: The Narrowing of the Exhaustion Requirement in *Ross v. Blake.*" *Administrative Law Review* 69, no. 2 (2017): 467–494.

Swearingen, Van. "Imprisoning Rights: The Failure of Negotiated Governance in the Prison Inmate Grievance Process." *California Law Review* 96, no. 5 (2008): 1353–1382.

Thatcher, David. "The Rise of Criminal Background Screening in Rental Housing." *Law and Social Inquiry* 33, no. 1 (2008): 5–30.

Thompkins, Douglas E. "The Expanding Prisoner Reentry Industry." *Dialectal Anthropology* 34, no. 4 (2010): 589–604.

Thompson, Joel A., and G. Larry Mays, eds. *American Jails: Public Policy Issues.* Chicago: Nelson-Hall, 1991.

Tokatlian, Juan G. "National Security and Drugs: Their Impact on Colombian-US Relations." *Journal of Interamerican Studies and World Affairs* 30, no. 1 (1988): 133–160.

Torruella, Juan R. "Ruling America's Colonies: The *Insular Cases*." *Yale Law and Policy Review* 32, no. 1 (2013): 57–95.

Tversky, Amos, and Daniel Kahneman. "Judgment under Uncertainty: Heuristics and Biases." In *Judgement under Uncertainty: Heuristics and Biases*, edited by Daniel Kahneman, Paul Slovic, and Amos Tversky, 3–20. 1982. Reprint. Cambridge: Cambridge University Press, 2008.

United States Department of Housing and Urban Development. "Office of General Counsel Guidance on Application of Fair Housing Act Standards to the Use of Criminal Records by Providers of Housing and Real Estate-Related Transactions." Washington, DC: United States Department of Housing and Urban Development, 2016.

———. *Housing Discrimination against Racial and Ethnic Minorities 2012*. Washington, DC: United States Department of Housing and Urban Development, 2013.

Valentine, Bettylou. *Hustling and Other Hard Work: Lifestyles in the Ghetto*. New York: Free Press, 1978.

Vatter, Miguel. *The Republic of the Living: Biopolitics and the Critique of Civil Society*. New York: Fordham University Press, 2014.

Ventura, Patricia. *Neoliberal Culture: Living with American Neoliberalism*. New York: Routledge, 2012.

Wacquant, Loïc. "Inside the Zone: The Social Art of the Hustler in the Black American Ghetto." *Theory, Culture, and Society* 15, no. 2 (1998): 1–36.

———. *Punishing the Poor: The Neoliberal Government of Social Insecurity*. Durham: Duke University Press, 2009.

Wang, Jackie. *Carceral Capitalism*. Cambridge, MA: Semiotext(e), 2018.

Warner, Judith Ann. *Women and Crime: A Reference Handbook*. Santa Barbara: ABC-CLIO, 2012.

Weare, Neil. "Why the *Insular Cases* Must Become the Next Plessy." *Harvard Law Review Blog*. March 28, 2018. https://blog.harvardlawreview.org/why-the-insular-cases-must-become-the-next-plessy/.

Western, Bruce, and Katherine Beckett. "How Unregulated Is the US Labor Market? The Penal Institution as a Labor Market Institution." *American Journal of Sociology* 104, no. 4 (1999): 1030–1060.

Williams, Patricia. *The Alchemy of Race and Rights*. Cambridge, MA: Harvard University Press, 1991.

Willse, Craig. *The Value of Homelessness: Managing Surplus Life in the United States*. Minneapolis: University of Minnesota Press, 2015.

Wilmot, Keith A., and Cassia Spohn. "Prosecutorial Discretion and Real-Offense Sentencing: An Analysis of Relevant Conduct under the Federal Sentencing Guidelines." *Criminal Justice Policy Review* 15, no. 3 (2004): 324–343.

Woodall, Denise. "Interrupting Cultural Constructions of the Criminalized Other through a Revised Criminal Activities Checklist Classroom Exercise." *Teaching Sociology* 45, no. 2 (2016): 161–167.

Wüschner, Philipp. "Shame, Guilt, and Punishment." *Foucault Studies*, no. 23 (2017): 86–107.

Yarborough, Marilyn, and Crystal Bennet. "Cassandra and the 'Sistahs': The Peculiar Treatment of African American Women and the Myth of Women as Liars." *Journal of Gender, Race, and Justice* 3, no. 2 (2000): 625–657.

York, Jillian C. *Silicon Values: The Future of Free Speech under Surveillance Capitalism*. London: Verso, 2020.

Young, Alison. *Imagining Crime*. Thousand Oaks: Sage, 1996.

Index

Abbot, Greg, 179
abortions, 179, 180
abuse: child, 176, 207n62; institutional power and, 149; of prisoners, 58, 79; sexual, 148, 156, 177
Acadia Healthcare, 52–53
accountability, 64, 148, 157, 175, 217n10
Acorns, 143
activism: judicial, 64, 134; racial/gender justice, 146; social justice, 146, 174; victims' rights, 66, 69
addiction, 33, 34, 35, 48, 52, 53, 54, 66, 84, 111
adjudication, 131, 132, 177, 185, 188; administrative, 21, 25, 54, 55, 57, 63, 68, 69, 118; of behavior, 143, 185; and cancel culture, 146, 154, 163, 172, 173, 187, 188; extralegal, 182, 183; of inmate grievances, 78; private or corporate, 1, 2, 20, 21, 22, 118, 120, 136, 143, 157, 184, 185, 186, 187, 188; process, 2, 57–58, 158, 173
ADT, 181
agricultural sector, 3, 27, 35, 194n10
Ahmed, Sarah, 157
Airbnb, 10, 15, 20, 26, 127–128, 140, 141, 143, 144, 163; antidiscrimination policy of, 127, 142; banishment by, 26, 118, 119, 120, 121, 123, 125, 126, 127–128, 129, 138, 142, 166; collateral consequences and, 124; employment relation and, 141; policies of, 123–125; racial discrimination and, 119, 129; sanction regimes and, 124; short-term rental market and, 122, 138, 139; target demographic of, 128–129; terms of service and, 141, 143

Airbnb magazine, 128–129
alcohol treatment. See drug and alcohol treatment
Alexander, Michelle, 35
algorithms, 49, 100, 118, 126, 159, 172; corporate decision-making and, 15, 119, 122, 124; criminal justice system and, 79
Allen, Woody, 177
Amazon, 42, 143, 146
American Airlines, 1, 2, 146, 147
American Apartment Owners Association (AAOA), 115
American Society for Industrial Security, 107
Americans with Disabilities Act, 213–214n70
America's Most Wanted, 90, 145, 152
Anderson, Elizabeth, 19, 140
Angola Prison, 196n25
Anslinger, Harry, 33
anticommunist sentiment, 32–33
antipolitics, 49, 186
Apple, 23, 51, 146; Hong Kong uprisings and, 6, 7
assault, 56, 67, 68, 146, 147; aggravated, 136; crime of, 1; as disruption, 1, 21; judicial, 28. See also sexual assault
authoritarianism, 7, 23, 31, 32, 34, 35
Autohost, 122, 139

background checks, 17, 106, 115, 123; criminal, 92, 112, 116, 123, 196; employee, 92, 108, 130, 109, 125; tenant, 112, 116, 125. See also consumer background reports
bad actors, 2, 20, 22, 26, 147, 151, 155, 188

241

lateral surveillance and, 146; as mode of justice, 147; popular justice and, 154, 155, 175, 187; post–juridical order of, 26, 175; as punishment, 154, 156; vigilante justice of, 152, 175, 181

cancellation, 146, 149, 155, 173, 187, 188; culture wars and, 153–154; personal consequences of, 177; poetic justice and, 148

capital: cultural, 184; economic, 5, 184; financial, 16, 75, 104, 116; legal, 184; political, 116, 129; social, 24; symbolic, 16, 24, 104, 116, 139, 184; transfer of, 185. *See also* human capital

capitalism, 10, 18, 37, 39, 42, 44, 46, 47, 65, 125, 140, 185; carceral, 54; China and, 7; disaster, 27; discrimination and, 46, 200n75; financial, 38; Jim Crow, 35; laissez-faire, 3; mass incarceration and, 37; penal system and, 10, 36, 47, 100–101, 140, 185; political ideals and, 7; racial, 5, 6, 36; social life and, 10

Capitalism and Freedom (Friedman), 8, 190n11, 204n33

Capitol riot, 220n16

Carter, Jimmy, 32

Castle Rock v. Gonzales (2005), 207n62

Chapelle, Dave, 147

Cheney, Dick, 28

Chicago School, 27, 29, 30, 90, 194n1, 201n94

Chile experiment, 27, 29

Chin, Gabriel, 12, 87, 88, 89

Chinese Basketball Association, 6

citizen, 1, 8–9, 11, 14, 28, 29, 31, 55, 57, 60, 61, 90, 135, 190n13; border policing, 182–183; bounty hunters, 180, 183; class, 76, 77; non-, 63–74; quasi-, 63–64, 138, 165; self-protection, 89–90, 91, 145–146, 181; victims, 63–74, 92

Citizen (application), 146

Citizen Defenders, 182, 184

citizenship, 1, 11, 14, 24, 25, 36, 42, 60, 64, 76; colonial, 61; criminal conviction and, 11, 14, 24, 95; criminality and, 73, 192n29; defining, 73; downsizing, 63, 72, 73; exercising, 1, 11; infantile, 73; measuring, 72; normative, 92, 102; participatory, 95; status, 108

Citizens United v. Federal Election Commission (2010), 24, 193n48

civic life, 24, 42, 73, 218n30

civic standing, 38, 80, 86

civil death. *See* death

civil liberties, 161

civil rights, 21–22, 85, 87, 88, 133–136, 146, 157, 158, 168, 173, 175, 183, 187; adjudication of, 143; Black Americans and, 29–30; circumventing, 110–118; limitations of, 38; loss of, 88; pursuing, 30, 135; transformation of, 134; violation of, 146, 158

Civil Rights of Institutionalized Person Act (CRIPA) (1980), 135

civil society. *See* Foucault

class, 8, 33, 40, 48, 70, 71, 76, 125, 127–129, 139, 193n46, 205n33, 209n18; aspirational, 139; conflict, 73; criminal, 77, 83, 103; non-optimized, 45; professional, 119; sexually suspicious, 20; under-, 35, 47, 54. *See also* working class

Clean Slate Act (2018), 129, 217n18

Cleveland.com, 130, 132, 133, 136

codes, 74; criminal, 73, 124, 137, 187; federal, 17; institutional, 167, 168, 171; internalization of, 169; legal, 154, 156, 175; regulatory, 17

Cold War, 31, 32, 33, 35

collateral consequences, 5–18, 85, 86, 120, 126, 130, 137, 138, 143; civil death and, 12; consumer background report industry and, 83; disenfranchisement and, 11–12; informal, 15, 121; privately administered, 10, 14, 15–16, 94, 120;

crime rates, 165–166, 186

Crime Scene: The Vanishing at the Cecil Hotel (documentary series), 152

Crime Victims' Rights Act (CVRA) (2004), 68, 69, 70

criminal defendants, 63, 120; challenges by, 88; impeaching, 216n3; intimidation of, 191n26; rights of, 56, 88; treatment of, 133, 137

criminal history, 16, 100, 111, 109, 125, 127, 129, 132; gun purchases and, 102; records, 103

criminality, 2, 21, 35, 43, 47, 72, 93, 102, 108, 112, 115, 125, 143, 165; Blackness and, 33; causes of, 99; concept of, 96; conflating, 118; excess of, 144; future, 121, 123; mass, 31, 37, 152; (non)citizenship and, 74; prior, 116; private government and, 145; question of, 73; racialized, 31, 196n24; rhetoric of, 116; stigma of, 139; transformation of, 92

criminal justice system, 3, 9, 10, 14, 19, 28, 30, 37, 66, 75, 85, 86, 87, 93, 96, 98, 102, 120, 145, 165, 167, 169; bureaucratization of, 91, 186; democratic norms/rights and, 64; expansion of, 18; failure of, 54, 148, 175; law and order and, 5; managerial expertise and, 137; operations of, 4; people of color and, 113; purpose/function of, 47; racial discrimination in, 115, 171; reform of, 94, 160; respect for, 80; success of, 20; transformation of, 30, 79, 96; trust in, 81

criminal procedure, 20, 80, 89, 120, 121, 136, 215n2; ambiguities in, 137

criminal records, 17, 85, 89, 113, 115, 120, 122, 125, 166; availability of, 110; fair treatment and, 130; impact of, 83; permanent, 137; perpetual risks of, 144; predictive logic of, 127; reliance on, 169; systematizing/streamlining, 102

criminals, 86, 165; Black, 200n84; as a defective condition, 92; legal standing of, 64; non-citizen, 63–74; screening process and, 108; slavery and, 57; as social enemies, 92, 93; social evaluation of, 70; treatment of, 10

Criminal Sentiment Scale—Modified (CSS), 80, 81

criminology, 95, 151, 165

CSS. *See* Criminal Sentiment Scale—Modified

cultural acceptance, 172, 187

cultural norms, 73, 158, 185; assimilation of, 140; medicalization of, 186; neoliberalism and, 186

culture, 25, 167, 183; law-and-order, 2; meaning/power and, 25; national, 72; of online rumors, 153; popular, 25, 148, 152, 188; punitive, 2; Reaganite, 73; woke, 163

culture wars, 26, 71, 147; cancel culture and, 159–164; cancellation and, 153–154; as popularity contest, 161

CVRA. *See* Crime Victims' Rights Act

Dardot, Pierre, 40

Davis, Angela, 35

Dean, Mitchell, 3, 189n2, 201n85

death, 217n10; civil, 12, 62, 89; social, 30, 62, 164

death penalty, 2, 12, 66

decision-making, 44, 125, 138, 142, 145, 187; ad hoc, 124, 126, 127, 131, 186; algorithmic, 119; ethical, 168; influence on, 126; political, 44, 166, 172; prosecutorial, 76

DeGeneres, Ellen, 147, 148, 149

De Giorgi, Alessandro, 84, 138, 218n30

DeLima v. Bidwell (1901), 60

Democratic Party, 23, 175

Deng Xiaoping, 7

deplatforming, 147, 160, 174

employment, 129, 141, 142; Black urban, 194n10; denial of, 89; law/rights and, 133; limiting opportunities to, 38; loss of, 88, 145, 157; mandatory, 85 enforcement, 17, 90, 180; child support, 105. *See also* law enforcement

Equal Employment Opportunity Commission (EEOC), 109, 110, 134, 135

Eskamani, Anna, 24, 193n48

ethics, 167, 169, 172, 173; practice of, 168; professional, 171

ethnocentrism, 149, 175

Etsy, 143

European Court of Justice, 130

Ewald, François, 199–200n73

exclusion, 165, 175; arbitrary, 17; communal, 19, 121–129; institutional, 118; mechanism of, 82; social, 84, 126

Expedia, 143

Facebook, 9, 19, 22, 23, 25, 51, 143, 144, 159, 163, 188, 194n7; removal by, 127; speech policies by, 126, 127

Fair Credit Reporting Act (FCRA), 17, 109–110, 122, 133; compliance with, 107; FTC and, 104; Section 604 of, 105, 106

Fair Housing Act (1968), 114

fascist states, planned economies and, 31–32

FBI, 11, 127, 152, 217n15, 220n16

FCRA. *See* Fair Credit Reporting Act

Federal Bureau of Narcotics, 33

Federal Rules of Evidence, 120, 215–216n3

Federal Trade Commission (FTC), 104, 212n61

Feeley, Malcolm, 64, 96, 98

felonies: conviction for, 9, 11, 12; non-violent, 12; pressing charges and, 75, 108; violent, 12

felons, 95; disenfranchisement of,

11–12, 13, 93–94, 102; law barring, 16; punishment of, 100

fentanyl, 53

Fifth Amendment, 68, 156

financial problems, 36, 51

fines, 21, 87, 88, 94, 97, 121

Florida, Chapter 961 (2020 Florida Statutes), 12

Forbes, 149, 159

Ford Motor Company, 140, 185

Foucault, Michel, 24, 31, 151, 155, 184, 185, 198n52, 199–200n73, 220n14, 221n23; actuarial justice and, 97; banishment and, 164, 165; Becker and, 199n73; capitalism/penitentiary and, 10, 47, 100–101, 140, 185; circulation of power and, 100, 165–166; civil society and, 46, 47, 200n78, 200–201n85; criminality and, 92–93; governmentality and, 3, 4, 39, 45, 46, 98, 101, 189n2, 199n73; infamy and, 149, 154, 171; neoliberalism and, 3, 32, 38–40, 45–46, 96, 199n73; punishment and, 149–151; statification and, 4, 101; theory of state and, 3, 4, 189n2

Fourteenth Amendment, 68

Fourth Amendment, 16

freedom, 7; of assembly, 77; economic, 8, 141; political, 8, 141; reducing, 204–205n33; religious 24, 76, 78, 206n11; of speech, 4, 6, 24, 76

free markets, 8, 9, 18, 139

free trade, 23, 27

Frenkel, Sheera, 22, 126

Friedman, Milton, 7–9, 24, 34, 43, 141, 190n13, 198n52; Chicago School Revolution and, 27; on freedom, 7–9, 204n33; on monopoly, 39; paternalism and, 8, 9; small government and, 190n11

Fugitive Slave Act (1850), 183–184

Fuller, Justice Melville Weston, 61

on, 144; criminal records and, 122; crisis, 51–52; denial of, 89; insecurity in, 53–54, 122; loss of, 145; market, 16, 110, 125; people of color and, 113; private, 15; projects, 111, 112; public, 50, 111, 112; search for, 210n26; short-term, 122

Housing First policy, Utah, 50

Houston Rockets, Hong Kong uprisings and, 6

HR Research Institute, 92

HRW. *See* Human Rights Watch

HUD. *See* US Department of Housing and Urban Development

human capital, 42, 43, 44, 45. *See also* Gary Becker

human resources, 109, 132, 134, 136, 157, 158, 163, 169

Human Rights Watch (HRW), 66, 67

Hume, David, 40

Hurricane Katrina, 28, 167

hustling, 138–139

hyphenated Americans, 33, 195n19

identity, 146, 160, 163, 215n3; collective, 40; marker of, 71; national, 72, 73; nationalism and, 9; social, 73; unstable, 33; victim, 154

Ikea, 15

Illinois State Penitentiary, 56

immorality, 73, 101, 140

Imperial Courts, 112

imperialism, 28, 58, 59

incarceration, 36, 82, 84, 98, 99; mass, 29, 30–31, 36, 47, 48, 65, 102, 111, 152; rates of, 37, 203n25

Indiana Women's Prison, 160

inequality, 40, 51; racial/gender, 45; structural, 125

infamy: cancel culture and, 155–156; intensity of, 154–155, 156, 159; model of, 147–159

infrastructure, 18, 19; criminal records, 103; education as, 42; human capital and, 43; market-based, 91; privatization of, 190n11

Instacart, 9, 139

Instagram, 9

Insular Cases, 60, 61, 63, 202n12

insurance companies, 45, 53, 186

internet, 132, 153, 154, 155, 158, 161, 188

Interstate Identification Index (Triple I), 37, 102

intervention, 32–33, 36, 37, 41, 99; environmentalist, 42, 44; in market by state, 38, 39, 42, 44, 45, 96, 200n75

Jackson, Robert, 102

Jacobellis v. Ohio (1964), 216n10

Jacobs, James B., 102, 213n63

Jim Crow, 35

job training, 45, 49, 166; participation in, 44; programs, 24, 48, 188

Johnson, Lyndon B., 32

Jones, Michelle, 160, 174

Jones Act (1917), 60

judgment: administrative, 55; collective, 155; ethical, 167, 168, 172; intuitive, 170; juridical, 154; moral, 5, 124, 132, 167, 168, 172; probabilistic, 170; psychological, 154, 155, 158, 164–173

judicial order, 46, 145, 175

jury trial, 60, 89

justice, 25; actuarial, 97, 98, 99–100, 165; administration of, 80; cancel culture and, 154, 155, 175, 187; contemporary, 186; gender, 147, 173; ideal, 156; modes of, 154; neoliberal social contract and, 18; Old West system of, 152; outsourcing, 157; popular, 152, 155, 173, 187; post-juridical mode of, 175; public perception of, 121; public-private, 4;

privacy, 69, 72; invasions of, 16;
protecting, 130; technology companies
and, 126
private interests, 19, 29, 89, 120, 154, 186,
202n99
private property: protecting, 181–182;
respect for, 129
private sector, 120, 166, 199n67; public
sector and, 87
privatization, 27, 31; of infrastructure,
190n11; of military, 28; of security, 91
probation, 73, 87, 88; terms of, 11, 85, 121;
violations of, 218n30. *See also* parole
productification, 25, 85, 188. *See also*
objectification
Professional Background Screening
Association, 92, 107
professionalism, 167, 168–169, 171
professional organizations, 25, 26, 107,
115, 155, 166, 169, 172; landlords and,
116. *See also* trade groups
property managers, 16, 116, 122, 139
prosecution, 29, 81, 217n15;
criminal, 56; policing and, 74–79;
professionalization of, 101; selective,
63, 102
psychological services, 99, 188
psychological treatment, 49, 81
psychology, discipline of, 165
public housing authorities (PHAs), 111, 112
public institutions, 19, 25, 54, 142, 173
public interest, 50, 68, 76, 101, 130, 132
public records, 14, 102, 103, 123, 133
public safety, 87, 88, 93, 94, 95, 99, 132, 181,
182, 187; promoting, 89; risks to, 103
public sector, 48, 117; private sector and, 87
Puerto Rico, 60; legal status of, 61
punishment, 10–11, 13, 17, 35, 79–80, 87,
90, 96, 98, 103, 118, 140, 145, 147, 159,
163, 164, 173, 184; actual, 149; ad hoc,
82, 117, 124, 185; administrative, 68;
of Black crime, 182; cancel culture

and, 146, 154, 156–157; collateral
consequences and, 87–89, 93, 99, 137;
corporal, 14, 82, 117, 185; cost-benefit
analysis for, 43, 97–98; debates about,
161–163; definition of, 88; effects of,
151; excessive, 100; kinds of, 138, 185;
legitimate, 174–175; limits and, 187;
material, 188; models of, 149–151,
155; by private companies, 1–2, 104,
121, 129–137, 145; proportional, 93;
public/infallible, 150; rehabilitation
and, 93; slavery as, 57, 150; symbolic
consequences of, 177; system of, 10;
techniques of, 104, 151
Punitive Society, The (Foucault), 10, 47,
92, 100, 149, 200n84, 210n27, 222n38
Purdue Pharma, 52

Quality Housing and Work
Responsibility Act (QHWRA)
(1998), 111
quasi-judicial: authority, 21, 135, 130, 136,
145, 157, 185; bodies, 26, 117, 120, 121,
135; expertise, 121; proceedings, 67, 83
Quickstay, 139

race, 8, 45, 70, 76, 79, 110, 113, 119, 127,
173, 174, 204n30, 205n33
racial slurs, 156, 159
racial subordination, 6, 37, 120, 151
racism, 8, 146, 147, 162, 175; consequences
of, 149; intentional, 114; shunning, 160;
structural, 81
Radiolab, 130, 131
rape, 21, 66, 67, 124, 136, 157
Rasul v. Bush (2004), 58
rationality, 4, 36, 96, 159, 163, 165, 166,
168; neoliberal, 3, 25, 50, 187
Ravenelle, Alexandrea, 138, 139
Reagan, Ronald, 71, 72
reasoning: administrative, 55; ethical,
167, 169; judicial, 55; legal, 172; moral,

Printed in the USA
CPSIA information can be obtained
at www.ICGtesting.com
CBHW030817190424
7138CB00005BA/488

9 780700 636594